The
Dot●Bomb
Survival Guide

The
Dot●Bomb
Survival Guide

Sean Carton

McGraw-Hill

New York   Chicago   San Francisco   Lisbon   London
Madrid   Mexico City   Milan   New Delhi
San Juan   Seoul   Singapore   Sydney   Toronto

To my beautiful daughter, Emma,
who taught me what really matters.

McGraw-Hill

A Division of The McGraw·Hill Companies

Copyright © 2002 by Sean Carton. All rights reserved. Printed in the United States of America. Except as permitted under the United States Copyright Act of 1976, no part of this publication may be reproduced or distributed in any form or by any means, or stored in a data base or retrieval system, without the prior written permission of the publisher.

1 2 3 4 5 6 7 8 9 0   AGM/AGM   0 9 8 7 6 5 4 3 2 1

ISBN 0-07-13779-4

This book was set in Life by MM Design 2000, Inc.
Printed and bound by Quebecor World/Martinsburg.

McGraw-Hill books are available at special quantity discounts to use as premiums and sales promotions, or for use in corporate training programs. For more information, please write to the Director of Special Sales, Professional Publishing, McGraw-Hill, Two Penn Plaza, New York, NY 10121-2298. Or contact your local bookstore.

 This book is printed on recycled, acid-free paper containing a minimum of 50% recycled, de-inked fiber.

contents

	Foreword	vii
	Preface	xi
	Acknowledgments	xvii
1	Lies, Damn Lies, and Business Models	1
2	The Customer? What Customer?	41
3	Fashion Victims and Supermodels: Push, the First Big Web Fad	73
4	The Perils (and Promises) of Software Products and Services Sold Over the Internet	103
5	Burnout: Short-Term Thinking = Short-Term Companies	133
6	Hype Bites Back: Marketing Disasters . . . and Success Stories	159
7	The Road to Hell Is Advertising Supported	189
8	Funding the Dream	221
9	Are We Learning Anything Yet?	247
	Glossary	257
	Index	265

foreword

mulch ado about nothing: no wonder ebusiness bombed

When was it exactly, I find myself wondering, that the publishers of the world decided I'd make a terrific book reviewer? I want to mark this date on my calendar with skull and crossbones. Because that was when an endless fleet of UPS and FedEx vans began arriving at my office with tome after tome of books these publishers think "I might want to take a look at." Sometimes they call me first. Must be a "permission marketing" thing. "Hello, Mr. Locke? I'm Traci Fobdoodle at Snodgrass & Sons, and we just published a book I thought you might want to take a look at." Uh-huh, I'm thinking. It wouldn't perchance happen to be a book about the Internet, ecommerce, and the New Economy, would it? "It's a really exciting book," Traci tells me, "about the Internet, ecommerce, and the New Economy." How did I guess? I must be getting prescient in my old age.

Nonetheless, I take 'em all. I have trouble sleeping these days—a bad conscience will do that to you—and I've found that a paragraph or two of such books is usually much more effective than Sominex. Plus, once you get the review scam going, it's a lot cheaper. They really started stacking up though. By last fall, I could no longer get to my desk through the mountainous piles of these, you know, real-

viii | foreword

ly exciting books. In a moment of rare insight, I ran the entire lot through a heavy-duty commercial garden shredder and blew the resulting mulch into my walls and attic crawl space. As a result, I have reduced my heating bills by a whopping 28 percent! Don't let anyone tell you there's no value in the hot air produced by business pundits.

But all that hot air did a lot more than keep my humble abode toasty warm during the long Colorado winter—it also managed to inflate the so-called New Economy past the bursting point. Hyped up on theory like a bunch of preschoolers mainlining Kool Aid and ogling new paradigms like teen girls who'd spotted Ricky Martin at the local DQ, an entire industry plunged headlong into collective insanity, worshipping at the altar of greed, money, and impersonal tech. The Internet was gonna change everything, right? Hoist the mainsail and full Net-speed ahead, mateys. The old rules don't apply anymore and there's plenty of loot for all!

Bullshit. People will always be people, and regular folks didn't give a hoot about the plans so many dot.com CEOs and stiff-backed golf-shirted MBAs had for them. While the Internet industry went on a 5-year bender, regular folks had their own lives to lead, their own priorities, their own friends to talk to. People didn't love the Net because it let them shop in their underwear. They loved the Net because it let them talk to other people, gave them a voice, and let them do their own thing in a public space that had never before existed. The Internet attracted people not because they got horny from the technology but because they could *connect.*

Why did so many dot.coms fail? How could so many have missed the obvious? How could so many (seemingly) smart people be so wrong? Were we all just insanely stupid? Was the New Economy simply the biggest scam in history? And who were these people writing this crap foisted on all of us? Did any of them actually use the Internet? Is there anything we can take away to make sure we get it right the next time?

The book you're holding in your hands just might have the answers to these questions. It's an exception to this sorry state of "business literature"—the biggest oxymoron to be visited upon our culture since jumbo shrimp and Valued Customers. The reason it's an exception is the exceptional writer who wrote it. Sean Carton is a Renaissance Man operating well ahead of the realization—which has yet to dawn on most—that there's a Renaissance under way. His involvement with the Internet has been phenomenally multifaceted and his output impossibly prodigious. Does he ever sleep? Does his physiology differ from that of normal terrestrials? Has anyone ever explored his rumored connection to Area 51?

Sean Carton founded and continues to manage several highly successful technology companies. This would be more than enough to keep most mere mortals out of trouble. But it hasn't been enough for Sean. He writes an endless stream of white papers, case studies, and reports—on subjects that range from wireless to Web development to online marketing to the latest niftiest software gadgets. Since 1998, he has published over 100 articles on the ClickZ network. Since who-knows-when, he's published thousands of shareware software reviews on *Cool Tool of the Day*. This is a guy who has gotten his hands dirty in the problems facing business. Impatient with armchair philosophizing, he's gotten under the hood and kicked the tires. He's also kicked a few asses along the way. This is a guy who's *engaged*.

And it's this engagement that makes all the difference. Innumerable authors and analysts have looked at the Internet and written voluminously about the potential and pitfalls of the medium. Thus all those delivery trucks at my door. Most, however, are wedded to highly conceptual models and frameworks—which unsurprisingly, turn out to be product-placement stealth ads for their consulting services. Additional charges may apply. The difference *The Dot.Bomb Survival Guide* brings to this sadsack display of turgid handwaving is a *feel* for the Net that comes only from full immersion. Sean Carton has lived and breathed the Web from Jump Street. His ideas about how to do business online—and how not to—are informed not by theory but by everyday practice. They're also informed by a sense of humor and breadth of perspective that are rare to find in any form of business writing. Evidently, someone forgot to tell Sean that books of this sort are supposed to be arid and boring and lame. Let's hope someone hips him to this immutable law of business before he writes the next one.

Then maybe I can get back to sleep.

Christopher Locke
Boulder, Colorado
June 2001

preface

I knew we were in trouble when the CEO called me up asking if I knew where he could sell his office furniture. Just 3 weeks before I'd been sitting with him at the offices of Women.com helping to negotiate an $8 million sponsorship deal. Things had gone well, the deal was nearly sealed, and the VCs were supposed to approve the first big round of funding any day.

Now he was trying to pawn his desk.

Oh, and offering me pennies on the dollar for the work my company had done for his startup.

It was spring, 2000. In the months that followed, many of the startups my company had been working to build or market started to fade and die. The nearly constant stream of entrepreneurs who hadn't gotten funding yet (but were looking for an agency to line up once they did) began to dry up. The Web industry media began to be filled with stories of once-huge companies going belly up or laying off workers. The stock market began to falter, and pundits began talking about a recession. I discovered FuckedCompany.com and started to read every day about dead and dying dot.coms. The magazines I read—*Wired, Business 2.0*, the *Industry Standard, FastCompany*—got thinner with every issue. People started whispering about the death of the New Economy.

xii | preface

What the hell was going on? Why had things gone so sour? How could companies that were worth billions just a year ago suddenly shut their doors? How could everyone have been so wrong about the growth of the Internet?

This book is the story of my search for answers to those questions. But before we get into how I found those answers, I want to tell you that I've come to one, unmistakable conclusion:

The New Economy is out of beta.

After a 6-year run of wild ideas, wild business plans built on those ideas, wild-eyed entrepreneurs, and even wilder spending by those looking to cash in on the forces ripping the economy wide open, we're now entering the painful period when the bugs are being corrected, the interfaces fully overhauled, and the first release getting ready for prime time.

It hasn't been easy. Vast fortunes have been gambled . . . and lost. Ideas that seemed ready to change the world are moldering on the scrap heap of failure. Dreamers and visionaries who enjoyed accolades previously reserved for conquerors are still reeling from being smacked down by an unforgiving marketplace.

Ever since the crash of April 1999 (and the subsequent carnage that followed), a lot of people and a lot of businesses that bet the farm (in some cases literally) on the Internet and the technologies that made it possible have had a rough time. According to WebMergers.com, over 592 dot.coms bit the dust since January 2000, setting over 70,000 people free to pursue other means of employment (to put it kindly). Along the way, the press has trumpeted the situation as the great dot.com downturn, the New Economy Crash, and the death of the Internet startup.

Sure, there have been a lot of casualties. Sure, a lot of money was lost. And sure, a lot of people are having a hard time recovering from a time when it seemed like every new idea was a world-changer, capital could be snatched up by anyone with a good business plan, and the world seemed new every day. But regardless of what's going on in the marketplace, the Internet isn't going away. The colossal changes to society brought about by the Internet are wide and deep, and they have permanently altered the way we interact with each other, how we do business, and how we think about the role of technology. We've built an amazing infrastructure over the past few years and have developed an incredible array of technology undreamed of a decade ago.

The growth of the Web has been amazing. As I write this, there are, by some estimates, over 2.1 billion Web pages online, with 7 million new pages being added every day. ACNielsen reported in May 2000 that nearly two out of three Americans over the age of 12 access the Internet, half of them going online at least once a day. Half of those users have purchased something online, and 86 percent regularly send and receive email. Forrester Research reports that approximately 50 percent of U.S. households have Internet access, and Grunwald and Associates report that the number of kids online has tripled to 27 million since 1997. One in five Japanese citizens (27 million people) access the Internet . . . 10 million from mobile devices. Internet usage is becoming mainstream in China. Over $24 billion was spent on retail ecommerce in the United States in 2000, according to Jupiter MediaMetrix, and they predict that amount will jump to $36 billion by the end of 2001.

When history looks back at the dot.com downturn, I suspect that most scholars will see that the explosive growth of the bubble—and its subsequent burst—was ultimately good for the economy and the world. The free abundance of capital, the incredible explosion of Big Ideas, and the many, many attempts at making a go at changing the world all have led to a New Economy and a new world. We can't go back.

But where do we go from here? How can companies who were looking at building their businesses through new rounds of funding survive the current drought? How can entrepreneurs who saw their Big Ideas go bust pick themselves up and move on to create new empires? What kind of future can hundreds of thousands of bright, young workers who cut their teeth in the New Economy look forward to? What can investors who saw their portfolios lose double-digit percentages over the last year look forward to? And how can businesses that made it through the downturn survive and build for the future?

That's exactly what we're going to try to answer in this book.

We'll start by examining some of the more successful (and unsuccessful) business models that made it to the Internet, looking at the companies that employed them and how they made them work . . . or how the model killed them off. We'll cover a whole spectrum from B2B exchanges to the "name-your-own-price" model popularized by Priceline.com to virtual communities and alternative advertising models in an effort to get to the bottom of what works online and what doesn't.

xiv | preface

Next, we'll examine the online customer and see how customer service and the online experience made or broke several major dot.coms. We'll dig into the statistics that reveal exactly who the online customers are, what they do online, and what they're looking for. Digging deep into the workings of ecommerce, we'll examine just how knowing the customer can mean the difference between life and death for online retailers and service companies.

Throughout the life of the Internet, various types of businesses and technologies have moved quickly in and out of favor. Fads have always been a part of the Net and will continue to affect the success and failure of companies. To get an understanding of which fads can sway marketplaces, the media, and whole industries, we'll examine the story of the first big Internet fad—push technology—and see what lessons we can learn from the biggest casualty and the most successful survivors.

While the media has paid an awful lot of attention to ecommerce and content sites, the whole arena of online products and services (and offline products that integrate with the Web) can tell us a lot about how to survive and thrive in the dot.com implosion. Taking a close look at the reasons product companies have struggled, the role of products in the digital age, the consequences of innovation, and the rise and fall of what Neil Klienman calls "The Beta Culture," we'll get a good understanding of why products succeed . . . and fail.

In Chapter 6, we'll explore how short-term thinking killed several prominent dot.coms and how companies that have taken the long view have prospered. With sometimes-astronomical burn rates and an overdependence on venture funding, many in the ecommerce sector ran out of money before they had a chance to start building a business. Why did this happen? We'll find out.

If there's one thing that's been a hallmark of the New Economy to this point, it's hype: wild promises and claims made through advertising and public relations. In some cases, this hype has been able to transform unknown companies into market superstars nearly overnight. In other cases overpromising and underdelivering has lead to some spectacular collapses. In Chapter 7, we'll examine the role that marketing had in creating and sustaining the New Economy.

Chapter 8 will examine the issues of marketing from the other end: the sites that supported themselves through advertising. At one time, ad-supported content was seen as *the* online business model. Content was king. Put up a site, get the eyeballs, and sell the advertising. Simple, right? Maybe not. We'll find out.

Finally, the dot.com boom never could have started without the venture capitalists who funded the flood of new startups. Between 1995 and the third quarter of 2000, almost $60 billion dollars (yes, with a *b*) had been pumped into new startups by VCs. We'll take a look at how the venture process works, how it changed, and what the prospects are for entrepreneurs looking for funding in the future.

There are a lot of scary stories in this book, but a lot of hope too. In every tale of failure, every step-by-step recounting of a dot.bomb's downward slide, there's a lot that the entrepreneurs, investors, and today's participants in the New Economy can take away to build their own new ventures. For every company that hit rock bottom, many others have seen what those that came before them did wrong and have retooled themselves for survival. This book will give you that view that you need to survive and thrive in the dot.com implosion.

The testing period's over. We've identified the bugs and have slowed down development to deal with them. The New Economy is out of beta. Get ready for version 2.0.

acknowledgments

First and foremost, I want to thank my wife, Lorna, and my daughter, Emma, for their endless patience and good humor during the writing of this book. This wouldn't have been possible without your love and support.

A big thanks also goes to Chris Locke for contributing the foreword to this book and for having so much faith in my work over the years. You rock!

I also want to thank my tireless research assistant and edge scanner Esha Janssens-Sannon. Her incredible ability to dig out the most obscure fact, statistic, and company reference contributed immeasurably to this book. Esha, thanks for putting up with me. I know it wasn't easy!

I'd also like to tip my fedora to Gareth Branwyn, my mentor, guide, sounding board, and cheerleader. I owe you more than you can know, bud!

Thanks too to my coworkers at Carton Donofrio Partners, who uncomplainingly picked up my ever-increasing slack during the production of this book. Well, OK . . . maybe you *did* complain, but I never heard it. Thanks!

Thanks also to Mark Walsh, Eli Barkat, Neil Klienman, Tom Gable, Hurst Lin, Trevor Villet, Paul Lee, Douglas Rushkoff, and xviii | acknowledgments

Terry Collison for submitting themselves to my interviews and/or contributing their sage wisdom to this book.

Finally, a huge thanks to my editor, Michelle Williams. Your poking, prodding, cajoling, sense of humor, and great advice made this book far better than it would have been without you!

lies, damn lies, and business models

If there's one thing there's been no shortage of since business started moving to the Web, it's business models.

Business models, those conceptual blueprints for doing business, have fueled the New Economy. Before the Internet, it seemed as if truly new business models were few and far between. Business—making money and building businesses by buying and selling goods and services—was fairly straightforward. Manufacturers made things. People bought them. Companies provided services. Other companies (and people) contracted for them.

Then the Internet came along and seemed to change everything.

now, everything is different

The biggest change brought about by the Internet and digital media was what Nicholas Negroponte called the move from "atoms to bits." Essentially, making business digital eliminated the barriers of time and space from transactions.

In an October 1997 piece in *Wired*, Negroponte laid out the changes wrought by what he called "being digital":

2 | the dot.bomb survival guide

> Being digital has three physiological effects on the shape of our world. It decentralizes, it flattens, and it makes things bigger and smaller at the same time. Because bits have no size, shape, or color, we tend not to consider them in any morphological sense. But just as elevators have changed the shape of buildings and cars have changed the shape of cities, bits will change the shape of organizations, be they companies, nations, or social structures. (*Wired* 5.10.)

But "being digital" wasn't enough to change the world of business without the global World Wide Web and the Internet. Once business moved into the digital realm and was given a global conduit, the world thought it would be fundamentally changed. There is no midnight in the digital world; business can be automated, transacted in a global Web 24 hours a day, 7 days a week. On the Web, there is no *there* there; moving a bit across the globe wired by the Web is just as easy as sending that same bit across your office local area network (LAN). People don't have to go to your store to buy stuff. They go to your website. Auctions don't have to take place in quaint barns. They can take place in real time within a global community of users meeting in a vertical place. Magazines and newspapers don't have to be shipped physically from place to place. They can be read in digital form by anyone who has the right gear. And because they never have to cross into the messy world of the analog, they can be updated instantly any time.

This move from atoms to bits has had a profound effect on the possible. With the traditional barriers of time and space removed, the fundamentals of business have changed. And though initially slow to respond, businesses have been looking to the Web to do things that haven't been possible in the physical world.

It makes sense. There are major differences that the Web brings to business:

1. *The Web is global.* It knows no national boundaries. The site you put up in Des Moines can just as easily be seen by someone in Brunei as someone in Buffalo. Distance doesn't increase cost. Any company that wants to put up a site instantly has a global audience.

2. *The barriers to entry are perceived to be relatively low.* Building a store on the Web has few of the messy physical restraints of building a physical store. Anyone with a simple text editor and access to a server connected to the Web can throw up a site in a matter of hours. In fact, most early sites were built in some early adopter's spare time. Books lined the store shelves declaring that you could teach yourself HTML in a week! CEOs saw their kids doing it and realized that their companies could do it, too.

3. *The Web is a many-to-many medium.* While the phone system provides a way to connect buyers and sellers worldwide, it is essentially a point-to-point system. One person can call only one person at a time (or a few others via cumbersome conference-calling systems). But when the transaction is over, it goes away . . . hang up and the connection's broken. The Web is always on, and it imposes no limits as to who can connect to whom.

4. *The Web allows automation of business practices.* Because the nodes of the Web are computers and computers can be programmed to perform tasks dealing with information and information is what is being transmitted back and forth across the Web, transactions can be processed automatically, without human intervention. Buying and selling doesn't have to involve human intermediaries; just fill out a form and let the program do the rest.

5. *The Web is a harshly accountable medium.* While TV and radio have to rely on statistical sampling based on measurements of a relatively small number of households in order to let advertisers know how effective their ads are, every click on the Web can be counted. Advertisers don't have to rely on suspect methods of measuring effectiveness anymore . . . now they *know.*

6. *Digital commerce can be disintermediated commerce.* Because the Web is global, always on, many to many, and automated, who needs people in the middle? Now buyers and sellers can transact business directly because they can find each other no matter where they are in the world. And if they want to do a transaction—bam! Just send a message and it is done.

For these reasons (and plenty of other, wackier reasons as we'll see in this chapter), the Web revolutionized how people thought of

4 | the dot.bomb survival guide

business. For content providers and advertisers, it was the first truly new medium since the advent of television 50 years ago. For people wanting to transact business, it was a truly new channel for connecting business to business. The Internet was going to change everything. The old rules didn't apply! Out with the old and in with the New Economy!

Yeah. Right.

As it turns out, while many new ways of doing business represented quantum leaps in concept, actually making these new models do what they needed to do—make money—turned out to be a little more problematic. These new models were wonders of conceptual business thinking, but the world wasn't always ready for a new way of doing business. Some startups failed because they based their business models on unrealistic expectations of marketplace performance, what Guy Kawasaki calls the "Chinese Soda" model (see sidebar "Choking on Chinese Soda, . . .") not taking into account factors such as marketing or distribution. Other models spawned companies that bit the proverbial dust because they assumed the world would change before it did . . . and they ran out of money waiting for the change to happen. Some dot.bombs blew up in the face of bad economic models that initially looked great on paper but didn't take into account the foibles of real human beings. And finally some died simply because they were just dumb ideas born in an era when anything seemed possible.

In this chapter we'll examine several popular business models and look at why some companies in these spaces failed while others thrived. We won't look at every possible model—there just isn't enough space in this book (or, God forbid, any other book) to examine all of them. We won't attempt to look at advertising-supported models as a whole here—Chapter 8 will cover that. And we won't look at ecommerce as a model unto itself . . . the next chapter will examine the real reason that many ecommerce models failed. But what we will look at is some of the innovative models wrought by the Internet (such as Priceline's "name-your-own-price" model, the B2B exchange model, online communities, and "pay-to-surf" advertising), how they came to be, who the casualties (and the victors) were, and where they may be going in the future.

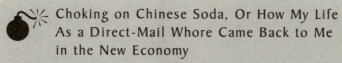
Choking on Chinese Soda, Or How My Life As a Direct-Mail Whore Came Back to Me in the New Economy

Guy Kawasaki of Garage.com calls the trap that many entrepreneurs set for themselves the "Chinese Soda" problem. Basically it comes down to making wrong assumptions about the size of a market and possible market share: "If there are a billion people in China and I can sell my new brand of soda to just 1 percent of them, I'll be rich!" Things don't usually work out that way.

In my dealings with new fresh-faced dot.com entrepreneurs, I got to see Chinese Soda thinking on a regular basis. What really amazed me was how similar their business plans were to the offers I used to write as a direct-mail copywriter. In my previous life I wrote "inserts," the direct marketer's euphemism for sales letters inserted into subscribers' newsletters. I worked for a company (which, in the interests of avoiding a lawsuit, will remain nameless) that specialized in selling new business opportunities. Month after month I would essentially try to sell subscribers on new business models guaranteed (with many, many caveats) to make them money in their spare time with a minimum of effort. Basically the pitch went like this:

> Today there are <INSERT NUMBER HERE> people who do <INSERT ACTIVITY HERE>. As a <INSERT JOB DESCRIPTION OF SERVICE TO THIS AUDIENCE> you can make <INSERT DOLLAR AMOUNT> every time you <INSERT NAME OF SERVICE PERFORMED> for one of these people. That's a total market of <MULTIPLY NUMBER OF PEOPLE BY DOLLAR AMOUNT>! Obviously, you'll never be able to do this for everyone, but if you could get <INSERT MILDLY PLAUSIBLE FRACTION> percent of that market, you'd be rich! Even if you could only get <INSERT SLIGHTLY MORE REALISTIC NUMBER> percent in your spare time, you'd still be making a great side income!

Truth be told, I'm not exactly proud of this, but the formula worked. People would buy the opportunity, swayed by the ever-so-rational-sounding argument. After all, who doesn't believe that he or she couldn't get some infinitesimally tiny fraction of such a huge market?

Of course, the problem with this argument is that it doesn't address some of the most important issues of building a business

6 | the dot.bomb survival guide

like marketing and overhead. Sure, you *may* be able to corner 0.5 percent of the market, but to do so you'd have to mount a national advertising campaign to reach those people, and the cost of that campaign could wipe out any trace of profit for years. And even if you got those people as customers, servicing them over a national territory by yourself would be impossible. It just doesn't add up.

But this kind of argument formed the basis of many dot.com business plans. And while any rational businessperson would have scoffed at the numbers before the advent of the Web, for many of the reasons outlined in the beginning of this chapter, the New Economy made arguments like this seem very, very plausible. Just advertise on the Web! Reach a global market just by throwing up a site! Service your customers via email! It's a sure thing!

Of course, as we'll see later in this chapter and throughout this book, it most definitely isn't a sure thing. Making money on your site means getting people to your site—not an easy task in the clutter of millions or billions of websites. And servicing those people once you get them requires more than just sending them an email or letting the automated CRM system handle the job—people want to talk to real people, and sending goods and services across the globe still requires shipping and travel . . . all of which cost money.

In the end, if it sounds too good to be true, it probably is, as many failed dot.coms found out.

B2B exchanges

The Web has the potential to radically change the way the world does business. All the elements that make the Web different—a global reach, 24/7 access, instant communications, and automated services—could conceivably streamline business processes, overhaul inefficient systems, and raise profits by decreasing the costs of doing business. The problem seems to be building enough critical mass over time to see the benefits actually occur. While many B2B exchanges have been born (and have died) in the past few years, a lot of the major players (such as Covisint, the auto industry's B2B super marketplace) still haven't come into their own yet. In fact, many B2B exchanges are still searching for chief executives with the know-how and vision to build them into thriving businesses. Why the holdup?

Generally, analysts are unanimous in their projections that B2B commerce and online business-to-business transactions will represent a huge market in the coming decade. The Boston Consulting Group estimates over $1 trillion in savings alone by 2010. The Gartner Group estimates that the global B2B market will represent as much as 7 percent of the total world economy by 2004 . . . a whopping $7.3 trillion. Jupiter MediaMetrix estimates that online commerce between businesses will reach $6.3 trillion by 2005. AMR Research, Inc., projects that over half of all B2B commerce in the United States will flow through B2B exchanges by 2004. We're talking a lot of money.

Most of the estimates of the B2B market focus on business-to-business exchanges, websites that link buyers and sellers in a particular industry together to facilitate their transactions. These transactions can take several forms. In one model, buyers post their needs to an exchange and wait for bids to come in from suppliers . . . the "reverse auction" model. In other versions, suppliers list their wares online in giant industry-vertical catalogs and wait for purchasers to either bid on their products (in competition with others) or pony up the money. The site then provides the necessary conduits for the transactions to occur—facilitating the letters of credit, billing details, and so on—and takes a cut of the transaction for its trouble. Everyone in the supply chain wins as suppliers see their acquisition costs decrease and the now-frictionless (or at least slippery-er) marketplace lowers all costs across the board as a result of fair and open competition. Everyone goes home happy: The supplier makes a sale, the buyer gets it for less, and the site owner gets his or her share for making the transaction happen.

It's easy to see why the prospects look so good to both industry and analysts alike. The concept makes perfect sense. CFOs and upper-management types love it. In fact, it's the common-sense *rightness* of the whole process that made the market explode originally. Currently, most analysts estimate that there are over 1,000 marketplaces operating on the Web, and more are being funded every day. Major industry leaders, initially skeptical, are moving to jump into the fray. Last year, Covisint—a joint venture by Ford, General

Motors, DaimlerChrysler, Renault, and Nissan—made a splash by joining forces to create an exchange with the potential for facilitating transactions of over $240 billion per year.

But at the same time that the future prospects for doing business online look rosy to most market watchers, many business-to-business companies are struggling to stay afloat. Funding for these ventures is drying up: 77 B2B exchanges were funded to the tune of $800 million in March 2000, but only 35 exchanges were funded for a total of $500 million between April and August 2000. These figures probably foreshadow a decreased optimism in the overall growth of the B2B exchange marketplace. In fact, while there are 1,000 exchanges today, some see a major consolidation on the way. Forrester Research predicts that by 2003 only about 180 "significant" marketplaces will survive.

Many exchanges have gone belly up. Two of the most widely publicized were Chemdex and Promedix, life sciences and medical industry exchanges operated by Ventro, a B2B marketplace builder (Figure 1-1). Chemdex and Promedix didn't hurt for big-name clients. Chemdex had signed on Bristol-Myers Squibb and SmithKline Beecham, and it opened for business in 1997 as the first exchange built by Ventro (www.ventro.com). The first "virtual marketplace" in its industry, Chemdex was financed by CMG@Ventures, and it targeted scientists and other small purchasers of chemicals as its primary market.

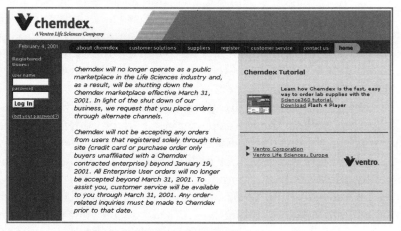

Figure 1-1.   Chemdex's "Goodbye" Page

Unfortunately, Chemdex didn't make it. Even though it had been sustained by venture funding and Ventro's one-time-high stock price of $243.50, the money quickly ran out. Ventro had sunk to a low of around $0.65 by May 2001. Before shutting down Chemdex and Promedix, Ventro had been hemorrhaging badly, reporting losses of over $75 million in the third quarter of 2000 as it struggled to make do with its low-volume sales. After the disappointing earnings, the company made the decision to shut down both Chemdex and Promedix, laying off nearly half their employees and taking a restructuring charge of approximately $410 million in its end-year results. And while Ventro is currently changing its business plan to move out of the operation of online marketplaces and into the service business providing software and expertise for the B2B exchange market, it is still hemorrhaging money and employees, in fact laying off 67 percent of its workforce in April 2001. But who knows . . . the new streamlining and redirection may work. After all, if you can't make money mining for gold, why not sell tools to the miners?

Another exchange that took a slightly different tack was BizBuyer.com, a site targeted to small- and medium-sized businesses. Its plan was simple: Charge a fee or $3 to $10 per bid for suppliers to participate in online reverse auctions. Buyers would get on the site, check out the products, and post their needs. Vendors would then bid for their business, and the site would forward the bids directly to the customer for consideration and purchase.

Things started well for BizBuyer.com, which raised over $69 million since its birth in 1998. While it stayed pretty much out of the limelight in the beginning, BizBuyer's profile was raised significantly by a December 1999 *Business 2.0* article that touted the company as "a digital yenta," praising it for its ability to let smaller businesses play in the game previously open only to major purchasers. However, the article did point out that how BizBuyer planned on making money was "unclear," an observation that was to prove prophetic.

In December 2000, BizBuyer.com shut down with $35 million left in its coffers (Figure 1-2). Its profits had fallen far short of expectations even though the venture firm Rustic Canyon had closed a round of funding for $64 million earlier in the year. The partners looked at the situation and decided to pull the plug while there was money still left to distribute to the investors. "We gave it our best shot," said Pat Lopker, CFO, in an interview for *LocalBusiness.com*, "and it's a tough job to get people to transact business on the Internet."

Figure 1-2. BizBuyer.com Says Bye-Bye

More than anything else, that statement alone sums up the problems that so many B2B exchanges are having, and will have. Getting business to change is tough, and while management might like it, not everyone is ready to jump onboard right away. Technology changes quickly, but people (and markets) change slowly.

A study published in January 2001 by the National Association of Purchasing Management (NAPM) and Forrester Research provides some of the best insight into the future of the B2B marketplace. Forrester and NAPM surveyed 368 purchasing executives and found that overall they liked the idea of transacting business over the Web via exchanges but they or their companies have been slow to get onboard:

- 48.4 percent said that they were in the earliest stage of using the Internet in their business.
- However, 87 percent reported that the Internet would be an important part of their purchasing plans during 2001.

- Nearly three quarters (73.4 percent) reported that they haven't seen any cost savings from the Internet.
- 92.3 percent have seen "no or minor change" in their procurement procedures as a result of the Internet.
- A mere 15.8 percent have purchased materials at online auctions.
- 19.1 percent have purchased through online marketplaces.
- Half (50.4 percent) collaborate with their suppliers online.

While B2B exchanges have gotten a lot of attention in the press, few companies seem committed to moving their business online immediately. They've got bigger problems. An A.T. Kearney study in July 2000 found that only 4 percent of 251 CEOs surveyed reported that ebusiness was "their main challenge." A mere 18 percent were interested in online auctions. But the interest *is* there . . . over the long term. In April 2001, a joint report from Forrester and the National Association of Purchasing Management found that 88 percent of U.S. businesses believe that the Internet is important to their purchasing process, and nearly 25 percent reported that they *have* seen cost savings as a result of doing business online. As the volatility in the marketplace continues, it appears (for the moment) that many companies are standing back to see what happens before they jump completely into the world of online marketplaces.

What do the failures of the past year and these studies say about the future of online B2B exchanges as a viable business model? Mainly that survival will mean weathering the storms until business can catch up with technology. As pointed out earlier, most analysts still see the sector as one with huge growth potential . . . over the next 10 years. Where that growth will take us remains to be seen (see sidebar "The Past and Future of B2B Exchanges").

The model makes lots of sense to CFOs and those who count the bottom line, but it may take years to break through the inertia of corporate America. Moving to exchanges represents a huge risk and a huge commitment of capital resources. It also represents a huge change in culture. Procurement has been conducted in more or less the same way for decades now. It may not be ready to change overnight . . . regardless of the benefits. In the meantime, it's the dot.coms that supply the services to all the companies building exchanges—CommerceOne and Ariba—that are raking in the money and weathering the storm. For everyone else, it's time to make sure that there's enough fuel to feed the burn rate until everyone else catches up.

 The Past and Future of B2B Exchanges: An Interview with Mark Walsh, chairman of VerticalNet

Q: What's your take on the state of the B2B exchange marketplace?

It's become bifurcated into two camps. The first is content, context, and community. The second camp is the platform and its role. But if you're a hammer, everything looks like a nail. Either software will drive the bus, open exchanges will rule, or closed exchanges will come to dominate the marketplace, or premium content will drive an advertising model.... It depends on where you're coming from.

Predictably, the technology folks believe that software will be the force that plays itself out. But it depends on what religion you worship at. The software companies currently enjoy relatively high multiples and approval from the analysts because everyone understands software. It's just about linking a value-added network into these software platforms.

The other people from industry news sources say that it's all about content. But I believe that it's somewhere in the middle. I've always believed in three rules: simple beats hard, cheap beats expensive, and open beats closed.

Q: Tell me about business models: What works and what doesn't? We've seen lots of sites go belly up depending on advertising.

The great line that I've always heard is that content-based and advertising-based models are the wave of the future ... and always will be. VerticalNet has a nice business selling advertising. We have an incredibly targeted audience that can command triple-digit CPMs (cost-per-thousand ad impressions). Nobody ever goes to solidwaste.com TWICE by mistake. They're all people that care about the specific vertical they're visiting. And from all that we're told, we're the biggest gorilla out there. We're very attractive to advertisers.

It's just one financial model. We've always believed that we should pursue whatever the hot model is at the time, but that success only comes from also having flanker brands and models to back it up.

Q: It seems that a lot of B2B companies died before they had a chance to succeed because they never lasted long enough to work. People change a lot slower than technology, and the people never had a chance to change their behavior to use the exchange.

It's never about the technology. Relationships are what matters. Relationships will never go away and can't be replaced by an inhuman interface. The ability to source vendors electronically has always been available . . . nobody used it. The relationship between the purchasing person and the vendor is the way life has always worked. We should never use the analog of consumer fungible goods in the B2B relationship . . . in the B2C relationship, we never thought the vendor added any value. But in most business situations we see that the channel adds value. The distributors are important people. They add value. But it's the mid-sized companies that are put under duress by the Net. They don't have the volume to bring down their prices, and they don't have the focus on relationships that the boutique shops do.

Q: But aren't exchanges inevitable? It seems like the executive management of companies should love these things because they can bring down costs and make purchasing a lot more efficient.

No technology has ever been adopted in the guts of the operation like the CTO thought it would. But you can see how people thought magic was going to happen immediately. That's what they were sold. There's a sales pitch that a lot of Net companies make. It's always got this slide with three clouds on it. Cloud 1 is labeled "today's world." Cloud 3 is labeled "the future." And the second cloud in the middle connecting today with the future is the miracle cloud labeled "miracle happens here." Everybody thinks there's a Santa Claus.

Q: What does VerticalNet plan to do to survive and thrive in the future?

Software is clearly the flavor of the month. But we've been in the software business for 2 years now . . . we just never told anybody about it. Now we're actively selling our VerticalNet Solutions software platform. It's winning contracts when it goes head to head with competitors. Why? Because cool code rules! We have the cool code and a lot of investment behind it. But at the same time, we're maintaining the basic content, context, and advertising business. It's a longer acceptance curve and an open environment to learn more about vendors. We thought that there'd be higher adoption rates more quickly, but that hasn't happened yet.

We're also into some big partnerships with consortiums . . . we're the single largest shareholder in Converge with a 20 percent stake. We believe that it's a good market. Of course some will flounder, but some will work really well.

We're maintaining the volume levels in our community business, and we're upping the volume in the software business. We're launching geography-specific verticals. We're doing a lot of cool stuff. The thing I like about our business is that we've always got three dials in front of us to turn to generate revenue, not just one like a lot of other companies in the space.

Q: Obviously, community is very important to the VerticalNet concept. How do you build community online?

Building community in the B2B space is a lot like building community in the consumer space: careers, information, comparing notes with other people. These are the basic characteristics. When I was at AOL, I used to tell Steve Case that AOL's best salespeople were loneliness and boredom.

In the B2B world, first you obviously have to add more business-specific content. Salary surveys, product information—all that stuff works. And when the community starts to kick in, you add product-specific information. The reason that the trade magazine business is so good is because a lot of what they basically print are press releases with new headlines. But people in the business love that stuff. They're looking for new information about their business. They read the trades because of the advertising. On VerticalNet, we put out a lot of information that's product specific. It's biased, but that's all that there is.

The second thing you have to do is normalize the product-specific information through a parametric search. People want normalized data so that they can log on and specify a search and find what they're looking for. You might not find it the first time, but a parametric search lets you narrow down the search so that you can find the three or four pieces of information you're looking for. But it's a huge job. We do a good job, but the person who figures out how to do it right will have a defensible franchise.

Information can be a problem, though. The Web has created an artificial churn of vendor lists because it's so easy to compare prices and services. Purchasers feel like they have to go for other vendors because their bosses can come in and ask them, "So why haven't you checked out Company X?"

Q: What advice would you give entrepreneurs thinking of starting a business today?

I keep seeing one big error: Don't get out of the Trojan Horse before you're inside the castle! Many of the business plans I see assume that the company can walk into an industry, say they're the Net guys, and change it forever. It doesn't work that way. You need to get inside and understand and wait for them to fall asleep. You can't say what you're going to do until you understand the intricacies. A lot of markets have inefficient systems because they like it that way.

Always raise 50 percent more money than you think you need. Never take the advice of VCs after they've given you the money. After that, you'll have to give them a spot on your board. Go out and get people that know what they're doing.

Q: What are the big lessons you've learned over your career?

Three things:

1. If something seems too good to be true, it is.
2. Hubris always gets its payback.
3. Believe it or not, you can always fall upward as long as you're willing to move geographically and are willing to bet your career.

But if you forget lessons 1 or 2, lesson 3 will never happen.

name your own price

Pioneered by Priceline.com, the name-your-own-price model reverses tradition by having the buyer submit an asking "bid" and then getting the seller to respond by accepting or rejecting the bid. If the seller accepts the bid, the buyer then has to make a decision in a preset amount of time (in some cases) or must take whatever price matches the one he or she set when bidding.

The name-your-own-price model was a breakthrough when it first appeared on the scene with the launch of Priceline.com. Here for the first time was a business model that was impossible without the enabling technology of the Net. The model allowed airlines to unload "distressed inventory" or unsold seats, it allowed car rental companies to unload unrented cars, and it allowed the consumer unprecedented pricing flexibility. It had the potential to revolutionize commerce as we knew it.

Priceline's original travel-focused model was quickly followed by an even more ambitious plan, a service called "WebHouseClub," which allowed consumers to set their own prices for groceries and, eventually, gas. Consumers would log on to the site, select products that they wanted, set a price point, see if their bids were accepted, and then go to the grocery store to buy the stuff at a discounted price.

The name-your-own-price model fit perfectly into a major consumer trend that had been accelerated by the Web—namely, putting control in the hands of the consumers. This trend had first been identified by the *Yankelovich Monitor*, an annual megasurvey of consumer behavior, and was heralded by the *Monitor* as a fundamental shift in the power relationships between producer and consumer: "We stand now on the brink of a fundamental shift of power: from producers to consumers, and from institutions more generally to individuals," said Yankelovich in the 1999–2000 report. "We are, in a sense, witnessing the end of consumer dependence."

This radical shift was seen everywhere. The most popular segments on the Web—travel, health, automotive, and auctions—were popular because they allowed consumers to get their own information, to get beyond the intermediaries such as travel agents and car salespeople who had previously doled out what they wanted the buyer to hear. Priceline and the name-your-own-price model fit perfectly into this trend.

Other models arose that attempted to give consumers control over their buying. Mercata.com, a group-buying site that allowed consumers to aggregate their purchases to get better prices, came onto the scene, coowned by Paul Allen's Vulcan Ventures who had invested more than $30 million in the concept. Unfortunately, it wasn't enough: Mercata shut down in January 2001 (see Figure 1-3). MobShop.com followed suit by opening up another site that allowed consumers to combine their buying power to get lower prices.

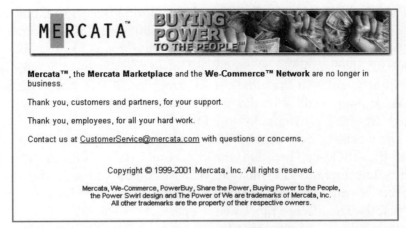

Figure 1-3. Mercata.com's Final Words on the Web

the rise and fall of Priceline and WebHouse (and Priceline's rise again?)

During the beginning of the B2C explosion on the Web, Priceline was the king. Starting with a venture-funded war chest of over $100 million, Priceline electrified the industry with its name-your-own-price concept. On the day it went public, March 30, 1999, Priceline shares soared to over $80 (from an asking price of $16), eventually ending the day at $69. From there it was up, up, up into the stratosphere beyond $100, making founder Jay Walker (temporarily) one of the richest men in the world. The money helped fund a now-famous $25 million ad campaign with William Shatner that, at times, seemed to be everywhere and provided Walker with the funds he needed to sink over $363 million into the company in a single year.

But Priceline's fortunes quickly turned for the worse. Revenues failed to materialize to expected levels, and losses continued to mount. On September 27, 2000, Walker lost his billionaire status as Priceline's stock plummeted 42 percent, taking his fortune of a mere $580 million along with it.

From the start, Priceline was losing money . . . lots of it. In the quarter ending September 1999, Priceline reported a total net income loss of over $100 million. One big drain on the company was the affiliated WebHouseClub, which was losing over $5 million per week. Walker himself poured over $179 million of his own money into the venture, but things weren't looking good. On October 5, 2000, Walker announced that WebHouse was shutting down. The announcement sent Priceline's stock dropping 38 percent to $5.81.

What happened? Why did WebHouse fail? Why is Priceline in so much trouble? Why couldn't the model work?

The most obvious reason is that the companies spent more money than they took in. That constant loss, combined with a downturn in the public markets, meant that Walker couldn't turn to the stock market to raise money to float a sinking ship. But that's just the symptom. The disease ran much deeper.

WebHouseClub was initially very successful in bringing in customers. The first week it was open, WebHouse signed up over 15,000 customers with many, many more to follow. People loved the idea. The problem was, the manufacturers didn't.

In theory, the manufacturers were supposed to make up the difference between what the store charged and what the consumer paid, much like coupons. If a bottle of ketchup normally cost $1.59 and the consumer "bid" $1.00 (and the bid was accepted), Priceline would refund the store the $0.59 difference. The draw to the manufacturer was that it could do away with coupons (and lead times associated with distributing coupons), reacting to market conditions instantly.

Unfortunately, not many manufacturers signed up. But to keep people coming back, WebHouse had to provide discounts on a whole range of groceries, not just the ones that had manufacturer support. As a result, WebHouse ended up subsidizing most of the purchases (most consumers saved between $4 and $6 per order), resulting in a constant bleeding of cash of over $1 million per week plus. The gas situation was the same. When the stock price was high (and Walker could keep pumping money into the company), there was enough capital to keep up the grocery pyramid scheme. But when the price dropped, there wasn't enough cash to prop up the concept. The center could not hold. WebHouse crashed.

Priceline is still hanging on by a thread, but losing money fast. In the third quarter of 2000, it was still showing significant net income losses of almost $192 million. And new competition from companies lies, damn lies, and business models | 19

like AutoByTel and CheapTickets is nibbling away at market share, though Priceline continues to surprise, booking a profit for the first time at the end of July 2001, keeping its stock on an upward trend.

But the biggest competition is coming from Priceline's former allies: the airlines themselves. Hotwire.com has garnered investments from six major airlines, including American Airlines, America West, Continental, Northwest, United, and US Airways, and it makes the process of buying a ticket easier than Priceline does. Instead of submitting a bid, waiting 10 to 20 minutes for a response, and counter-offering if necessary, Hotwire allows users to enter their departure and destination locations, specify a date and a few other details, and sit back to wait for a ticket price. Hotwire does all the work by searching its database for unsold inventory. For consumers who just want to book tickets without the guesswork, Orbitz.com (which shares investors such as United Airlines with Hotwire.com) functions as a full service travel site . . . with the backing of some of the biggest air carriers in the United States. While this approach has some competitors concerned about antitrust regulations, consumers seem to like the approach . . . over 175,000 had registered by the time the site had launched.

And that, in the end, may just be the crux of Priceline's (and WebHouse's, and Mercata's, and MobShop's) problems. People are used to simple pricing, especially Americans. Consumers don't, as a whole, haggle on products or want to work overtime to save a few (perceived) pennies. For most people, the benefits don't outweigh the hassles it takes to get the savings . . . mildly irritating when bidding on items costing hundreds of dollars (airline tickets) but ridiculous for groceries. It just ain't worth the trouble. Time is money, and most folks didn't feel that the time they spent looking for lower-cost goods and services was worth the time.

While Priceline's approach does fit the trend of consumer control identified by Yankelovich, it also runs counter to one of the other trends identified in the study—the desire for more fun. When asked if they "need to get more pleasure out of life," 81 percent of the respondents in the survey answered "Yes!" Of course, what the other 9 percent's problem was remains a mystery.

In the end, after the novelty wore off, making people do too much work to save money might just be the problem that killed

20 | the dot.bomb survival guide

WebHouseClub and may have mortally wounded Priceline. Other companies that required consumers to bid and wait haven't fared too well either. Mercata.com, Allen's group-buying site, shut down on January 5, 2001. MobShop dropped its consumer business 10 days later, reportedly to focus on B2B applications for group buying. It's not just enough to put consumers in the drivers' seats for a bargain. You have to get them there in a hurry without a lot of bumps in the road.

virtual communities

Virtual communities have existed practically since the first time one computer could be connected to another. In the early days of the PC revolution, computer bulletin board systems (BBSs) allowed users with modems to dial in, read postings from other users, post messages of their own, download files, and, in some cases, chat in real time with other users. Long before the Internet became a household (or boardroom) word, BBSs dotted the virtual landscape of cyberspace, disparate nodes in a newly emerging global information network.

Then the Web came along. All of a sudden a medium was born that unified all the disparate communities into a common interface. In the past, users who wanted to participate in Usenet discussion groups, talk in live chats on IRC, fight virtual dragons in any one of hundreds of MUDs, or build their own spaces on a MOO had to download special client software and go through the gyrations of finding and connecting to a server. Now with Web browsers acting as universal interfaces to the datasphere, users can participate in discussions simply by logging on to a site and pointing and clicking in a familiar environment. At the same time, AOL's marketing department started blanketing the United States with those all-too-familiar discs, signing up users at a dizzying pace, and introducing them to the myriad chat rooms and discussion boards on the service.

As more and more communities started to link into the Web (either by "Web-ifying" their interfaces or providing easy links to their servers), and the Web started to become more commercialized, the Big Question arose: How are we going to make money with this stuff? AOL, CompuServe, and the WELL provided one model: subscriptions. But the Web was rapidly evolving into a "free" medium, and people were fast getting used to not paying for anything. And while these virtual communities basically ran themselves after they got started, they still needed techies in the background maintaining the hardware and software as well as a marketing budget to get people to come to the site. Critical mass was everything.

In 1997 John Hagel and Arthur Armstrong of McKinsey & Company published a book that seemed to provide the answer. *Net Gain, Expanding Markets Through Virtual Communities*, published by the Harvard Business School Press, soon rocketed to the top of the biz-book charts. It posited that virtual communities weren't just good for bringing people together for social reasons. They were also good places to sell people stuff. Their version of the virtual community brought customers together into communities of interest, communities that would be drawn together by content and commentary and, by extension, would make ready consumers of the goods and services that bound them together. "Community," they predicted, "precedes commerce."

Like Seth Godin's later book on "permission marketing," it was one of those shockingly obvious (but previously unvoiced) concepts that struck a loud chord in the hearts and minds of New Economy visionaries. It made perfect sense: Get people together in one place, get them to talk to each other, fuel the fires with content, and then sell them things based on their already-indicated interests. Along the way, advertising targeted to the eyeballs of those visiting the site would provide a steady source of income to the host. Not only were community sites bound to be "sticky," keeping visitors enthralled for a lot more time than typical content sites, but ads could be targeted based on the topics being discussed on the site. Bingo. Instant business model. The race was on to build virtual communities in order to reap the expected commerce that would follow.

COMMUNITY RECEDES FROM COMMERCE

Actually, the first venture-funded experiment in community building was already underway and faltering by the time *Net Gain* came out. Founded by WELL ("Whole Earth 'Lectronic Link," one of the first

22 | the dot.bomb survival guide

virtual communities) denizen and visionary Howard Rheingold, author of the influential book *Virtual Communites*, ElectricMinds (www.minds.com) was launched after Rheingold defected from the WELL in 1996. Rather than taking the subscription model of the WELL, ElectricMinds decided to drum up revenue through advertising and the innovative technique of "inverse publishing"—selling ideas from the site's members to traditional media.

Seeded with $1 million and later gathering another $10 million in venture capital, ElectricMinds began to falter after SoftBank withdrew an offer of $500,000, spooking other investors. By June 1997, ElectricMinds was showing signs of running out of cash. Its advertising and inverse-publishing models had failed to bring in enough money to keep the company running, and Rheingold started to look for a buyer to bail it out. It had switched its business model to providing community services to other sites (foreshadowing a trend to crop up later in 2000, as ad-supported sites started to have problems), but even after landing IBM as a client, things looked grim. In July 1997, Durand Communications (which ran CommunityWare, another community/messaging site) acquired ElectricMinds for an undisclosed sum. ElectricMinds is currently "closed" due to "the shutdown of [its] current host, Webb Interactive." There's no word when or if it'll ever be back.

At the same time that ElectricMinds was on the way out, a whole new crop of community sites was just starting up, utilizing new business models and garnering investment dollars that made ElectricMinds' paltry $11 million seem like chicken feed. These new kids on the block would later rocket to stock market fame with atomic-powered IPOs and buyouts by the big portals.

The failure of ElectricMinds (temporarily) pointed out the dangers in relying on advertising . . . you had to sell a lot of ads to a lot of people to pay the bills. Achieving critical mass—getting enough folks to come back enough times to generate the necessary impressions for enough ad sales—was tough when you offered something that wasn't all that different from what folks could find for free on numerous sites, on AOL (as part of their fee), and on Usenet. Instead of competing with free services, these new community sites provided free access to something that had previously only come at a premium—home-page space.

Before home-page and community sites TheGlobe.com, Tripod.com, Xoom.com, and GeoCities.com came along, Web users who wanted a home of their own had to pay for Web hosting on their own or get it for free from their school or business. And since anyone who wanted to be anyone in cyberspace needed a home page, everybody wanted one. The free home-page sites allowed anybody who signed on to cough up some personal info, play with a few free tools, and soon have a site online indistinguishable from a site they may have paid for . . . except for the advertising.

Free home-page sites let users make a Faustian bargain of access for advertising. Users who hosted pages on these sites allowed them to deliver advertising banners through "pop-up" windows, framesets, or embedded banners. The community site got revenue through ad sales, the user got a free site. Everyone was happy, especially the investors. By April 1998 when GeoCities went public, half of the 10 fastest growing sites on the Web were community sites, according to MediaMetrix. GeoCities' IPO rocketed 120 percent on opening day, giving the site a market cap of over $1 billion. Later that year, in December 1998, Xoom.com closed up 145 percent on its opening day. But the big star that year was community and home-page site TheGlobe.com, which closed up 606 percent on its opening day in November—the second-largest first-day gain ever. Even though these sites were showing big losses (TheGlobe had lost over $11 million before it went IPO), nobody cared. In 1998, communities were the Next Big Thing.

With dollars like these floating around, the big portals started to get nervous. Envious of AOL's ability to hold on to customers by providing everything from information to community to commerce, Lycos, Yahoo!, and others were starting to view home-page communities as one way of locking in a permanent user base and attracting new eyeballs. Lycos was one of the first to buy in, snapping up Tripod.com for $58 million in stock in February 1998. It took a little longer for Yahoo! to come around, but when it did, it was big: In January 1999, Yahoo! acquired GeoCities in a deal worth $4.5 billion (yup, *billion*) in stock, a figure many analysts attributed to TheGlobe's stellar IPO.

A year later, at the beginning of 2000, the home-page and community sector didn't look very healthy. TheGlobe.com had gone

24 | the dot.bomb survival guide

through a disastrous attempt to portalize itself by adding content to its home page. It didn't work, and by the beginning of 2000, TheGlobe had returned to its roots, moving back to free home pages and community and licensing its technology to other sites wanting community. It was an attempt to turn things around by doing what it knew best. As cofounder Stephan Paternot told *ClNet* in a January 2000 article, TheGlobe.com had gotten into trouble by "trying to be a portal, and a mediocre portal at best. . . . What we can win at is if we're known as a community site. The real money generator here is in the long run, by signing up six or seven major sites."

In the meantime GeoCities wasn't performing up to its multi-billion dollar expectations. While the acquisition had provided an immediate 63 to 64 percent boost in reach, the payoff proved elusive. Most analysts, from Forrester's Chris Charron to Piper Jaffray's Safa Rashtchy, agreed that Yahoo! had paid a lot more for the personal publishing site than it was worth.

But GeoCities is now part of Yahoo!, the biggest property on the Web, and it is, for the time being, still holding up. GeoCities' had Yahoo! to fall back on—many of the others in the sector didn't. The Crash of 2000 wasn't so kind to many, devaluing Xoom enough to be swallowed into the greater bulk of NBCi and causing TheGlobe's stock to plummet to its current price, hovering around $0.19 per share and resulting in its delisting from the NASDAQ in April 2001. With over 80 percent of its revenue coming from advertising, TheGlobe has been particularly hard hit by the dot.com downturn. It has continued losing money, ending the third quarter of 2000 with a total net income loss of $16.6 million. In October 2000, TheGlobe laid off 41 percent of its employees in an effort to save over $4 million. In April 2001, TheGlobe laid off an additional 31 percent in an effort to save $8 million for the year. Finally, in August 2001, TheGlobe.com shut down its community and small-business Web hosting company, laying off 49 percent of its workforce as it scouted for "partners" or someone to buy what was left of the business.

While the big home-page, chat, and community sites labored under the yoke of trying to rake in huge amounts of traffic by appealing to everyone on the Web, other community sites cropped up hoping to corner niche markets, especially the fast-growing crop of teen eyeballs. These sites knew that they couldn't compete in terms of raw traffic, but the kid/teen market was pretty big and expected to get a lot bigger over time. How could they go wrong?

Kibu.com was probably the most ambitious. Funded in February 2000 with $22 million raised in part by Netscape and Silicon Graphics cofounder Jim Clark, along with Excite@Home chairman Tom Jermoluk and the Kleiner Partners venture fund, Kibu.com jumped into the fray in February 2000, going toe to toe with kids' sites Snowball.com (content and community network), Alloy.com (ecommerce), and Bolt.com (community and commerce).

While the competition was tough, all the numbers coming from the analysts seemed to point to a market that wouldn't quit. In 1999 consultancy Computer Economics predicted that there would be over 77 million kids under 18 by 2005. Market research firm Simmons had discovered that the number of teens online had doubled between 1996 and 1998. Jupiter MediaMetrix projected that kids would be spending a total of $1.2 billion online by 2002. NFO Interactive had even found that 52 percent of kids had asked their parents to buy something they'd seen online. The teen market looked like a sure thing.

Kibu decided to focus on what seemed the most lucrative part of the teen market: girls between 13 and 18. With high amounts of disposable income and (it assumed) a gregarious nature, Kibu's chat rooms and content were sure to draw in a highly desirable demographic for its advertisers. Higher ad prices and sponsorships were sure to follow.

Unfortunately, they didn't, and Kibu struggled from the beginning. In September (a mere 7 months after announcing its original funding), Kibu threw in the towel and returned the remaining money to its investors (Figure 1-4). Citing "Kibu's timing in the financial markets" as the reason, the site quietly shut down after launching kibupeople.com, a site that showcased the now-ex Kibu employees. Some thought the closing was premature and represented skittishness on the part of Jim Clark, who resigned from his board position at WebMD later that month. Others thought that the investors were overreacting. "The fact that they wanted their money back after a few months is telling in itself," whispered one anonymous backer to News.com in September 2000.

Figure 1-4.   Kibu Gets Sucked into the Dot.Bomb Blackhole

Why did Kibu go bye-bye? The official statement contains the usual excuses: "Unfortunately, Kibu's timing in financial markets could not have been worse. With public and private markets for consumer Internet companies showing no signs of life, Kibu's managers and directors concluded that Kibu's significant financial assets and employee talent would find a better return elsewhere."

Translation: We got in too late in the game to go IPO, know that we don't have enough cash to sustain us with what we've got, and the big boys want their money back before it is all gone. Oops! In reality, ad revenues and ecommerce revenues weren't adding up fast enough. Combined with the ever-popular "market conditions" excuse, Kibu was doomed.

SIXDEGREES FROM PROFITABILITY

But in the world of business models, few were more inventive (or more reviled) than sixdegrees.com. A prime example of the network effect, sixdegrees.com was originally designed to literally network everyone in the world together through the connections they had with other people. Based on the assumption (popularized by the "Six Degrees of Kevin Bacon" drinking game) that everyone in the world is within six relationships from anyone else, sixdegrees was started with a small contact list supplied by CEO Andrew Weinreich. Members of the list were asked to register on the site and add 10 of their friends to the list.

By September 1998, sixdegrees had over 1 million members, with 10,000 to 12,000 new people signing on every day. Though the service initially took hits on privacy issues, sixdegrees claimed that it provided only general demographic data to advertisers, the site's primary source of revenue. In April 1999, in an effort to add additional revenue streams, sixdegrees branched out into the new "guru services" market by adding a "servicefinder" auction. Here, users could list their services and allow other users to bid on them, and sixdegrees would receive a cut. It didn't get a lot of use.

Other attempts at diversifying its business model followed. An agreement with ShopNow.com in August provided sixdegrees' members with access to ShopNow's ecommerce engine to build their own shops on the site. Another August agreement matched Uproar.com's game shows with sixdegrees in a cross-promotion deal.

Life at sixdegrees was good. Up until the end of the year, sixdegrees had spent only a reported $150,000 on promotion and had actually taken until October 1999 to bother picking an ad agency. It was a virtual marketer's dream come true, a site whose very business model sustained itself, growing exponentially with each member and actually acquiring more value for its users the more people it signed up.

YouthStream Networks thought the situation was too good to pass up. In December 1999, YouthStream, a company that marketed to college and high school students, acquired sixdegrees for $125 million in stock, getting 3 million members and a major investment from News Corp. in the deal. The idea was to jumpstart YouthStream's embryonic mybytes.com teen community site with sixdegrees' traffic and expand the business through additional community and content features.This was quickly followed by a flurry of additional alliances and deals with other teen-oriented Web properties. YouthStream also began to work out a business-to-business model, supplying its software to outside clients looking for connection technology (supplied by sixdegrees) or community

28 | the dot.bomb survival guide

features in its ongoing struggle to make money. In the quarter ending September 2000, YouthStream posted a loss of almost $28 million on revenues of $10.8 million. It had consolidated sixdegrees.com and mybytes.com at the end of August to try to create "the ultimate college online destination."

During this time (perhaps signifying an increasing desperation in the company), sixdegrees started to turn up the heat on its members, badgering them with emails that were difficult (and some say impossible) to unsubscribe from. "Pure spam" was how one former member described it in an angry post on dot.bomb site FuckedCompany.com.

At the end of December, YouthStream was in trouble from its continued losses, losses attributed to site development and marketing of sixdegrees.com and teen.com (another site run by YouthStream). At the same time, YouthStream's stock had dropped from $32 in January to around $2. It vowed to drop its burn rate to approximately $1 million per month in the coming year and claimed to have $40 million in the bank.

Unfortunately for sixdegrees, these last-ditch efforts weren't enough. On December 8, 2000, YouthStream announced that it was "writing off" sixdegrees and its ASP business Sodalis in an effort to stem the losses from maintaining these businesses and returning to focus on its core business: campus marketing (Figure 1-5). Judging from the message boards on FuckedCompany.com, few people were sad to see the site go. Since it had relied on getting friends to sign up friends, many people had become upset over the years when their friends added them to the site's database, instantly making them a mark for the site's email advertising.

"Thank God these f***s are shutting down," read the first post on the site. "My friend (an AOLer, of course) recommended me to them like two years ago . . . I'm not sure if I responded or what, but I did nothing for two years; didn't order anything, didn't sign anyone up or seek to meet anyone." A common complaint among those who'd signed up for sixdegrees . . . including your humble author.

This (and another 197 comments) wrote the epitaph for the company that was originally designed to bring people together. Now, after 3+ years and millions of dollars blown, nobody was sad to see it go.

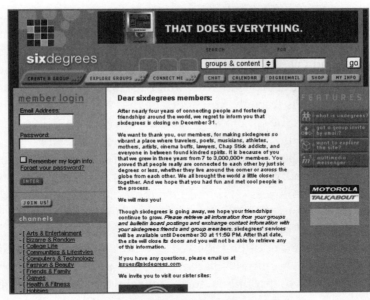

Figure 1.5. Sixdegrees Says Goodbye

CAN'T WE ALL JUST GET ALONG?

Building communities online is tough, as the dot.bombs littering the sector have discovered. Communities don't just happen when somebody puts up a site designed to attract users interested in a specific topic. Maintaining community means more than just maintaining technology. It also means dealing with human factors such as loyalty, trust, continued interest, and all the dynamics that go into building messy human relationships.

The network effect also comes into play, creating a unique chicken-and-egg scenario for many online communities. People won't post or contribute until they see others doing the same thing, and you can't get discussions started without people participating. Some communities like ElectricMinds employed trained online hosts to keep conversations going. "They invite people, they introduce people, they keep conversations moving," explained Rheingold when asked about his hosts in a 1997 interview, "and if there's trouble, they deal with it." The problem is that hiring hosts to shepherd the conversation costs money. And spiraling costs is just what brought so many online communities down.

30 | the dot.bomb survival guide

Getting people to contribute to communities is tough, too, especially when what they're contributing goes beyond chatter or discussion boards. A recent study by Xerox's Palo Alto Research Center found that 70 percent of users of the Gnutella peer-to-peer file-sharing system didn't share files with other users, and over 90 percent refused invitations to chat. Apparently taking is a lot easier than giving, and giving is the lifeblood of communities.

Many of these dot.bomb online communities died when they ran out of money. The expected advertising and ecommerce revenues never materialized to the levels that would support, in some cases, hundreds of employees and millions of dollars of development. Getting kids to buy stuff has become particularly difficult in a climate where kids' privacy is so zealously protected; in order to place an order, children are often required to enter personally identifiable information that requires a parent's permission. In addition, kids need credit cards to buy online, further placing another barrier in the way of easy ecommerce. Other communities built around commerce have had similar problems, finding that people who are there to meet and talk aren't there to shop.

Communities that have thrived, combining social interaction with ecommerce, have done so by addressing demographics that naturally want to combine content and commerce. eBay, for example, has had a stellar ride over the past few years, posting constant gains and unwavering profits for the past couple of years. And even with employing over 1,000 people, eBay's margins have been hovering around as much as 18 percent during the same time period. With 16 million registered users and over 4,500 categories of merchandise, eBay continues to stay alive, thrive, and make money.

Is eBay a community? You bet it is. Users interact with each other, rate each other, buy from each other, and even give back to the analog world community through charity auctions and other types of giving. Many eBay users stay connected to their community in real time through wireless and PDA auction alerts, living "in" the community as they go about their "real lives."

Why does eBay work? One answer may come from a study conducted by McKinsey and MediaMetrix in 2000. In their "All Visitors Are Not Created Equal" survey, the analysts identified six distinct types of Net users: *simplifiers* (those who shop for convenience), *surfers* (those on the hunt for new and exciting content), *connectors* (newbies who chat and send greeting cards), *bargainers* (users who like community and bargains), *routiners* (consumers of news and financial information), and *sportsters* (consumers of sports and entertainment content). eBay owns the bargainers: The study identified half of eBay users as belonging to this category.

It also doesn't hurt that eBay has huge brand recognition, some surveys placing it in the top three recognized online brands. Much of this has happened by word of mouth and through the press, as fanatical eBay users have turned on their friends to the bargains they find online, an increasingly important channel for new customers according to Opinion Research Corporation International (ORCI), which found that ecommerce traffic is particularly driven by word of mouth—more than any other consumer sector. It's tough to underestimate the impact that eBay has had on the Web at large—when Microsoft starts putting auction-tracking functions into its new browsers (as it did in a recent release of *Internet Explorer*), you know you've got a winner.

The future of online communities as a model is going to depend on the ability of the remaining communities to keep their user base up while looking for sources of revenue beyond advertising. Communities that hoped to be all things to all people—either through their connections to portals or through their own "portalizing"—are in for a world of trouble. In February 2000, a Forrester Research study predicted that the ad share of the portal market would drop to less than 1 percent by 2004. Some niche sites are continuing to thrive—just take a look at the number of users on many of the financial chat sites, and watch the impact of a few choice postings on a stock tip board as it sways the market—but combining community and commerce is going to be difficult unless these community startups can control their spiraling burn rates.

pay-to-surf

In the classic Ponzi scheme, investors recruit other investors with promises of huge returns. And there are huge returns . . . for the early investors who are paid from the money siphoned off of the suckers who get into the pyramid late. As long as money keeps pouring into the scheme, it can stay afloat. Turn off the cash, and the whole thing collapses.

That's essentially what happened to the short-lived "pay-to-surf" model cooked up by AllAdvantage.com and copied (in modified form) by several now-dot.bombs. An elegantly simple business model, AllAdvantage.com paid surfers by the hour to look at ads served up into a bar that stayed on their screen as they browsed the Web. The more time they looked at the ads, the more money they'd make.

But that wasn't all. Looking back at the virtual marketing successes of Hotmail.com and (at that point) sixdegrees.com, CEO Jim Jorgensen and his Stanford B-school cofounders added a twist designed to dramatically lower the cost of acquiring new customers: For every person that a member brought into the fold, that member would get an additional 10 cents per hour on top of the 50 cents he or she was already getting. In a classic multilevel marketing (or pyramid scheme) fashion, AllAdvantage.com would populate itself.

How would AllAdvantage.com make money? Two ways: advertising and selling the vast amounts of information it had collected on its members' surfing habits. Advertisers would be attracted by the company's ability to target users with razor-sharp precision, and marketers would line up to drink at the infomediary's unstoppable fount of consumer knowledge.

When it launched on March 30, 1999, AllAdvantage set a modest goal of 30,000 members in its first quarter. At an estimated average of $6.49 per month per user (for a total of $194,700 in payouts), profit should have been right around the corner. It had raised an astounding $135 million in venture capital from Softbank Capital Partners (and others) and looked poised to become the Next Big Thing.

It worked. Too well.

By the end of its first 8 months it had over 2 million members. Instead of the relatively small quarter of a million dollars or so it had expected to pay out, its member payments skyrocketed to over $40 million. Some members claimed to be making thousands of dollars per month because of their recruiting efforts (some turned to mass-email spam to build their "downlines"), though most members received between $10 and $30.

While money seemed to flow out of AllAdvantage at an astounding rate, income wasn't pouring in as fast. By the end of the first quarter, AllAdvantage had made less than $10 million in revenue. According to a Fortune.com article that called AllAdvantage "The Dumbest Dot-Com," AllAdvantage's costs per surfing hour per member totaled 60 cents, a figure "more than a television network gets for showing a viewer about 30 commercials," wrote Mark Gimein, "in an hour of TV."

The situation only got worse as time went on. At the same time that AllAdvantage was falling into financial ruin, the advertiser's budgets were falling, causing ad rates to plummet.

AllAdvantage filed for an IPO in February 2000 hoping to raise the cash to stay afloat. That summer was particularly cruel, forcing it to pull its IPO and reduce the amount it paid out to members. Before its collapse, AllAdvantage.com switched to a sweepstakes model, but the change came too late to lure deserting users from other sweepstakes sites that were seeing a huge boost in traffic (iWon.com was listed in the top 20 sites in September). By December, AllAdvantage.com saw its user numbers decrease from 2 million in June to just 547,000. It had laid off over 300 people in 2000 in an effort to stem the tide, but nothing was working. AllAdvantage.com was doomed.

On February 1, 2001, AllAdvantage.com closed its doors (Figure 1-6). No surprise to anyone familiar with the company. The *San Francisco Chronicle* noted its passage with a simple headline in its "Business Digest" section that read, "All Over for AllAdvantage."

Is the pay-to-surf model doomed, or was AllAdvantage.com merely a victim of its own success? Clearly, people like the idea of possibly making money by surfing the Web; sweepstakes site iWon.com was number 3 on AdRelevance's list of top properties in December 2000, clocking in with 2.56 billion impressions (third only to Yahoo! and MSN). Sean Kaldor, VP of ecommerce strategies for Nielsen/NetRatings, told *ClNet*'s News.com that he sees great promise for the model, provided it's done correctly: "Every site that's implemented some kind of sweepstakes promotion giveaway has attracted a lot of traffic. Greed in terms of gambling and sweepstakes . . . works very well online. [But] it is not easy to execute on that; not everyone does a great job."

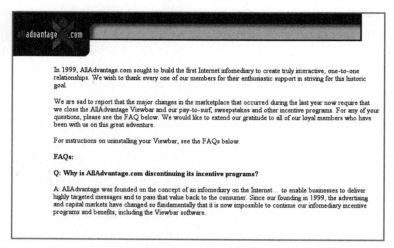

Figure 1-6. AllAdvantage's Goodbye Page

Across the board, Web ad revenues may also be on the way up, though not at the rates they were during the height of the boom. Forrester Research predicted in January 2001 that ad spending will grow to $63 billion by 2005 as more advertisers shift marketing budgets to the Web. As agency media buyers become more sophisticated, information offered by infomediaries may become more attractive based on the successes sites like Yahoo! and Amazon.com have had with targeting commerce and advertisers to usage patterns.

But do ads that are seen only by users being paid to watch them really do their job—namely, drive traffic to sites in order to create customers and build brand recognition? It's doubtful. Not only are many companies that require consumers to trade advertising access for service plagued by spoofers who use any number of readily-available software agents to fake usage (and make money or keep the service active), but the very model calls into question the value of the audiences who use the service. Advertising only works when it's seen by the right person, when it's targeted to the correct audience. If an ad isn't targeted, it's wasted. Unlike broadcast media, the Net can be an extremely efficient medium, delivering advertising and commerce to far smaller niches at lower cost than could be reached in other media. It's not just enough to have eyeballs . . . you have to have the *right* eyeballs.

finding the right model: lessons learned

For all the failures laid out in this chapter, there are plenty of successful new business models. As painful as it has been for all the employees and investors in the dot.bombs mentioned above (particularly the employees), each failed dot.com means another lesson learned. We're moving out of beta. We're shaking out the bugs.

We've probably barely begun to scratch the surface of the possibilities of online business. After all, the industry is only 6 to 7 years old. Television really took about 20 years to find its legs, and we're still discovering new ways to make it work as a business. Has the killer model for the Web arisen yet? Probably not.

But if you look at all the models that have worked, you'll see that they have one thing in common: They've provided the most value to their users for the least amount of cost, either psychological or financial. In addition, the ones that took off the fastest were the ones that made an offer that was both cheap and easy. eBay and Yahoo! are two examples: Both require little investment for their users and provide substantial value. On the other hand, if a model can hang on for the time it takes for users to adopt it, a high-value model that involves more substantial cost can survive.

Customer inertia can be a killer. Many companies in this chapter may have eventually succeeded had they been able to weather the storms of the markets until they reached a critical mass of users. They may have provided high value for their users, but the psychological or financial costs involved slowed their pace of adoption. While, of course, other factors (primarily marketing) can gravely affect the pace, all things being equal, people will first adopt what's most beneficial and least expensive.

This cost-value relationship is represented in Figure 1-7, "The Adoption Inertia Chart." Basically, the higher the cost and the lower the benefit of a new technology or product, the longer it will take for a population to adopt it. Business-to-business exchanges, for example, represent a high-benefit/high-cost proposition that will take longer to play out. On the other hand, a site like Yahoo!, which manages to be easy to use and free while providing a high value for its users, is quickly adopted by those who experience it. A site that has a high psychological cost (it's difficult and stressful to use) and a low perceived benefit (it sells things that you can buy at any local mall) may never take off.

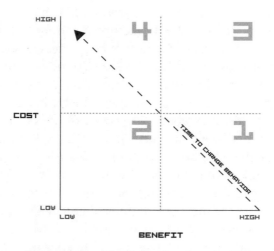

Figure 1-7. The Adoption Inertia Chart

While the play of cost to benefit provides the framework for discussing the merits of various online business models, it obviously doesn't tell the whole story. What other lessons can we learn from failed business models? Here are nine that take into account both the winners and losers in this chapter:

1. *It's not about the size of the market. It's the size of the market you can reach.* Remember the Chinese Soda story? While business plans built on estimates of garnering some small percentage of the market are seductively simple, they're also deadly for their seductiveness. Sure, millions of kids are going to come online. Sure, they're gonna spend billions of dollars. That doesn't necessarily mean that they'll spend them on *your* site. As many communities found out, building the virtual Field of Dreams doesn't guarantee that anyone will come. And even if you've got a huge marketing budget, it doesn't mean that anyone will come back. A bigger share of a smaller market that's actually reachable via advertising, marketing, and public relations is better than a miniscule target in a large population virtually unreachable without megabucks of marketing.

lies, damn lies, and business models | 37

2. *Grow organically.* Probably the biggest sin that most of the dot.bombs in this chapter committed was that they got too big, too fast. They looked at a datapoint that represented the sharpest point of the adoption upslope and extrapolated into the stratosphere. As websites and PC manufacturers alike are discovering, saturation can happen and the pace of adoption of new technologies eventually does slow down. Most sites thought that they had to be the biggest and the fastest in order to win the race to market dominance. Along the way they forgot that businesses actually needed customers and revenue to sustain themselves.

3. *"Internet time" is a myth.* Get over it. One of the most common expressions in the early days of ebiz was that "6 months of real time equals 1 year of Internet time." Just as Internet protocols compressed information for speedier transmission, conventional wisdom assumed that time was compressed. Things moved fast. The Web never slept. We had to be on top of our businesses 24/7, growing faster than our competitors who were clawing their way in front of us in a mad rush into the frontier. In retrospect, the concept that businesses had to be first or be dead was wrong. Many who were first are gone, some aren't. Many who came later are still around. In the long run, success came more from being smart.

4. *Beware the power of an industry aroused.* As Priceline and many independent B2B exchanges are finding out, as "old economy" industries start to wake from their lethargy and discover that their power is being siphoned off by brash young upstarts, they're going to fight back. Large established businesses have deep pockets and aren't as subject to the whims of the stock market (or, worse, venture capitalists) to fund new businesses. Hotwire.com is one such attempt in the airline ticket realm, and Covisint is the auto industry's answer to the various B2B marketplaces that tried to usurp it. If you've got a plan that means going up against a giant, be prepared to duck.

5. *Look for your niche . . . and fit into it.* The days of megaportals are probably over. Not only is starting one difficult and prohibitively expensive, but advertisers are increasingly looking for niche buys as they (finally!) come to the realization that the Web isn't TV. Niche plays that take advantage of a previously unfulfilled

38 | the dot.bomb survival guide

need in a tightly defined population are much easier to start and grow due to the natural word of mouth that exists in these communities. Selling advertising becomes easier too, but such advertising must be sold to advertisers that can benefit from microtargeted niches. But start small, growing the business to fit the niche rather than expecting the niche to grow to fit your burn rate. Ask ex-members of Kibu, sixdegrees, and other niche-based sites for advice on what *not* to do.

6. *Ask yourself: Can this be done only online?* Though it sounds intuitively obvious (and circular), the Web is good for business models that best work on the Web. How does the business that you run (or are planning to run) gain value by moving online? In the case of something like eBay, it's obvious: eBay couldn't exist without the Web. On the other hand, generic ecommerce models have a much harder time justifying themselves in this age of megamalls. Adding value through net-effected features like customer ratings (such as Amazon.com pioneered) means creating something that just can't be done in any other way.

7. *Investment is not income.* Yes, this is Business 101, but the stories of so many of the dot.bombs in this chapter show that a lot of folks never realized this simple fact: For a business to grow and survive, it actually has to sell something, not just be good at getting people to invest in it. Eventually those investors are going to want to get their money back. The only way that's gonna happen is if the company's worth something. That can happen only with actual customers and actual sales. If, like AllAdvantage.com, your model can run only when it is constantly infused with cash, it's a bad model.

8. *Inertia kills; change takes time.* One thing that folks touting "Internet time" forgot was that new models require people to change their behavior to use that model. Moore's law doesn't translate to people. Deeply held processes, habits, and cultures take a long time to change. If your model requires people to change their ways, be prepared for a long haul. This doesn't mean it's not going to work, just that it'll take time.

9. *People want things easy, relatively good, and they want them NOW!* There are reasons that, in our health-obsessed society, people keep buying prodigious amounts of fast food: It's cheap, easy to find, tastes good, and can be had in mere seconds. Trends

in consumer behavior consistently point to instant gratification and ease of use as defining characteristics of American culture. If you want to reach Americans, don't make them work for it too much. Don't make the process confusing. And get them what they've bought right away. There's a reason that OneClick ordering has made Amazon.com so successful. There's a reason that FedEx rules the delivery world. There's also a reason that Priceline is having trouble and WebHouseClub and Mercata are gone.

the customer? what customer?

> Profit? Are you kidding? We're in Amazon.com mode.
> —Stuart Skolman, founder of now-defunct video rental and sales site Reel.com

Of all the dot.bombs, none held as much promise (or exploded as loudly) as the ecommerce sites. On the surface, they seemed like sure winners. Take an affluent global audience with money to burn, and combine with a business model that seemed inherently efficient. Toss in 24/7 access, sit back, and collect the money. A store on the Web didn't require any employees to run the counters, or real estate, or building any buildings (heck, it didn't even require building more than one site!). It didn't even require any inventory—just take the orders from the customers, place an order to the manufacturer, and let FedEx take care of the rest. Credit card payments would eliminate the messy requirements of cash, and measurement technology would allow the Holy Grail of retailing—true one-to-one customization—to tailor the experience and the products so that each customer got exactly what he or she wanted. The Internet was growing at an exponential rate, and it would only be a matter of time before those that were first to market had things locked up. Sure, there'd be a buildout period when profits would be elusive, but with the size of the market and the ability to sell so easily, those that dared to dream big would be able to reap unheard-of profits.

42 | the dot.bomb survival guide

Unfortunately for many, things didn't exactly turn out that way. For too many companies, the huge sales projections and efficiencies never materialized. Even with the huge war chests they had assembled through venture financing and the capital markets, many dot.bombs simply ran out of money chasing difficult-to-find customers. Others, whose extravagant ad campaigns brought millions to their sites, had a hard time converting browsers to buyers. Many who had discounted the physical world of brick-and-mortar retailers found out that it was real-world requirements of shipping and fulfillment that was their Achilles heel. Still more found out that while computers could take care of taking the orders, the real people using their sites wanted real people to talk to when things went wrong. Those real people cost a lot more money than many dot.bombs had projected in their tidy business plans. Ecommerce turned out to be a lot harder than many people thought. The rules of retailing really hadn't changed . . . they had just been translated to cyberspace.

What caused the collapse of so many online retailers? For many, the excuse was "market conditions." In their waning days, most blamed the downturn in the stock market for their demise, citing lack of capital as their main reason for cutting their losses and closing up shop. Even after burning through hundreds of millions of dollars, many were still looking for that lifeline that would pull them over the hump and into the promised land of profits.

But was lack of money really the problem? Superficially, yes. Many ecommerce retailers simply didn't have enough to keep their huge operations running. But a lack of money from a stock market that had suddenly turned an unsympathetic back to their dreams wasn't really the problem. It was the symptom. Lack of customers was the real reason so many went out of business.

Simply put, the story of the big ecommerce failures has more to do with misunderstanding and mistreating customers than it has with business models or economic forces. Sure, some companies were run into the ground by entrepreneurs who wanted to go public, make a quick buck, and cash out . . . but we'll hear more about them in Chapter 5. The majority of ecommerce companies were run by people who sincerely wanted to run a business, who thought they were doing the right thing, and who believed in the dream. But they also believed that the Internet had changed everything. And that's

the customer? what customer? | 43

where they were wrong. While the Internet may have changed the way goods are sold, it didn't change the nature of the people who bought those goods. People were still people. And misunderstanding what people wanted when it came to products and services (or having no idea what they wanted in the first place) is the real reason so many sites went under. The story of the ecommerce dot.bombs is about the failure of knowing and serving the customer.

The reality is that ecommerce isn't about technology. It's about people.

the online customer

Who's online? What do they do? What do they want? Amazingly, that's some of the easiest information to discover. There have been scores of studies about Internet shoppers and their habits. Unfortunately (it seems), few etailers took the time to read them, and ultimately died. To understand what killed the dot.bombs, we've gotta understand who they were trying to sell to.

WHO IS YOUR CUSTOMER?

In the United States, the online population is beginning to look a lot like the rest of the population. According to *The UCLA Internet Report, Surveying the Digital Future,* a study of 2,096 Internet users and nonusers, almost 67 percent of Americans use the Internet either at work, school, or home (or all three). Of these, nearly all (78.6 percent) have used the Internet for more than a year. While the stereotype of the typical Net user is well-educated, middle- to upper-income, young-adult males, the truth is far different. Approximately 53.1 percent of those who use the Internet have only a high school education, and 60 percent of adults using the Internet have incomes between $15,000 and $49,000. More women than men use the Internet as a whole, though users between the ages of 16 and 45 are more likely to be male than female. Women with children have more access to the Internet; 70.2 percent of women with kids use the Net versus 56.6 percent of women without children. Of those that aren't online, the older they are, the more likely they are to say that they plan to get online sometime in the near future. Other studies report similar numbers.

44 | the dot.bomb survival guide

The Strategis Group estimates that there are currently over 101 million users online in the United States, a number slightly smaller than the UCLA study but still nearing 50 percent of all Americans.

Gaps still exist in the online population, particularly among inner-city African Americans. A recent FleetBoston survey of inner-city residents in Boston; the Harlem and Brooklyn neighborhoods of New York; Hartford, Connecticut; and Newark, New Jersey, found that 56 percent of adults with incomes of $40,000 or less knew little or nothing about the Internet, though most (80 percent) said that they'd like to know more. Only 42 percent said they had computers at home, and 32 percent said they had Internet access. According to this study, race is one of the main predictors of computer usage, with 64 percent of African Americans and 55 percent of Hispanics polled not owning a computer compared to 42 percent of Europeans.

Even though there are some slight disparities when it comes to race, overall the U.S. Internet population is pretty mundane. Internet users aren't the braniac technogeek rich wizkids they're often portrayed to be in the media. They're regular folks, with, it turns out, fairly mainstream habits and concerns who need to be treated the same way brick-and-mortar retailers have served them for years.

WHAT DO YOUR CUSTOMERS DO?

When it comes to what people do online, most of them seem to be getting work done or searching for information, not seeking entertainment. When the Jupiter Annual Demographics Survey (published in 2000) asked respondents if they considered the Internet to be a useful or entertaining use of their time, most (48 percent) said that utility was their main concern, followed by entertainment (36 percent). When Jupiter probed further and asked people what they were actually doing on the Internet, the most popular responses were using search engines, researching products and services, gathering info on local events, using online directories, and reading the news (Table 2-1). *The UCLA Internet Report* found similar patterns of behavior. People go online for information, interaction, and, increasingly, to buy things. They're not necessarily interested in flashy sites, fancy graphics, and entertaining extras. They're goal directed, and they're seeking utility over entertainment.

the customer? what customer? | 45

Table 2-1. The Top 10 Most Popular Internet Activities

Surfing or browsing the Web	81.7%
Using email	81.6%
Finding hobby information	57.2%
Reading news	56.6%
Finding entertainment information	54.3%
Buying online	50.7%
Finding travel information	45.8%
Using instant messaging	39.6%
Finding medical information	36.6%
Playing games	33.3%

turnons: why people buy online

What makes people want to buy online? While many etailers focus on price, service seems to be a big driver. A Bain & Company/Mainspring study in May 2000 found that most of the online profits were being driven by shoppers looking for brand or convenience, not necessarily price. In fact, they found that shoppers they labeled as "bargain hunters" were the least profitable segment of all. And while a Yankee Group survey published in August 2000 found that 39 percent of shoppers reported that cost was most important, 32 percent reported that service was the most important factor in making the decision as to whether to buy online. Jupiter's *Profile Management* report published in 2001 confirmed these earlier findings, reporting that websites where customers found features that made it easier for them to buy—such as stored personal info— and stores that focused on customer service had increased levels of repeat purchases. Clearly, customer service and ease of use are vital to ecommerce success, which is ironic in light of so many failed etailers' efforts to compete on price.

People don't tend to browse a lot of sites while shopping online. Instead, if they're browsing (such as searching for a gift), they tend to limit their searches to a few sites. During the holiday season of 2000, the Gartner Group found that 87 percent of consumers bought all their holiday gifts at only three different sites. David Schehr, research director for Gartner's e-Business Service Group,

46 | the dot.bomb survival guide

explained their findings by pointing out how goal directed online consumers are. "Consumers don't yet see the Web the same way they see a shopping mall, as a place to stroll, browse, and window shop in search of gifts," said Schehr. "Consumers continue to show that they use sites they are already familiar with, and in most cases for only those things they've come to expect at the sites. Other research we've completed shows that consumers don't usually think of the sites they use as one-stop shopping locations but more as specialty stores for selected categories" (*Gartner Holiday Survey 2000*). Clearly, brand recognition (or at least brand familiarity) matters.

On the other hand, if they know what they want, consumers aren't averse to getting out and shopping for the best price. Jupiter's *Fake It, Don't Make It* vision report points out that 53 percent of online buyers visit more than three sites before making a purchase. Its *Retail Differentiation* study found that 46 percent of buyers purchase because a site makes it easier to compare prices and products.

To surviving etailers, understanding the differences between these behaviors is vital. If people know what they want, they're shopping price (and visiting lots of sites to do so). If they don't know, they're going to limit themselves to a few sites they're comfortable with. For goal-directed consumers shopping for commodity items (books, CDs, software, etc.), price matters. Gift buyers (or consumers on a shopping spree for themselves) are looking for sites they are familiar with where they can consider brands they recognize. Both groups are looking for excellent customer service.

turnoffs: what keeps browsers from becoming buyers

What prevents people from buying? Privacy and security concerns are still a big issue: 91.2 percent of the respondents told *The UCLA Internet Report* that concerns over credit card security kept their wallets closed, followed by worries over privacy, shipping charges, difficulty in assessing products, shipping delays, and a lack of face-to-face contact. The experience itself is a big issue, too—in The Yankee Group's August 2000 survey of consumers, most people reported that they didn't buy because they couldn't determine the quality of the merchandise they were being asked to buy. And even if they decided to buy something, over a third ditched the sale because they had trouble navigating the site, and nearly a quarter bailed out when the site took too long to load. As we'll see later on in this chapter, the customer experience became THE big issue leading to the demise of several high-profile dot.bombs.

Ironically, while many ecommerce retailers sought to impress users and drive traffic through spectacular graphics and high-tech features, many of these features actually contributed to driving away customers. A Boston Consulting Group study found that four out of five online purchasers have experienced one purchase that failed due to site errors, 48 percent of which were attributed to long download times due to large graphics or other "extras." But were etailers listening? It didn't seem like it: dot.bomb MotherNature.com's CEO Michael Barach told *The Industry Standard* in July 1999 that "high-tech, gee-whiz stuff will do some things, but what really [drives sales] are things like bigger graphics."

experience matters

The problem with most of the failed online retailers is that they didn't sell enough stuff to enough people enough times. As we'll see later in this chapter, their expenses were always far in advance of their earnings. While the market was good, the engine kept running, fueled by seemingly limitless (at least for a while) cash from investors. A lot of that money was fed into infrastructure and operations: the site, the servers behind it, the shipping, the warehouse, and the employees to keep everything running. But, in most cases, a huge portion of the spending went to marketing, splurging on lavish campaigns to drive eyeballs to the site. Unfortunately, most of those browsers never became buyers. No buyers, no income. No income, no company.

As we've seen, there are plenty of reasons that people don't buy, but most of them can be lumped into the category of customer experience. And not just experience on the site—that's one assumption that led many dot.bombs to their downfall—but experience after the sale. Customer support, shipping, fulfillment, returns . . . all these

48 | the dot.bomb survival guide

things weren't always part of the neat and tidy, technology-driven plan. Ironically, that's what mattered most in the end.

CUSTOMERS AND BRANDS: IT'S THE EXPERIENCE THAT COUNTS

Big advertising campaigns were designed to build brand, defined by most etailers as name recognition. Having a "brand" meant that people knew who you were, knew what you sold, knew how to find you on the Web. But brand is bigger than that. It's a promise, a covenant between company and customer, and the sum total of the experiences that anyone who comes into contact with that company has. It's the feeling a customer gets that turns into loyalty and repeat sales. Brand has to be more than a logo.

Traditional retailers have known this for a long time whether they've said it out loud or not. The experience matters as much as the other more rational, tangible aspects of the contact between company and customer. That kind old lady greeting you at the door of Wal-Mart is just as much a part of the Wal-Mart brand as the smiley face in the ads or the big red letters in the logo. The experience of browsing unhassled among the stacks of a Borders bookstore is just as much a part of the brand as the name of the store. The way a customer service representative greets you on the phone when you call L.L. Bean is just as important as the look and feel of the catalog in your mailbox. The funky flair of a Ben & Jerry's ice cream store is as much a part of the brand as is the easily identifiable tubs of tasty ice cream in the grocery store. And the cool stuff that Virgin Atlantic hands out to its transatlantic travelers says "Virgin" just as much as the logo.

Brand happens every place where a company touches the outside world. That brand can be communicated in print advertising, on the radio, or in TV commercials. Brand is also embodied in the way a store looks from the roadside. Most BestBuy's would be identifiable whether or not the logo was stuck to the side of the building or not. The brand is communicated by the customer service rep that answers the phone or the clerk ringing up the sale . . . for good or ill. And brand is even communicated by the ecosensitive packing material used by shippers or the nifty little pads and goodies that Amazon.com throws in the box with many orders.

This place where brand is experienced can be thought of as the "Contact Zone," that virtual space that exists where company intersects with customer (Figure 2-1). Brand isn't a cute mascot, as Pets.com found out. Brand is the total experience.

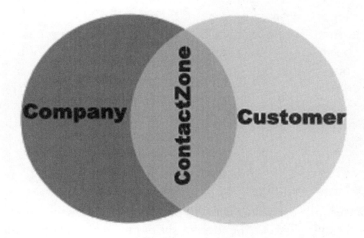

Figure 2-1. The Contact Zone

But nowhere is a brand communicated as clearly as on the Web. On the Web, your site *is* the brand. Unlike any other communications medium, the Web is the one place where all the different elements of your brand can come together:

- Customers experience a brand through the look of the site, by the way the brand is communicated through graphic design.
- Brand is communicated through the transactional, interactive portions of the site, such as the product search function, the shopping cart, and the product recommendations.
- The way products are experienced on the site also communicates brand. It's enhanced by superior product display and information.
- Customer service is also a big part of the brand experience. How customer service is handled via the Web says much about a brand to its customers.

Not every business understands this. I once sat on a panel at a conference where we were discussing brand in the digital age. One of

50 | the dot.bomb survival guide

the panelists was a nice young woman from a major Web consultancy who eagerly accepted a question from the audience. "How does your company handle branding on the Web?" asked a middle-aged man obviously trying to make sense of all this cyberstuff. "Very well," she answered, chiming up proudly. "We make sure that our clients' logos are on every page of their site!"

Yeah, right. When customers are loyal and become repeat buyers, it's not because they like the logo. That may be one part of the experience, but it's just one part. Overall, what drives customer loyalty (and profits) is a brand built of the superior experiences delivered to its customers. The only way to do that is to know the customers, understand their motivations and their concerns, and then address them head on. Only then do browsers become buyers.

THE ECONOMIC IMPACT OF CUSTOMER EXPERIENCE

As pointed out earlier in this chapter, bad experiences mean abandoned shopping carts. Abandoned shopping carts mean no sales. No sales mean no profits. A pretty simple equation.

An Activmedia study of March 2000 verified this when it found that overall, online shoppers are more concerned with the products a site sells and the site selling them than they are with the price of those goods. Sure, people want a fair price but not necessarily the lowest price . . . if that were true, shopping bots like MySimon.com would have put Amazon out of business years ago. What keeps people coming back to Amazon isn't necessarily price (though discounts certainly help), but the experience. Customers receive recommendations they can trust, on-time shipping, accurate inventory reports, and goodies thrown into the box.

The signs were there from the beginning. Back in 1998, ecommerce research firm Common Good estimated that the "customer experience gap" may have cost etailers as much as $3 billion due to lost sales. In addition, high-volume sites could reap as much as $10 million in revenue simply by upping the conversion rate one-tenth of one percent. In its *Holiday 2000 Online Shopping Report*, Common Good reported that nearly $15 billion would be lost during December unless improvements were made to customer service.

Loyalty is the key to profitability. Customer acquisition costs are usually fairly high online, but once you've got the customers, they can become profitable if they don't have to be constantly reacquired. Each time a customer comes back on his or her own volition, the revenues he or she generates reduce the cost of acquisition until, finally, the cost of acquisition is paid back and the margin on the sale finally becomes profit.

In retrospect, it's easy to see how bad customer experiences can light the fuse on a dot.bomb. It's not enough to drive customers to the site . . . that's the expensive part. The profit doesn't come until they've been back several times over a year or more. Several of the dot.bombs we'll look at later in this chapter didn't last even that long.

THE ELEMENTS OF EXPERIENCE

So if it's the brand experience that counts when it comes to making profits, and if that brand experience is made up of all the things that happen when the company touches its customers, what is the best way to break down that experience into its constituent parts in order to analyze what went wrong with many ecommerce dot.coms? In order to analyze the experience, let's break down the total customer experience into its steps:

1. *External brand identity.* The ads. The press. The goofy mascot. The first place that many people experience a company is through the media. How well that experience works influences if and when people decide to go to an etailer in the first place.
2. *Usability.* How easy is the site to use, to navigate, to find products, make selections, and pay for the purchases? Usability encompasses the navigation, graphic design, and interactivity of the site.
3. *Product selection.* What products are available? Are they in stock? Are they known brands? How much do they cost? Are there hidden costs? Questions like these go through the minds of consumers as they shop.
4. *Buying experience.* What's it like to buy? Can the transaction be completed without glitches? Does the site remember customers when they come back?

52 | the dot.bomb survival guide

5. *Customer service.*   Can customers get live help online? Is there a phone number and a rep waiting to talk to customers? How are returns handled? How can customers handle complaints?
6. *Fulfillment and shipping.*   Are goods delivered on time? Are they delivered at all? How? How much does shipping cost? From the time that the customer clicks the "order" button to the time the product is unpacked, brand is communicated through the experiences that people have actually had in getting the stuff they've bought.

All of these elements make up the customer's experience of an ecommerce site, and each one of these elements represents a point where you can turn off a customer. Each of these elements also represents a place where things can go *right*, turning that one-time customer into a profitable, loyal, satisfied customer.

dropping their end of the sofa: Living.com and Furniture.com

On the surface, selling furniture online looks like a sure thing. While it amounts to only 1 percent of the total furniture market of $201 billion, the online market was estimated to be over $2 billion. The customer demographic perfectly matched the affluent Web buyer: an average of 38 years old, 72 percent white-collar professionals with median household incomes of $77,729. And home furnishings have traditionally enjoyed high markups and traditionally good margins.

So why have online furniture retailers had such a hard time on the Web? Furniture.com blew through over $70 million in venture capital before shutting its doors in November 2000. Living.com spent all of its $41 million before dying on August 15, 2000. What caused so much money to be spent so fast for so little return?

The answer is customer experience—*bad* customer experience. While both sites were well designed and technically sound (at least when it came to serving Web pages), both suffered from severe problems with fulfillment, shipping, and customer service. Both struggled against the power of the manufacturers they needed so desperately on their side. Both struggled to sell items that were difficult to experience online and, as a consequence, difficult to buy. And both quickly bled themselves to death trying to attract customers by selling items for less than it cost to acquire and ship them. They both did a good job attracting customers—Furniture.com was, for a time, the most trafficked site in its category—but they had major problems holding on to them. Furniture.com and Living.com are our first object lessons in what happens when companies neglect to serve the people they need the most: their customers.

FURNITURE.COM: WHEN BROWSERS DON'T BECOME BUYERS

Furniture.com got its start in June 1998 when long-time furniture guy Steve Rothschild launched Furnituresite.com as a way to tap into the (seemingly) soon-to-be exploding online furniture market. His initial plan was to market his family's 50-year-old furniture company, Empire Furniture Showroom, using the Web to streamline his business and eliminating the need for inventory by allowing him to electronically submit orders to manufacturers who would then drop-ship to the customers. But the vision for the venture soon got a lot bigger than Rothschild had originally envisioned. Within 6 months, Rothschild had been replaced by Andrew Brooks, a 37-year-old marketing whiz from Bertelsmann. With a pedigree that included a Harvard MBA and stints at BMG Direct and Channel One Network, he seemed to be the perfect candidate to transform the little furniture company that could into the Amazon.com of home furnishings.

Immediately Brooks moved into action, moving the company's headquarters to a plusher neighborhood, overhauling the website, and raising more than $13 million in funding. He put the money to work immediately, securing the Furniture.com domain name for a hefty 1 million bucks. By June Furniture.com had launched a national $5 million advertising campaign, a figure that eventually exploded to almost $30 million as Furniture.com worked overtime to drive users to the site and raise more money.

It worked. CMGI signed on in June to the tune of $35 million, helping to bankroll Furniture.com's rapid expansion. By the end of the year, Furniture.com had pulled in 2 million unique visitors and had net sales of $10.9 million (but with losses of $43.7 million), rocketing it to the top of its category. By the beginning of 2000,

54 | the dot.bomb survival guide

Furniture.com was the most popular home decor site online. All signs screamed "big IPO!"

In January Furniture.com filed the papers for an IPO with underwriter Goldman Sachs. The company hoped the offering would fuel expansion further by bringing in at least $50 million. It seemed reasonable . . . the company was estimating over $20 million in sales for the first quarter of 2000. But perhaps Goldman Sachs saw the writing on the wall: Another big Internet IPO might have problems in a crowded marketplace. It pulled out right when Furniture.com started to run out of money, triggering a layoff of 12 percent of the company in April. In May 2000, with prospects for an IPO looking grimmer by the day with the market still reeling from the April crash, Furniture.com started to try to conserve capital by stopping payment to several of its creditors. At the end of the previous quarter, it had posted a loss of $3.1 million in total net income. Things didn't look good.

By June the company continued to lose money and Furniture.com was desperate for capital. Three executives and a top engineer left, and the company was forced to lay off 41 percent of its remaining staff—80 people. Just as things were falling apart, CMGI stepped in again with a $27 million injection of cash, and the company planned to get itself together again. It yanked the now-doomed IPO plans and prepared to retool. However, the losses continued to mount, and the investors decided to pull the plug. By September Furniture.com had racked up $22 million in sales. It wasn't enough. On November 6, 2000, Furniture.com announced that it had laid off 76 of its remaining 88 employees and would soon be shutting down for good.

So what went wrong? With all the eyeballs Furniture.com was driving to the site, it should have been able to convert more browsers into buyers. All told, the company had burned through over $75 million bucks from January 1999 until November 2000—enough money, it would seem, to keep most furniture stores alive for a good long time.

To find the answer to Furniture.com's demise, you need to look off of the site and to the part of the customer experience that happened after the sale—the shipping, fulfillment, and customer service the company offered.

Furniture.com was a "virtual" company in that most of its shipping and fulfillment was handled by the manufacturers who supplied the products. Dealing with more than 200 different manufacturers would have been a logistical problem in itself even if the systems had been working, which they weren't.

In July 2000 *News.com* ran a special feature called "Apart at the Seams," a hard look under the hood of Furniture.com. What they found was order-tracking systems so inadequate that there was no way for the company to tell whether items had been shipped or were still sitting in a manufacturer's warehouse. Customer service reps had no way to answer customer inquiries, and customers had no way of knowing where their furniture was. It's irritating enough when this happens with a $20 CD order . . . it's a lot more annoying when nobody knows where your $2,000 couch is.

According to *News.com*, customers were waiting a long time to receive their orders, some as long as 8 months. When customers called customer service to find out the status of their orders, the reps, having no way to track the orders, would have to feign computer errors, offer to give the customers their money back, or cancel their orders. Some Furniture.com internal estimates reported unsatisfied customer rates as high as 30 percent . . . death to any retailer.

Furniture.com knew it had problems and needed to get more customers. It started offering free shipping as a way of enticing customers, a move that ultimately led to bankruptcy. While small housewares items can be shipped via well-managed channels such as UPS or FedEx, bigger items such as tables, couches, and chairs often had to be shipped via specialized shipping companies at huge costs. Some items cost more to ship than what the customer paid for the item in the first place. Furniture.com publicly estimated that shipping costs amounted to 30 percent of sales.

Customers weren't silent about their problems, either. While it's impossible to estimate how many dissatisfied customers told their friends about their experiences, the New England Chapter of the Better Business Bureau racked up over 120 complaints during Furniture.com's last year of operation. Not a good sign for a company so dependent on customer goodwill (Figure 2-2).

Figure 2-2. Furniture.com's Bankruptcy Announcement

In its drive to build its business and sales, Furniture.com forgot the most important lesson of all—if you don't have customers, you don't have sales. In the end, few (except the employees) were sad to see Furniture.com go. Tim Mullaney of *BusinessWeek* listed the site on the top of his list of "bygone sites I'm happy to see go" in a January 2001 article on failed dot.coms.

"The lesson," wrote Mullaney. "Keep your promises . . . promises of customer service were writ on air: When I logged on to their instant messaging support line, I was on hold nearly long enough to read a copy of *Sports Illustrated*."

You can bet that most customers didn't wait that long.

LIVING.COM

Living.com's story is sadly similar to Furniture.com's. It was started by a father-son team with a lot of combined business experience looking to tap into the growing online furniture market. Father Andrew Busey had spent 37 years in the furniture business, and son Jay had already sold a successful Internet business before starting Living.com. They quickly raised approximately $41 to $70 million

the customer? what customer? | 57

(accounts vary) from investors including Benchmark Capital and Starbucks. At the time, these investors were enamored of the promises of streamlined operations and direct selling offered by the Internet. Amazon.com also signed on early, agreeing to list Living.com as its exclusive retailer of home furnishings in exchange for payments of $145 million over 5 years.

Unfortunately for Living.com, furniture manufacturers weren't as willing to sell directly because it meant undercutting their own brick-and-mortar retail base. As a result, Living.com was only able to sell about 20 percent of the manufacturers' brands most physical retailers carried. In addition, its ordering and fulfillment systems, which tied into their manufacturers' systems, were just as bad at tracking orders as were Furniture.com's. Efforts to improve the system proved costly. In a *New York Times* article about the company's demise, one manufacturer recounted how Living.com spent an estimated $200,000 or more trying to integrate its old system with the company's new Oracle database.

Additionally, Living.com was often delivering damaged furniture. Cracked tables, broken lamps, split headboards, and damaged desks resulted in return rates reported to be as high as 30 percent . . . a costly problem when shipping back a return could cost as much as shipping the product out in the first place.

Living.com died on August 15, 2000. Amazon removed the "home living" tab from its website menu. Two hundred seventy-five employees were out of jobs.

Even if Living.com and Furniture.com hadn't been plagued by shipping and customer service problems, the small selection of known name brands was probably a big contributor to their demise. Given the virtual nature of the Web and the perceived barriers to entry, many dot.coms still have a hard time convincing their users that it's safe to use their credit cards to buy online (a concern shared by 91.2 percent of consumers, according to *The UCLA Internet Report*). Well-known name brands provide a shortcut to consumers, one that says "Yes, the product you're about to buy is a known quantity . . . you'll get what you think you're going to get." While this feeling is a factor in sales of lower-priced items, it becomes a much bigger problem when delving into the confusing, expensive world of furniture. Unless people can buy a brand that they're confident in,

58 | the dot.bomb survival guide

they're not going to buy it unless they can bounce on the couch, try out the bed, or recline in the chair. The problem is one of information, information that can be gathered only from physical contact with the product. It's easier just to go to a local store where you can actually see what you're about to spend thousands of dollars on and buy it . . . even if the price is a little higher.

selection kills

Another etailer who suffered from a lack of brand selection was Eve.com, an online cosmetics retailer that actually prided itself for its lack of ties to major manufacturers. Cofounder Varsha Rao told *The Industry Standard* in April 2000, just 6 months before Eve.com closed up shop, that "it remains to be seen whether customer service will be truly objective if there's a brand behind the site," referring to Estée Lauder's purchase of Eve.com's rival Gloss.com.

For Eve.com, having a brand or two behind the site would have made a huge difference. Launched June 14, 1999, and founded by Ivy League MBAs Varsha Rao and Mariam Naficy and backed by superstar incubator Idealab!, Eve.com promised to "change the way women everywhere shop for cosmetics."

Starting with 50 exclusive brands and later expanding its selection to over 120, Eve.com combined content with commerce, offering professional advice along with content on the latest fashion and cosmetics trends. The site even signed on cosmetic artist Victor Longo to create a monthly makeover series. Eve.com seemed to have it all.

All except Estée Lauder, Lancome, and many other major cosmetics brands that make up approximately 70 percent of the total market. Because it operated without these products, Eve.com had to make do without such well-known heavy hitters as Clinique and Bobbi Brown, mainstays in the cosmetics business.

This didn't seem to bother the founders, who, after being dubbed "DotCom Divas" in a book by Elizabeth Carlassare of the same title, were quoted as predicting that "Eve.com's ability to secure exclusive deals with suppliers . . . is working to lock out rivals."

And the rivals were coming in fast and furiously. Estée Lauder purchased Gloss.com in April 2000, and competitor Sephora.com was backed by fashion-giant LVMH Moet Hennessey Louis Vuitton SA. Procter & Gamble also put its own stake in the ground with Reflect.com, a high-touch site backed by more than $80 million in venture capital. In fact, Eve.com was operating in a crowded marketplace of more than 100 online cosmetics retailers, according to NPD Group, a market research company that watches the cosmetics industry.

Expected sales never materialized, and by October 2000, Eve.com fell to its competition, closing down on Friday, October 20, laying off 164 employees. Eve.com would later sell its remaining assets to its competitor Sephora.com. The company's parting press release cited "fundamental industry issues related to product supply" that would "preclude the company from achieving acceptable levels of profitable growth in cosmetics alone." Bill Gross, Idealab! chairman and major shareholder, blamed the ubiquitous "market conditions" when asked about the closing in a November 2000 interview in the *Los Angeles Times*. He believed that it wasn't Eve.com's lack of known brands or sales that led to its demise . . . it was that nobody believed in it enough to keep throwing money at the idea (Figure 2-3).

Figure 2-3. Eve.com's Tombstone on the Web

60 | the dot.bomb survival guide

"Eve's closing is a very interesting story," Gross told *Times* reporter Karen Kaplan. "It's about how much cash is required to get to profitability and what the trade-offs are. We set out to build a business in the beauty area, and our goal was to make it the Number One company in that space. We succeeded in doing that, and the site was doing about $1 million a month. It's not that the company has fundamentals that don't allow it to get profitable. . . . The problem in this climate is that no one is willing to fund the company."

What Gross didn't say was that it may also have been about the size of the industry. While the total cosmetics market amounts to $30 billion annually, the NPD Group recently estimated that the total online market might amount to only 1 percent of that, perhaps rising to 5 percent of total industry sales by 2004. Hardly the stuff of Amazon.com-sized companies.

Like Furniture.com and Living.com, Eve.com suffered from a lack of brands from which customers could choose. And, like the furniture companies, Eve.com also tried selling items in a medium that has a difficult time communicating the qualities of the products it is trying to sell.

Cosmetics are all about aesthetics—the subtleties of color, texture, how it feels on your skin, how it smells. Like furniture, most people prefer to try cosmetics before purchasing them, hence the tried-and-true methods of providing testers and consultants behind department store cosmetic counters. Without knowing the brand of a tube of lipstick or vial of perfume, the experience provided on the Web does little to provide the sensory information needed by the consumer to drive the sale of a product.

Some cosmetics retailers have tried to solve the problem by providing prepackaged groups of products arranged around a theme or mood. Reflect.com tries to create custom cosmetics for users by making new users wade through a series of questions designed to match them up with their perfect fragrance. Questions such as "What kind of house are you" are designed to get at the soul of a user's personality. Other etailers (such as the now-defunct BeautyJungle.com) eschew straightforward and "boring" interfaces such as alphabetizing their products and instead lump them into "fun" themes such as "Elite Street," "Virtual Spa," "Nature Zone," and "Global Chic."

Does this problem doom cosmetics sales on the Web? Probably not, though those sales may have more to do with niche products and restocking of products that people have already purchased in a brick-and-mortar store (. . . unless a company knows how to keep its costs in line with growth—see FragranceNet's story in Chapter 6). As more and more brick-and-mortar companies come to dominate the Web—Wal-Mart, ToysRUs, Sears, and BestBuy all held positions in the PCData's top 100 websites in December 2000—etailers who aren't able to provide some sort of analog to the physical experience of buying may see their market share slip.

Experience matters.

the costs of customer loyalty

Getting people to come to a site is one thing. Getting them to come back is another. Since it costs money to get them to come to a site in the first place, it's logical to assume that every time they come back after that initial visit helps pay back that acquisition cost. Loyal customers become profitable customers.

And it's the lack of profits that killed so many ecommerce dot.bombs. Unlike advertising, ecommerce sites can't just survive on visitors. To make money, they have to translate those browsers into buyers. And the longer they keep those buyers coming back, the more profitable they become as customers. The value of repeat customers is significant; as much 53 percent of total online revenues comes from repeat customers according to Emarketer.

Bain & Company/Mainspring conducted a landmark study of the profitability of customer loyalty in early 2000. It surveyed 2,000 online consumers, asking them how frequently they shopped at various sites in three separate categories: apparel, groceries, and consumer electronics. The researchers then did the math to discover how repeat visits—customer loyalty—translated into profits. The results are very instructive, especially when seen in the context of some of the dot.bombs in the ecommerce sector.

What they found was that there was a direct link between repeat customers and site profits. They also found that it often took a lot longer than conventional wisdom held before a new customer became a profitable customer. For example, the study revealed that long-term shoppers of apparel not only were more profitable customers, they bought more, too. The average repeat clothing customer spent 67 percent more in the third year of visiting a site than in the initial visit. Tenure makes a difference in the grocery industry, too—grocery shoppers spent 75 percent more in their third year than in their first.

Yes, *years*. It takes a long time for a person to start spending the money necessary for a site to become profitable. Many of the dot.bombs in this chapter (and a lot of dot.bombs in general) weren't even alive for more than a year and a half. In this sense, it is possible to blame the downturn in the markets. Many businesses couldn't get enough capital to hang on long enough to reach profitability. Of course, this doesn't explain how such short-term thinking ran the companies into the ground. But it does say that the horizons for profitability were a lot further away than most businesses thought.

The same Bain & Company/Mainspring study actually identified the profitability horizons. In apparel, a retailer had to retain a customer for 12 months before he or she recouped the acquisition costs. Online grocers had it even harder—with smaller margins and higher operating expenses, the average online grocer had to retain a customer for 18 months before he or she became profitable. In "Internet years," that's a long, long time. Longer than many investors, spooked by the markets and hungry for profitability, were willing to stomach.

While businesses on the Net can take an extraordinarily long time to reach profitability, that time also increases the "network effect," as more satisfied customers refer more people to sites. Bain & Company/Mainspring found that satisfied apparel purchasers referred 3 other people to the site after their purchase . . . but after 10 visits they'd referred 7 people. Consumer electronics purchasers satisfied with their experiences referred an average of 13 people after they'd purchased 10 times. Long-term customers equal more customers and more profits—the formula for success.

To get those customers, you have to know them. To create repeat customers, you have to treat them well. Not only do you have to

the customer? what customer? | 63

know your customers, but you have to also understand how they buy and adjust your business accordingly.

One business that struggled with this since its inception in 1998 was Bigwords.com, at one time the top college textbook retailer online. From the beginning Bigwords seemed to understand the college market. The outlandish promotional stunts (which included dressing up employees in wacky costumes to canvass college campuses) and marketing know-how from major investor WPP Group (the owner of agencies Young & Rubicam and Ogilvy & Mather Worldwide) helped propel its traffic into the millions for some months. A cash infusion of $30 million from the group of investors led by WPP and NBC in June 2000 helped the site reel in over 800,000 users in August of that year. The money also helped it grow fairly quickly, moving into a new state-of-the-art distribution center in Kentucky during that summer.

One thing it hadn't counted on from the beginning was how cyclical the student market was—kids buy textbooks at the beginning of the semester. Sensing that sales weren't going to be as high as it projected (one employee told *The Industry Standard* that the company was hitting only 10 percent of its projections), it decided to evolve into a media site for college students with original content and apparel in order to draw a year-round audience.

But it was too late. With a total of $14 million in sales for 2000, Bigwords decided to shut down in October 2000. On its site, it blamed "the powers that be" and directed creditors to where they could file their petitions (Figure 2-4).

Low sales be the powers that killed Bigwords. The low sales came from customers who had no loyalty to the site—and no reason to be loyal. With a plethora of other college bookstores competing with Bigwords, including Efollett.com, which brings together 627 campus bookstores, students were shopping for the best price on what were essentially commodity products. Bigwords could get the users at the beginning of the semester, who were shopping for price, but it couldn't hold them. It spent so much money on infrastructure (so much that it had to lay off 100 workers in Kentucky during the peak of the textbook-buying season) that it couldn't hold out long enough to build up a loyal customer base.

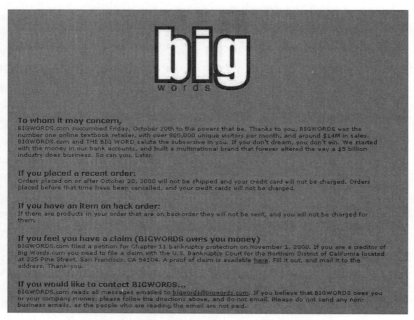

Figure 2-4. Bigwords Blames "The Powers That Be"

College students are loyal to their local college bookstore because, well, it's the *local* store. It's convenient, associated with their school, and right in front of them every time they walk through the student center. Not only that, but most college bookstores don't make their profits on books—most make their money on apparel and other items with the college logo on it. In fact, Sherry Natoli, marketing director for a company that's helped put 350 campus bookstores online, was blunt in her assessment of the economics of the college textbook industry during an interview in *The Industry Standard* in July 2000: "If the bookstores only sold textbooks, they could not stay in business."

It's the repeat buyers that keep those businesses running.

wireless: bonanza or boondoggle? ask the consumer!

It's been hard to miss the hype surrounding the wireless Web. Fueled by analyst reports that project huge growth in wireless Web users in the next few years, pundits everywhere have been touting wireless as the Next Big Thing. Analyst estimates have been exuberantly grand: The Yankee Group estimates that there will be over 1 billion global users for wireless Web technology by 2003; IDC predicts that wireless Web access will surpass desktop by the same year, and the Strategis Group predicts that 60 percent of U.S. users will access the wireless Web by 2007. Content providers and wireless carriers have responded to these lofty projections with a dizzying array of products. Most are information based: wireless news alerts, stock quotes, headlines, and updates. Others are more transactional: travel information, movie availability, and event ticketing. "*Mcommerce*," the term for purchasing and using wireless devices, has become the new buzzword du jour and is projected to become a $1.2 billion market in the United States by 2005, according to Datamonitor. Marketers have also jumped on the bandwagon with various schemes to push advertising, coupons, and location-based offers to consumers' cell phones as they browse the mall or shop in grocery stores.

Many in the industry see the potential of wireless as mirroring that of the Web, only now we know how to do things right. We've learned from the mistakes of the past, and now we are able to market and sell to consumers carrying the Web around in their pockets without committing the errors that have plagued so many on the desktop-based Web.

Maybe. Maybe not.

One of the major differences between the wired Web that we experience on our desktops and the wireless Web that we experience on our cell phones is the experience. While the desktop Web runs on high-powered, multimedia computers in windows that allow us to multitask, switching our attention between the Web and our work, the wireless Web is usually experienced on small screens using text-based browsers that require our undivided attention. There are other differences, too. Table 2-2 highlights those differences.

Clearly, there are big differences in the user's experience. In fact, the experience is so much different from the desktop Web, so limited due to technology, that Web usability guru Jakob Nielsen was inspired to call the wireless Web experiences "miserable" in a

66 | the dot.bomb survival guide

report published in July 2000 (see sidebar "Wireless Advertising and the Problem of Usability").

Table 2-2. Desktop User's Experience versus Wireless User's Experience

Desktop Web	Wireless Web
Average 17-inch screen size.	Small screen, 1.5 inches or so.
Multimedia capabilities.	Text only (in U.S.).
Multitasking: Users can do more than one thing at a time.	Users can view only one thing at a time.
Always on.	Users must initiate connection.
High bandwidth.	Low bandwidth.
Full control over experience.	Limited control over experience.
Messages can contain attachments.	Messages cannot contain attachments.
Fixed location.	Mobile.
Fairly well defined standards for data.	Few standards between phone manufacturers.
High hardware cost.	Low hardware cost.
Low ongoing costs (access priced at a flat rate).	High ongoing costs (charges by the minute).
One-to-many communications.	One-to-one communications. Users are used to talking to only one other person at a time.
Continuous access.	Interrupt driven. When the phone rings, the user answers it.
Simple data entry.	Cumbersome data entry.

Wireless Advertising and the Problem of Usability: A Story from the Field

In order to prepare for a talk on wireless I was giving at the ClickZ B2C Email conference in mid 2000, I went in search of wireless marketing success stories. After searching in vain on the Web for real results (I found plenty of promises but no actual numbers), I posted a question to ProfNet, a service that allows journalists to ask questions of PR professionals. My request was simple: Does anyone have any wireless case studies?

The silence was deafening. Even though ProfNet is read by thousands of people, I got no case studies. Sure, I got plenty of PR folks touting their new wireless tech, but when pressed for results, nobody had any.

That was a story in itself, and I wrote about it in my weekly column on the Web marketing site ClickZ (www.clickz.com). I titled the article "No News Is Bad News for the Wireless Industry." I wrote about how, despite the hype and promises made by the nascent wireless advertising industry, nobody had any real successes to talk about.

Now *that* drew a response! Within hours after the article went online, my inbox was flooded by flacks angry at me. "So I missed your response!" read one email. "That doesn't mean we aren't doing anything!" Most of the other responses I got weren't as kind.

Even so, when pressed for results, only a few companies ponied up the numbers. I received a tremendous amount of information from 24/7's European wireless advertising group that showed some promise. And then I got a lead from a guy in the United States who hadn't had such an easy time. This person was president of a large college marketing company who had recently partnered with one of the wireless ad serving companies to test out a promotion on college campuses. On paper, the promotion looked like a sure winner: College students were mobile, were comfortable with technology, had cell phones, and had cash to spend.

"It was a disaster," the company president told me. When I pressed him for the reason, he told me that it all came down to usability.

"Most of the kids didn't even know who their carrier was and weren't able to sign up for the service. And of the ones that did, most didn't know how to use the messaging features on their phones. They saw the blinking message light, but they didn't know how to read our ad. We're not going to do this again soon."

While the idea may have been sound, it failed because no one knew how to use the technology. Usability killed the sure thing.

68 | the dot.bomb survival guide

The wireless Web is different than the wired Web. Even discounting the physical manifestations of the experience—the screen size, the bandwidth, the fact that it's text based—the very fact that the wireless Web is mobile brings up a lot of issues as to what is applicable in this new context. If the experience of using the wireless Web is so different from using the desktop Web, why are so many of the applications being offered merely stripped-down versions of what's available on the desktop Web? Do people even want this stuff?

The Context-Based Research Group designed a study in mid-2000 that discovered what people around the world were actually doing with wireless and what they wanted from the experience. Rather than go out and survey people (like most studies) and find out what they say they do, it observed and then interviewed people to find out what they *really* did on the wireless Web. Tapping into a worldwide network of anthropologists, Context placed researchers on the ground in nine different cities in six different countries: Beijing, Hong Kong, Tokyo, Stockholm, Paris, London, San Francisco, Los Angeles, and New York. The study was designed to get a global perspective by going out to places with heavy wireless Web usage (such as Stockholm) and places where the wireless Web hadn't penetrated as much (such as Paris). Each researcher went out with a camera, a notepad, and a series of interview questions. They hung out in places where people traditionally used mobile phones—transition spaces such as building lobbies, train platforms, and airports. When they observed people using a mobile device, they watched for a moment to determine if they were using it for voice or for data, snapped a picture or two to record the context of the interview, and then moved in to find out what people were doing with the technology. In the end, Context collected over 200 hours of interviews with 150 participants.

While most of the promise of the wireless Web (and most of the applications being developed for it) seem to assume that what people want is more information, the data indicated that the opposite was true. In addition, the study revealed that the biggest barriers to acceptance aren't necessarily cost or applications but education, especially in the United States—people didn't know how to use the technology!

Overall, most of the applications and services that people around the world want from the wireless Web are far removed from the news headlines, stock quotes, alerts, and ads being proposed by the industry. The study found that what people want is directories and guides, information that they can turn to in order to get directions, find entertainment, or just a place to eat lunch. Many users across the world reported that they wanted to be able to communicate directly with their friends using text, a practice that's been by far the most popular usage of wireless data services in Europe to date. Additionally, many users expressed a desire to be able to control home appliances remotely, see and transmit video, and access the services they need when they're on the road.

But, above all, people want education. They want to know how to use the technology that's being handed to them. In Sweden, where the aging population was targeted by wireless carriers who promoted wireless through adult education and "edu-marketing" activities, usage shot way up and has received near universal acceptance. If wireless is going to take off in the United States, the carriers are going to have to know what their consumers want: education and guides.

Wireless provides an opportunity to avoid many of the mistakes made on the Web by ebusinesses, namely, ignoring the needs, desires, and behaviors of our customers. Rather than blindly trying to throw things at the marketplace and have them stick, businesses are close enough to the beginning of the industry to take the time to discover what people want. And what they want isn't more news headlines.

how to survive:
the four pillars of customer experience

If there's one thing to learn from the dot.bombs in this chapter, it's that not understanding your customers—and what makes them come back—is fatal in the world of ecommerce. Instead of just tossing up a bunch of features and hoping they stick, know your customers *before* embarking on a new direction. Clearly, if we build it, they won't necessarily come. To survive, etailers must focus on the four pillars of customer experience: adding value, providing information, building an effective brand, and providing excellent customer service.

70 | the dot.bomb survival guide

ADDING VALUE

Knowing your customers means understanding how the Web fits into their lives and not assuming that *your* site is going to become the center of their universe. Online shopping behavior is very goal directed. Unlike shopping in the physical world, the opportunities for enticing customers into impulse buying are few and far between.

Etailers must take note of this behavior and design ways to address it by adding value to the online transaction. That's where personalization and recommendation engines can come in. Amazon's system of offering suggestions based on user preferences or other shoppers' buying practices is a perfect solution, often driving up sales by breaking through the clutter of the Web to assist buyers in finding selections to their liking. Rather than being perceived as "selling," it's perceived as helpful, further enhancing the experience.

PROVIDING INFORMATION

It's also important to realize how little information people have to go on while shopping online. Bandwidth limitations lead to product photographs that are pale representations of the physical object. And while print catalogs can rely on the quality of the paper and production to add to persuasive power of the beautiful pictures, everything on the Web has the same "feel" in terms of the medium it's viewed through. Adding comprehensive product information, customer testimonials, and live customer support can help alleviate these issues.

BUILDING BRAND

Brand is important, too, as Eve.com, Miadora, and the various defunct online furniture etailers discovered. But not brand as status. Because of the limitations of the Web, brand must be seen as a way to compress information delivered to customers, as a way of communicating value. If people know a brand and what that brand represents, they're much more likely to spend their hard-earned cash on it than on a brand they don't know. It's this phenomenon that also explains why commodities such as books, CDs, and DVDs sell so well online—they're known commodities. People know what they're getting. The aesthetics, performance, reliability, and support for a

the customer? what customer? | 71

CD aren't the critical issues that they are for expensive items such as couches.

PROVIDING CUSTOMER SERVICE

Customer support after the sale is just as vital (if not more vital) than the experience that leads to the sale. Most ecommerce sites are not performing well in that area. The Gartner Group "Etail Eservice Functionality Study" published in August 2000 found that out of the top 50 sites surveyed, 100 percent failed to achieve a ranking of "excellent" or even "good" in customer service.

The economic impacts of customer service are difficult to measure. Estimates of the cost of customer service range from $3 billion in lost revenue (Bain & Company/Mainspring) to $6.1 billion lost to poor customer service (Datamonitor, "The U.S. Market for Internet-Based Customer Service"). That's a lot of money that many dot.bombs could have used to stay alive.

While there's no way to guarantee success, one thing is clear: If you don't have customers, you don't have a business. Knowing those customers and providing them with what they need will go a long way to getting them to come back long enough to begin making a profit.

fashion victims and supermodels: push, the first big web fad

> The Internet is full of fads, and I think push was the biggest of them.
> —Jim Clark, chairman and cofounder of Netscape,
> *San Francisco Chronicle* June 30, 1998

In 1996 and most of 1997, there wasn't a hotter technology on the planet than push technology. The media anointed it as the successor to television. Investors jumped at just about any startup with "push" in the business plan. Industry analysts far and wide told us that no longer would we have to search for information . . . no, sir-ree! In the future, "intelligent agents" and "knowbots" were going to scour the Web for us, looking for information we wanted, delivering it in tidy packages to our desktops. Push-tech applications like *PointCast* and *BackWeb* were going to keep us informed, 24/7, scouring headlines, reading the news wires, and delivering content in TV-like "channels" that we'd view through popups, screensavers, or continuously fed desktop crawls. Even Microsoft got into the action with its "active desktop" capability that was going to feed our desktops with Web pages we "subscribed" to on a continuous basis.

But push wasn't the only fad that went bust. Several others followed (or are following) in its wake.

Consumer portals were another early model touted as THE way to online success. Every site you entered wanted to know you, wanted your personal information, your content preferences, your favorite

74 | the dot.bomb survival guide

means of information delivery. In exchange for your personal data, you would be treated to highly targeted data sure to fulfill your every information need. News. Stocks. Sports scores. Industry info. Directions for dancing the *macarena* (this was a few years ago, remember?).

Free email was another big fad. After Hotmail's early runaway success, it seemed that free email couldn't fail. Who could argue with free? Soon everybody from your insurance carrier to your bank to American Express was offering free email accounts to customers.

Predicting the demise of television was another popular pastime in the early days of the Web. Pundits far and wide envisioned a time when animated shorts delivered over streaming media were going to replace the now seemingly content deficient world of those mere 90 or so cable channels you received with a gazillion razor-targeted streams of homegrown and commercial media over ubiquitous broadband connections. We're still waiting.

In the world of B2B, the idea of "disintermediation" may have moved beyond fad status and into religion. After all, it sounded great to cost-conscious businesspeople. No more middlemen. No more distributors. No more markups. The Net was going to connect buyers and sellers directly through online exchanges that took a salami-thin cut of the transaction as a kickback for facilitating your new global relationships. In the end, it turned out that the supply chain was a lot more complex than originally thought.

Free ISPs were another big trend predicted to revolutionize the way we used the Web. The proposition was simple: In exchange for a small piece of your valuable desktop real estate (onto which were going to be placed an endless stream of virtual billboards) and your vital data, you'd get a free Internet connection for as long as you wanted it. Unfortunately, while the vision was compelling, the infrastructure was more expensive than projected and the ad revenues a lot less than many hoped for.

And do you remember when everyone was going to fire their IT staffs and trust all their enterprise applications to application service providers (ASPs) in distant locales? Save time! Save money! It's the future!

If there's one thing the Net industry's been susceptible to since the beginning, it's fads. While the push craze was one of the most visible (and fast-burning) fads to hit cyberspace, there are plenty of other hype-fueled, fad-driven ventures around today. So why have so many smart folks gotten caught up in the throes of fashion, throwing good money and talent on ideas that seem bonkers in the cold hindsight that time (and a slumping stock market) has granted us? Stupidity? Lack of business sense? Mass hypnosis? Aliens?

Blame Netscape.

As noted earlier, Netscape's IPO hit the world of technology and finance like a bomb. All of a sudden, something that seemed like a neat (if geekily niche) idea was making millionaires out of 20-something nerds. Who could have foreseen it? Not the analysts. A mere 6 months before, people were still questioning whether or not the Internet would ever catch on and questioning the validity of a company with no revenues that gave its software away for free. Not the VCs, though you'd better believe that the Netscape IPO was a major wakeup call. And not the public. To most of them, the Internet was still something that their weirdo tech friends played with. Netscape's IPO turned everything upside down. Suddenly, if one unknown, nutty idea could make gobs of money, who was to say that The Next Big Crazy Idea wouldn't?

the difference between a fad and a revolution

In some ways, the story of the Web biz is the story of fads and fashion. Somebody would have an idea, somebody would be nuts enough to fund it, it'd hit big, and other investors, inventors, dreamers, and entrepreneurs would look to see how they could cash in. Sometimes it would flop. Other times, the "fad" would revolutionize the way we live.

By definition, fads are short-lived, much-hyped themes that start small, make a big splash, and then quickly go away. Revolutions change the world and keep going. The question for all of us, whether we're starting a new venture, funding one, going to work for one, or just trying to determine whether or not to invest our hard-earned dough in one, is how to tell a fad from a revolution. How do we fine-tune our radar to differentiate hype from reality?

As we'll see in this chapter, companies that were born in fads and narrowly averted failure often morphed into successes . . . slowly. In

76 | the dot.bomb survival guide

fact, once the limelight faded, many of the surviving companies in this chapter have continued to develop revolutionary technologies. They focused on what they do well and they re-tooled, and they are ready to provide a framework for some evolutionary advances. And the ones that died provide object lessons in what happens in the world of fashion victims.

kill your tv

In all fairness, few folks at the time had any reason to doubt that push technology was going to be the Next Big Thing. It made a lot of sense. At the end of 1996, The Yankee Group predicted that Internet Broadcasting would bring in $5.7 billion in revenues by 2000, though only $10 million had been realized by early 1997. Never a publication to shun technohype, *Wired*'s breathless predictive cover story "Push!" in March 1997 (*Wired* 5.03) was, in retrospect, both a stunning example of the folly of overreacting to a short-term boom fed by a new technology and a remarkably prescient view of many of the forces still shaping the Net today. The boom in push technology brought about in part by media hype and the explosive success (and subsequent implosion) of companies like PointCast provides a good example of what can happen when technology becomes fad . . . an industry jumps on the bandwagon.

In late 1996 and early 1997, *Wired* wasn't alone in its advocacy of the new push technology. Much of the business press, just starting to catch the Internet fever, began to tell us that the first big breakthrough in the commercialization of the Internet had arrived, and its name was "push." Noting how push's broadcast model was similar to TV, *The Wall Street Journal* trumpeted the arrival of push technology by declaring that the Internet "has been a medium in search of a viable business model. Now it has found one: television." Soon after, the *Houston Chronicle* called push "a fundamental shift that promises to spur the development of electronic commerce and re-shape the balance of power in the technology and media industries."

Essentially, push reversed the metaphor of the Internet (one where users *pulled* information from websites by pointing, clicking, and following links) and turned it into something a lot more like television . . . something we were all used to and for which there was a proven business model.

Push brought the Web to you. Instead of typing URLs and chasing after information, data would automatically come to you based on your preferences and location. Forget about searching in vain for distributed information on the Web—push would bring it to you through your TVs, cell phones, cars, Internet appliances, and pagers. It was to be the revolution that would finally propel the Net out of the realm of technophiles and geeks and into the lives of every consumer. Advertisers were going to love it for its pervasive reach and accountability; consumers were going to love it for its effortless stream of useful information, and business was going to love its amazing breadth of applications. Marrying the boundless connectivity of the Net (with its ability to microtarget users) with the couch-potato-friendly semirecumbent ease of television, push was going to change everything.

Kevin Kelley and Gary Wolf, authors of the "Push!" article, described a whole taxonomy of push:

1. *Push-pull media.* Push media selected by the user in response to a current task:

    In the middle of wandering through a Web site on Eskimos, you suddenly switch to push and watch *Nanook of the North.* Or while doing a spreadsheet for next year's budget, you get interrupted with an on-the-spot packaged report of an oil spill in Chesapeake Bay. Or while zoning out with *ER,* you suddenly wonder if you too might have rickets, and so you click on the button in the corner of the screen to pull up an autodiagnostic questionnaire on the disease. This is push-pull media. ("Push!" *Wired* 5.03.)

2. *Low-intensity networked media.* Media that interact with current conditions or with the position of the user to subtly offer information, suggestions, or help:

    You are standing on a street corner in an unfamiliar city where you are attending a convention. On your PDA, you stare at a map of a city. It looks like rain. The weather icon starts blinking. Droplets pepper your glasses. On the map, tiny umbrella icons appear showing stores within a two-block radius that sell rain gear. This carefully tailored mix of instruction and mer-

78 | the dot.bomb survival guide

chandising is environmental push media. Low-intensity networked media. ("Push!" *Wired* 5.03.)

3. *Always-on networked media.* Accessed through a TV-like client that displays a constantly changing stream of data:

You are in your study, answering email from the office, when you notice something happening on the walls. Ordinarily, the large expanse in front of you features a montage generated by SCI-VIZ—a global news feed of scientific discoveries, plus classic movie scenes and 30-second comedy routines. You picked this service because it doesn't show any of the usual disaster crap, yet the content is very lively, a sort of huge screensaver. Which you usually ignore. But just now you noticed a scene from your hometown, something about an archaeological find. You ask for the full video. This is always-on, mildly in-your-face networked media. ("Push!" *Wired* 5.03.)

4. *Ambient push media.* Information supported by advertising that appears in many or all of the media technologies we use:

You are driving your car, using the heads-up map display on the windshield to find your way around a strange city. It works wonderfully, helping you get to your appointment on time. Real-time display is expensive, but you're not paying for it. It's "free." You pay by renting a little piece of your brain to the Krakatoa HeadsUp Advertising Corporation, which beams clever poetic messages twice an hour. They are little rhymes, and no matter how hard you try, you cannot get them out of your head. But they beat getting lost, and the maps are detailed beyond belief. Including weather reports. This is ambient, low-intensity push media. ("Push!" *Wired* 5.03.)

5. *Intense networked push media.* Passive information and/or entertainment that we sit and watch—basically, TV activated by a link:

You are skipping through footnote links, researching the diaries of impressionistic painters, when you come across the letters of van Gogh's brother, Theo. The next link holds the documentary film *Vincent*, a feature-length saga about the painter's last years based on his accounts. You click. An hour and a half (and US$3) later you resume surfing. This is intense networked push media—for that 90 minutes, you did not steer at all. ("Push!" *Wired* 5.03.)

6. *Immersive push media.* Information/entertainment we watch, delivered based on preferences or the actions of an intelligent agent:

> You sit down at your big screen and send your bot out to the DreamWorks server. Give me something 45 minutes long, you tell it. Something funny. You know what I like. Something I can interrupt while I make some phone calls. OK, start. This is in-your-face, immersive, experiential push media. ("Push!" *Wired* 5.03.)

The ideas outlined above make sense. What went wrong?

The hype-gap killed push. As the first big Internet fad to go bust, push set the pattern for many of the now-dead fads to follow:

1. Visionaries imagine a technology that uses the Internet in a totally new way.
2. Entrepreneurs and engineers develop technology demonstrations and build business plans around these ideas. Investors, always looking for the next Netscape, pour in money.
3. Following the first-to-market mantra, barely beta versions of these products are released via the Net to an eagerly awaiting consumer marketplace.
4. Early adopters, drawn to the lure of the new and correctly recognizing the potential, eagerly download and install the software.

The industry is in motion:

5. Pundits and members of the press (often neophiles and visionaries themselves) write glowing reviews of the technology and prognosticate that this Next Big Thing is going to change the world.
6. Advertisers, eager to find a new channel to the public, jump onboard.
7. Content providers see a new opportunity and start retooling to take advantage of the new tech.
8. Regular folks jump on the bandwagon next, spurred into action by a fear of falling behind, technoenvy for their early adopter friends, and glowing stories in the press.

80 | the dot.bomb survival guide

Then the problems start:

9. The technology doesn't work as promised.
10. Sloppy beta-version code crashes computers and browsers, and other technological problems crop up during the public beta test.
11. Consumers, brought up in a world where products worked or were quickly returned, begin to uninstall the unstable software and spread bad word of mouth. Many realize that they never really needed this stuff in the first place.
12. The media, stung by their embarrassing early endorsement, begin writing backlash articles.
13. Investors pull out.
14. Early capital dwindles, burned away in a furious rush to be first.
15. Advertisers look for greener pastures.
16. Revenue falls.
17. The industry falters.
18. Those that survive begin to retool their business models and issue press releases about their new "strategic direction."

Some make it. Many don't, dying an untimely death as funding runs out or merging with bigger, more established companies in a frenzy of consolidation.

As we look back now with 20/20 hindsight, it's easy to see this pattern repeated over and over again during the history of the Web. But to truly understand how these kinds of fads can sweep an industry, we need to look at PointCast, probably the first beneficiary (and later victim) of fads played out on Internet time.

PointCast

PointCast began in 1992 as PED Software Corporation, a company that sold a product called *Journalist* that allowed CompuServe and Prodigy members to create their own newspapers from a variety of online information sources. But it wasn't until February 1996 that PointCast leapt into the spotlight with the release of the *PointCast*

Network (PCN), an application that allowed users to specify content "channels" and receive constant news updates via the Internet.

Hot off the blocks, PointCast was backed by some major industry heavies. Netscape founder Marc Andreessen accompanied PointCast chairman Chris Hasset to the kickoff press conference, vowing to modify the next version of the Netscape browser to work with PointCast's software. EDS signed on as an early partner, along with content providers from CMP Publications to *The Boston Globe*. Advertisers were eager to sign up, too—the first version of *PointCast* debuted with ad agreements with Twentieth Century Fox, Fidelity Investments, and Saturn.

PointCast 1.0 featured six channels of content: News, Companies, Industries, Weather, Sports, and Lifestyles. Once the software was installed in a personal computer, it would periodically query the main *PointCast* server and pull information down to a customized screensaver/client application. Up-to-the-minute information was also pushed to the program, providing constantly updated stocks, sports scores, celebrity sightings, and weather reports.

From the beginning, *PointCast* represented a radical break from the traditional Web paradigm. Rather than displaying information in a browser, *PointCast* depended on its own client application to display information in a format that very much looked like Bloomberg TV today. Headlines provided links to full articles, moving news tickers provided a constant stream of data, and multimedia areas provided a more television-like experience for both viewers and advertisers. *PointCast* looked like something that was going to change the world . . . exactly what its creators set out to do (Figure 3-1).

"The *PointCast Network* represents the natural marriage of broadcast and the personal computer," said Christopher Hassett, in an initial press release. "We've combined the power of the Internet with the convenience of broadcast news to give users current, personalized news and information without wasting valuable time searching, surfing, and sifting through the Internet. This is the news format for the 21st century." In a later *Los Angeles Times* article, Hassett even went so far as to say that the service, targeted mainly to professionals at work, "makes you a more valuable employee to your company."

82 | the dot.bomb survival guide

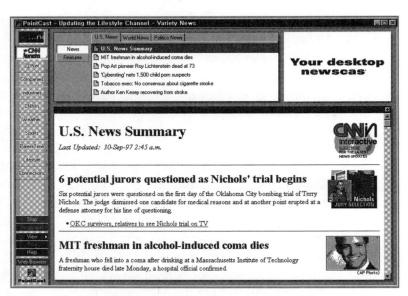

Figure 3-1. *PointCast*'s Revolutionary Interface

To advertisers (the companies who were going to supply the revenue to keep PCN in operation), the message was broadcast. This thing wasn't that geeky, scary Web browser that people were still nervous about. Your ads didn't have to look like low-budget postage-stamp banners. Heck, people didn't even have to *go* to *PointCast* to see your ads: If they weren't using their computer, content would just pop up on the screen! Nope, this was the first wave of convergence that was going to change the way that we used the Web.

The tech world loved it. Dave Winer, a columnist for *Wired*, called *PointCast* "the most compelling application I've ever seen for a personal computer." Andreessen promised that *PointCast* "would take the Internet to new levels." *Ad Week* lauded *PointCast* for "taking advertising beyond the online banner." Some pundits even saw *PointCast*'s model as the one destined to make money. Stephen Lynch, of the *Orange County Register* predicted, "Don't think *PointCast* isn't making money. The animated format is perfect for short, silent movie advertisements while the news rolls, and small logos tell you who—from Prodigy to Quarterdeck—sponsored the service today. Not exactly inventing the wheel, but at least it will keep PCN rolling."

Users ate it up. While PointCast's higher-ups had predicted they'd have a million viewers by the end of 1996, it only took until August before they'd topped the 1 million mark, gaining as many as 250,000 new users per month. Noticing the rapidly expanding medium, advertisers were ponying up as much as $50,000 per month for a spot, making a revenue stream of $2.5 million per month a distinct possibility.

Investors were eager to jump on what looked like the next Netscape. By August, heavy-hitters such as GE Capital, Knight-Ridder, Times Mirror, Adobe, and Compaq (led by Morgan Stanley) had committed to $36 million in financing, an amount that seems amazingly small today for a company enjoying as much hype as PointCast.

Competitors started to get worried, too. By the third quarter of 1996, Microsoft announced that it was developing a similar technology (which later became *ActiveDesktop*), and Berkeley Systems (publishers of the then-ubiquitous *Flying Toasters* screensaver) announced plans to jump into the fray with its own push-technology screensaver. Other companies like Intermind, Tierra, Sourcecraft, MyWay, and iFusion (all now out of business) followed suit with their own versions of push technology.

And then the Monday Morning Syndrome hit.

All over the country, corporate networks were being brought to their knees every Monday morning when *PointCast* users returned to work, fired up their computers, and began to download the *PointCast* updates they'd missed over the weekend. Over 70 percent of *PointCast*'s users were on office networks (a good thing, too, when updates over a 28.8 modem could take as long as 30 minutes) and companies began to notice the drain that *PointCast* put on their infrastructure and on their employees.

"It's the Web site from hell," complained an anonymous IS manager from a large database company in the San Francisco Bay area when interviewed for an October 1996 article on *PointCast* in *The San Francisco Examiner.* "It's mesmerizing for users and counter-productive for our infrastructure."

Corporate America began to respond to the pressure. Hewlett-Packard initially "discouraged" the use of *PointCast* on its internal networks and later banned it, a move followed by many other com-

84 | the dot.bomb survival guide

panies. PointCast responded by tightening up its network code and releasing a network proxy server called *iServer* in October 1996, billing it as "the first broadcast system for corporate intranets." It never really caught on.

But these problems, and repeated consumer reports of software crashes, didn't dampen PointCast's push for glory. By May 1998 it had filed with the SEC for a July IPO led by Lehman Brothers, Inc., BT Alex. Brown, and BancAmerica Robertson Stephens, intending to sell up to 4.3 million shares at an initial price of $11 per share. This would raise an initial market capitalization of $235 million.

The IPO was a gamble. Earlier in 1997, NewsCorp had tendered an offer of $400 to $450 million for PointCast. But the market was hot, and PointCast had been pulling in millions of dollars a quarter in ad revenue, though by the time of its SEC filing, revenues were down to $5.1 million from $7 million the previous quarter.

There were other, more insidious problems, too. PointCast's churn rate was at 100 percent by the time it filed for its IPO, as it lost as many users per month as it gained new ones. Investment Guru Adam Lashinsky reported that most users who left were doing so after 3 months because of poor performance and reliability.

PointCast knew it had a problem, too. In its IPO filing, it noted that the churn rate would be an issue in continued growth and profitability: "The failure by the company to reduce attrition levels and increase its installed viewer base would have a material adverse effect on the company's ability to increase advertising revenues, which would have a material adverse effect on the company's business, financial condition and results of operations."

With all of these issues, an initial public offering began to look like a no-go. On July 15, 1998, PointCast pulled its IPO. It had accumulated $58.6 million in losses and reported that it would keep losing money "for the foreseeable future." PointCast reported that it would seek "partnerships" to stay alive.

While PointCast was pulling its IPO, other Net companies were going through the stratosphere. Broadcast.com's IPO rose over 200 percent, temporarily giving it a market cap of over $1 billion (even though it had lost $6.5 million on $6.9 million in revenue by the time of the IPO). Search engine maker Inktomi raised over 275 percent from its opening price. VeriSign tripled its offering price, rising from fashion victims and supermodels | 85

$14 to $42.50, and ISP Exodus saw its shares jump from $15 to $42.94.

All of a sudden, push, the darling of the press a year ago, was seen as a has-been, a failed technology that was fundamentally flawed from the start. Touted as the new paradigm when it began, PointCast was now seen as missing the paradigm shift entirely. "You use it for a few weeks, and then you get bored with it. The Internet paradigm is pull, not push," observed Jupiter analyst Patrick Keane, summing up PointCast's problems in an August 1998 *Rocky Mountain News* article. In the same article another analyst, Ira Machefsky of Giga Information Group, pointed out the folly of PointCast's earlier rejection of NewsCorp's offer of $400+ million. "They were stupid to turn that down . . . I don't know what they were smoking then."

PointCast began looking for partners to pull it out of its slide. It soon settled on a consortium of Baby-Bells, a group it was led to by new CEO David Dorman, ex-CEO of Pacific Bell. Soon, plans were drawn up for a broadband service to compete with AtHome, a service tentatively called "Newnet" and funded by the likes of Microsoft, US West, Bell Canada, Bell South, and Bell Atlantic. The group intended to invest $400 million in the service, purchasing PointCast for $100 million for use as a consumer-friendly front-end. The players signed a letter of intent on December 16, 1998, and the partners set a launch date of April 1999 for the service. They also sunk $15 million into PointCast to keep it afloat in the meantime.

The year 1999 arrived with little progress. Impatient with the delay (and eyeing the future in WebTV), Microsoft ditched the group. The rest of the group tried to get SBC Communications to join, in order to fill the gap, but it never happened. At the beginning of March, Dorman bailed. By mid-March the partners declared the deal dead. In April PointCast laid off 220 employees.

In May, Idealab! entrepreneur Bill Gross stepped in when Launchpad Technologies (a startup funded by Idealab!) acquired PointCast for $7 million in cash and stock. By August, LaunchPoint debuted its first product with *PointCast* technology, a toolbar called *EntryPoint* that delivered news, stocks, and weather to users' screens. A far cry from PointCast's 4-megabyte, computer-hogging application, *EntryPoint* is a 700K application that behaves itself with other desktop applications.

86 | the dot.bomb survival guide

In October 2000, EntryPoint (formerly LaunchPoint) merged with the Internet Financial Network to create Infogate, releasing a desktop toolbar that offers personalized news and stock alerts as well as search functions. In November 2000, ex-PointCast CEO David Dorman became president of AT&T.

push different

PointCast offers an object lesson in what happens when a not-ready-for-prime-time technology collides with credulous hype and fails to deliver on its promises of revolutionary content and experience. Not every company that began during the push craze failed to make it to the twenty-first century. Several companies from the push goldrush (though they're quick to call themselves "knowledge management companies" today) looked at the marketplace, saw what was coming, retooled their technology, forged the right partnerships, and reinvented themselves. Their lesson of surviving the first big bubble—push—is one that many companies hanging by a thread today can learn from.

Marimba and BackWeb (though arguably not as visible as they were in the push era and certainly not as high priced) offer good examples of companies that have ridden the peaks and troughs of a fad into the future. From the beginning, they were designed to be different than PointCast. They'd seen the problems that PointCast had as a network hog and responded by releasing software that was much friendlier to the corporate LAN and modem-based users. Channels were smaller, with few (if any) Net-choking multimedia ads. BackWeb, in particular, made a lot of editorial hay out of its UDP-based Polite Agent technology that watched user activity and downloaded bits of its InfoPaks when the computer wasn't being used.

In addition, the business models were different. Rather than relying on the already shaky advertising model, both BackWeb and Marimba gave away the client software for free and charged heavily for the back-end "server" package. BackWeb started by charging between $10,500 and $100,000 annually for servers and distribution.

The user experiences were different, too. Both systems ran in the background and popped up content when it came across the channel. Neither screensavers nor desktop applications (though they did have desktop application environments), these programs delivered content in various formats right to the users' desktops as they were working.

And the biggest difference (and the one that probably contributed most to their survival) was that both Marimba's and BackWeb's systems didn't rely on a single arbiter of content distribution. While *PointCast* modeled itself on an old-style centralized TV network (its moniker, *PointCast Network* [PCN] set that metaphor from the beginning), both *BackWeb* and *Marimba* fashioned themselves as open technologies that could be used by any developer or content provider. Nobody had to strike a deal with these two companies to get in on the party. Just buy the server and development software, develop content, and start publishing. Rather than being a channel, both *Marimba* and *BackWeb* were like the Web itself: a medium, a channel for distributing information.

Let's take a look at how they got there and where they're going.

BACKWEB

By the time *BackWeb* launched in September 1996, *PointCast* had already defined "push" to the public. *BackWeb* wanted to redefine the marketplace—not an easy task for a space that had become crowded with "me-too" push technologies and industry hype.

"Setting its sights on establishing a new medium for proactive, 'one-to-one' online communication, BackWeb Technologies today introduced a breakthrough technology designed to fundamentally change the way companies do business and the way customers interact via the Internet," declared its opening press release on September 16. "Called *BackWeb*, the new client/server system will enable companies to build direct, continuous relationships with customers and provide customized content based on their specific areas of interest."

Started the year before by BRM Technologies, an Israeli Internet company that also launched *Checkpoint Software*, BackWeb's off-the-valley founders were bucking the trends from the beginning. But their roots hadn't stopped them from making inroads into the some-

88 | the dot.bomb survival guide

what insular U.S. tech community. At the time of the launch, BackWeb had already signed up Infoseek, Ziff-Davis, *The Wall Street Journal*, Mecklermedia's *iWorld*, General Motors, and Earthweb as content providers, and it had lined up development partnerships with CKS New Media, Utopia Inc., and Kaufman Patricof Enterprises.

Because *BackWeb* was envisioned from the beginning as an open system for distributing information and multimedia, the launch included both a Sun/Solaris-based server (with an NT version soon following) and a *Windows 95* client. A Macintosh version and *Windows 3.1* version was promised by the end of the year.

Industry response was relatively cool, though at the time, user interest was high. A *Fortune* article the following month credited BackWeb for stepping ahead of the push pack by actually releasing software. However, the content available on *BackWeb* was charitably called "tough to love."

Content problems aside, by the end of the year, BackWeb had secured its second round of financing. An investment group, led by GS Capital Partners II (an affiliate of Goldman Sachs) and including both U.S. and Israeli investors, pulled together $13 million in equity financing to kickstart the business. Things were looking good. *BackWeb*'s user base was swelling every day, and companies as diverse as The Weather Channel, The Patricia Seybold Group, and *The Jerusalem Post* had signed on to provide news and other content channels to *BackWeb* users.

But in January 1997, BackWeb took a turn that was to set the stage for the continued growth of the company. Up until this point, push had been seen mainly as a way of providing customized information to Internet users. Granted, that information was more targeted and personalized than what they could get at the time by surfing the Web, but it was still just information; news, stocks, sports scores, and technology commentary made up the bulk of the offerings. Then BackWeb signed on with antivirus software maker McAfee, and everything changed.

McAfee was (and still is) the leading provider of antivirus software. Normally purchased as a protection/repair shrinkwrapped software package, McAfee's software sought out and killed viruses by checking for their unique signatures based on McAfee-designed virus definition files. Users who wanted to make sure that their software was able to stamp out the latest virus could, by installing new definition files, keep their immunity up.

But getting new virus definitions required users to download them from the McAfee website, something that a lot of home users (and plenty of corporate users) often neglected to do until it was too late. With new viruses coming out seemingly every day, staying current was vital for anyone connected to the expanding Web of information that offered new opportunities for infection with each new download and email attachment.

Instead of waiting for users to get the files themselves, McAfee decided to bring the new virus protection software to its customers. Utilizing *BackWeb*'s capability to push various types of content across the Internet, McAfee's Home SecureCast service automatically pushed updates to customers as they became available. It was a success. The following month, BackWeb launched its first corporate edition of McAfee's software—the Entreprise SecureCast system.

As the year progressed, BackWeb continued to expand its network of partners. In March 1997 BackWeb partnered with Microsoft to provide push technology for Microsoft's new *Internet Explorer 4.0.* In addition to pushing content to Microsoft's browser, BackWeb also agreed to create a Microsoft Explorer channel on its network and to adhere to Microsoft's new channel definition format (CDF), a new standard for Web broadcasting.

BackWeb continued to add new content, but by the beginning of 1998 the push bubble had burst. *PC World Online* published a poll that revealed that only 8 percent of people wanted to get information pushed to them. Ross Rubin, an analyst at Jupiter MediaMetrix, declared in a February 1998 *New York Times* article "Push has gone from the most popular buzzword of 1997 and late 1996 to something verboten in business plans." PointCast and other push companies were starting to feel the pinch. Nobody said "push" anymore. The new buzzword was "knowledge management."

But that didn't stop BackWeb from going public. On June 8, 1999, BackWeb opened at $20 and ended the day a bit down at $19.69 . . . not an auspicious beginning for a public company whose IPO was backed by tech-stock titans Goldman Sachs, Lehman Brothers,

90 | the dot.bomb survival guide

and Wit Capital (among others). The investors saw a great future in push technology and what they called "personalized broadcasting." "Personalized broadcasting is a true Internet 'killer app,'" predicted Joseph Gleberman, managing director of Goldman Sachs.

BackWeb pushed on with its strategy to partner with content providers of all sorts. In January 2000 BackWeb inked a deal with RealNetworks to use its technology to deliver CD-quality sound samples into the RealJukebox player. Yet, most of the growth was in the B2B world. By February 2000 BackWeb's technology was being used to deliver data and software inside major corporations.

Ericsson was using BackWeb's technology to deliver news and pricing information to over 120,000 VARs worldwide. NEC tapped BackWeb to deliver product info to its global network of 8,000 dealers. Sage Software and Computer 2000 were using the product to deliver updates to their networks, too.

And then on April 14, at one time trading as high as 58⅛, BackWeb ended the day at 15¾, beginning a downward trend (along with the rest of the market) that continues as I write this (currently BackWeb's at 0.54). But BackWeb continued to press on. With a patent on its Polite Push technology, BackWeb has continued to retool itself as a provider of B2B infrastructure. In June 2000 it signed on with KPMG to provide the backbone technology to the consultancy's *eWorkforce Solution*. The next month BackWeb and ADP got together to create a network to keep salespeople in ADP's dealer service group up to date on the latest sales and product info and launched a service with online content syndicator FILMSPEED to deliver Hollywood Feature Film content.

These and other deals have kept BackWeb afloat long after the demise of many other push companies. But like the rest of the companies born in the early years of the New Economy, life hasn't been easy. Its 2000 fourth-quarter results showed a loss of 11 to 14 cents per share on revenues of around $7 million.

But there is cause for optimism. Looking forward to the business applications of push, analysts are starting to smile on the possibilities of a system that can get software to a large number of users simultaneously. IT infrastructure growth is expected to continue, with Jupiter MediaMetrix predicting global B2B spending to grow from $2.1 billion in 2000 to over $80 billion in 2005. Customer

Inter@ction Solutions picked BackWeb's desktop messaging software as one of its Products of the Year for 2000.

What does BackWeb's future look like? Considering the current state of the economy, it's hard to tell. It recently signed a $9.2 million contract with one of its existing partners and expected to see the revenue come in during 2001. "We believe that critical communications infrastructures will continue to be a priority, and we are confident in our superior technology and competitive positioning in the market," said CEO Eli Barkat (see sidebar "The Long View") when announcing the company's fourth-quarter downturn. But the downturn in the tech sector has been tough on BackWeb. Even though Lehman Brothers rated the company a "buy" in January, declining sales in the IT sector forced BackWeb to lay off 25 percent of its workforce in the second quarter of 2001.

The Long View:
An Interview with Eli Barkat

Eli Barkat has been everything from a celebrated paratrooper in the Israeli army to a successful venture capitalist (with BRM Technologies, Ltd.). But since cofounding BackWeb in 1995, he's used his skills to guide the company from a startup during the heady early days of push into a successful $40 million company and a leader in its industry. How did he do it? In this interview he describes the beginnings of BackWeb, where it's going, and how new entrepreneurs can learn to build new ventures with the right combination of planning, strategy, and financing.

Q: Tell me about the history of BackWeb, how you got to where you are now and what you learned along the way.

BackWeb began in late 1995 with a vision. We wrote on a whiteboard: "There will come a day when business will realize that the Web is too passive. They'll need a reliable and practical business infrastructure. The idea of sending an email and praying that somebody got it wasn't going to work. Push was the answer.

In late 1996 we came out with a communications infrastructure. At the time, the media demand was for consumer content, and for the first 6 months our revenue came from companies that thought that PointCast was going to eat their lunch. But we figured out 6 months into 1997 that we'd better dramatically change our focus away from selling to media and to the intranet market at the time. Even though our revenue was doubling every quarter, I noticed that a lot of new companies were buying into the technologies, but I didn't see a lot of existing companies asking for more. It was time for a change.

I came to the board and said that we needed to change the business model; everyone thought I was a lunatic. Success isn't about great tech or ideas, but about timing. We decided to change at the right time.

Look at Palm. They won because they entered a mature market, one that Apple had already worked to develop with the Newton. This was about changing our model at the right time.

Push made sense because it is very intuitive. All of us spend too much time searching for information and surfing websites. There was nothing wrong with the model. There was something very intuitive about the value. But the leaders in the industry were wrong about the amount of time it would take to work.

The push market was beginning to have problems, and when we figured out where the problem was, we said, "Let's take the technology to where the market's ready, as an infrastructure." We went to where the market was more mature.

Q: What is BackWeb doing right now to survive and thrive in the current business climate?

Right now, we're working with Cisco, Nortel, and others. Companies that have critical information that's timely and need to have it understood. We're pushing new product announcements, information into call centers, and we're doing well in reseller communities. Executive communications applications, too. . . . We know that the biggest communications problems that executives have is with their own employees. Our product helps solve that problem.

Q: What do you think has made BackWeb successful?

What made us successful? The timing of the market and a different view of what was going on than some others.

On the technology front, the other major issue was one that PointCast created. You just can't use the standard networks and clog them up with technology. We came up with our patented PolitePush technology that senses the network's downtime and sends the information through them. Seventy percent of networks are always idle.

It's about timing. It's about critical information. It's about PolitePush. We've grown to $40 million in sales, and we have 200 customers in the Global 2000.

Q: What advice would you have for entrepreneurs looking to start a business today?

The last 6 months have changed everything. It's becoming clear that building a startup is not a business for kids anymore . . . it's a business for professionals. It's not about raising money. It's about raising money from the right places. The cycle from idea to IPO is going to move from 2 to 3 years to 5 to 6 years. It's a much larger commitment.

I'd advise people with new ideas that the days of technology now and business model later are done. Make sure you have a good plan. Get good developers and salespeople. Get back to where we were 5 years ago . . . back to real business models.

Q: Tell me more about raising money. What should entrepreneurs look out for as they seek sources of capital?

Over the last couple of years, everybody in the world has created a funding facility for startups. Angels and everybody with an MBA from someplace created a VC fund because no matter where you put the money, you hit a goldmine. If you're just starting out, you should go to the professionals with proven experience, people who will fund you through the hard times.

There's always an uphill after a downhill. You need people who can support you through that, that understand it's a long-term business. Make sure they're willing to put in the money when you need it again.

The VC community created and paid for Internet time. The sense from the VCs was that all you had to worry about was market share . . . and let's figure out everything else later. They were telling entrepreneurs to raise money as fast as you can to grab market share before the market closes. They created an environment in which all that was important was the press release, that if you spend more money, you will eventually make more money. What you create is a cost structure that isn't sustainable over time. There were a lot of people pushing me to do that, too. But one day they'd be measured by fundamentals, and changing the fundamentals is tough. If you don't build it based on the fundamentals, you're in trouble. Change is hard.

Let's start being reasonable.

MARIMBA

Like BackWeb, Marimba's story is a similar one of a push company reinventing itself from the ashes of a dying industry. However, while BackWeb has kept a relatively low industry profile, slowly building business and rising and falling with the market, Marimba's star has left a spectacular trail across the sky of the Internet marketplace through its arc . . . though it's currently suffering the devalued fate of many early Internet startups. Its up-down survival story shows how even survivors can get burned (but can still press on).

Marimba launched its first product in October 1996, almost exactly 1 month after BackWeb. The company, started by four original members of Sun's Java team (all of whom contributed $15,000 apiece to fund the new company) and headed by the soon-to-be tech star Kim Polese, Marimba's *Castanet* used a radiolike metaphor (complete with "tuner" and "transmitter") with a Java backend to deliver nearly any kind of digital data across the Internet.

From the beginning, the emphasis was on open development and a wide range of content. "Using *Castanet*, developers can now build and easily deploy full-featured, media-rich applications over the Internet that are unrestrained by platform dependency, limited bandwidth, or the traditional HTML browser framework," declared the opening salvo in the press release announcing its launch. "Without these limitations, developers can now create compelling, differentiated content and applications by leveraging the processing power of the personal computer to incorporate capabilities such as animation, audio, newsfeeds, simulations, and more—all without the need for huge amounts of immediate network bandwidth."

Pretty heady stuff. Marimba's *Castanet* was out to break the mold of the Web. Rather than focusing on information as every push technology up to this point had done, *Castanet* was designed from the ground up to deliver applications and deliver them in Java, which at that point was nearly a religious obsession among its proponents and heavily promoted by its creator, Sun.

Polese wasn't shy about predicting what *Castanet* could do. "Imagine a personalized financial portfolio app that notices your investment trends, informs you of new funds, dynamically creates what-if scenarios as new information arrives, sends constantly updated market data, and can be used offline. Or, an evolving adventure game that developers can morph in real time by adding new worlds or new characters—transforming the game into an ongoing revenue stream. This is what the next generations can be like."

Her infectious enthusiasm and nonstop evangelism (along with some nice industry contacts) caught the interest of some big players early on. From the beginning, Apple, AT&T, Macromedia, HotWired (*Wired's* online network), Netscape, Sun, and CPM all announced that they were exploring uses for this new technology. In a November 1996 article, Jesse Freund of *Wired* magazine saw it as the next stage in the new Internet: "The Internet is about to undergo a new stage of evolution, one that could threaten the browser market while making the Net look a lot more like TV—TV possessed with interactivity and intelligence, of course."

To understand the interest in *Castanet,* you have to understand what a leap it was from what had come before. While most Internet technology up until this point had been designed to deliver information to users (and some technologies, like *BackWeb* were evolving to do more), *Castanet* was designed for a future world in which the PC on your desktop functioned in a networked world of constantly changing information. No longer would applications be able to exist as islands, cut off from the rest of the metaverse. Rather, tomorrow's applications would be constantly infused with new data, updates, and intelligence delivered via the Internet.

Marimba's product caught on fast. By June Apple had announced that it would be part of its new OS 8 operating system (along with *PointCast,* by the way). By August Microsoft was teaming up with Marimba to propose an XML-based Open Software Description to provide a data format in which software components could talk to one another and swap resources. Playing both sides of the battle lines in the so-called Browser War, Marimba also announced an initiative with Netscape to develop a new industry protocol called DRP (distribution and replication protocol) to "improve and optimize the efficiency of the Internet." In fact, Netscape would later incorporate Marimba's technology into its own browser, using it to power its *Netcaster* software.

There was no doubt about it, Marimba was setting the standard for buzz. Thomas Dolby (an electronic musician who made his mark in the eighties with his hit "She Blinded Me with Science") called CEO Polese "Silicon Valley's answer to Madonna." The company had grown from 4 to 70 employees and had bagged 300 customers. *BusinessWeek* was calling Marimba "a silicon valley sensation," stating that "as more companies use the Web to reach customers and employees, technology like Marimba's will be in great demand." Forrester Research was predicting that the Web-software management market (which Marimba dominated) would be worth $400 million by the beginning of 2000.

The money flowed in. By the end of September, Marimba had raised $14.5 million from an investment group led by Compaq Computer and including Lehman Brothers, PeopleSoft, National Semiconductor, and Deutsche Morgan Grenfell Technology Group, among others. But Marimba's success (and Polese's hyperbole-fueled rhetoric and some key defections) started to attract detractors. In Chris Nolan's June 22, 1998, "Talk Is Cheap" column in the *San Jose Mercury News*, an unnamed investment fund manager whispered that he thought Marimba might have problems: "When people leave before their options vest, you know there's a problem. There is no other interpretation."

Polese fought back. "There are people who simply are jealous and spread gossip and lies," she countered. "Those people who you are talking to [about Marimba's problems] know nothing about our products. Nothing."

But unnamed industry insiders weren't the only ones sniping at Marimba. Michael Wolff, author of the popular book *Burn Rate, How I Survived the Gold Rush Years on the Internet*, pointed to Marimba when asked about Internet fads in a 1998 *San Francisco Chronicle* article: "The sun shines brightly on a selected place for a concerted moment and then it passes. If you don't cash in you're fucked. . . . Everything in this market's about timing, timing, timing . . . It's all about promise, hype and heat—not about business performance. PointCast and Marimba's time came and went."

Marimba was about to prove him wrong. Very wrong. On April 30, 1999, Marimba went public at $20 per share. By the end of the day the IPO had risen 204 percent to $61, giving Marimba a (temporary) market capitalization of $1.4 billion. Kim Polese's $15,000 investment had made her and the other founders multimillionaires.

Investors were so excited to buy in that Morgan Stanley, the underwriter for the IPO, was able to knock up the opening price twice from $13 to $15 and later from $16 to $20.

The financial press was optimistic about Marimba's success. In June 1999, *Fortune* declared, "While Marimba's not going to sport a $10 billion valuation, it's also much less likely to flame out as some of its highflying IPO brethren undoubtedly will." But, at the same time, *Fortune* predicted that Marimba may have some rough times because "in the twisted logic of the Net, its business may be too solid."

They were right. By August, Marimba's stock had slipped to around $25. But it would rise again, at least for a little while. In the meantime, Marimba kept pressing on, refining its software and building new alliances (Figure 3-2).

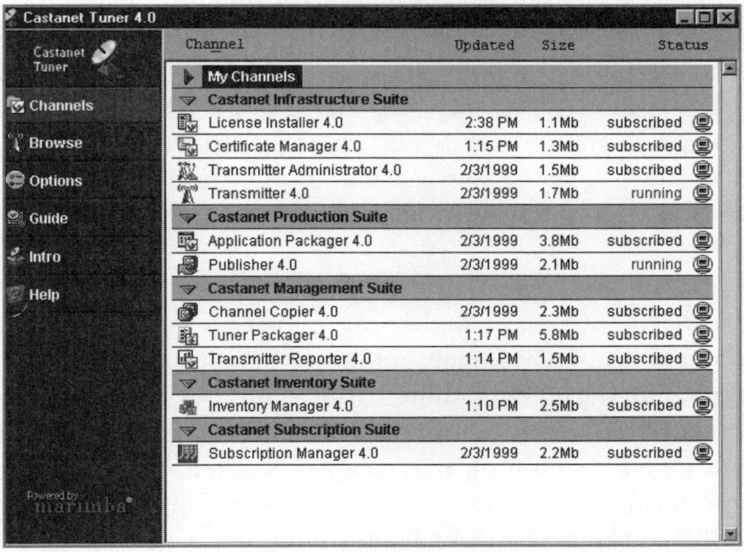

Figure 3-2. *Castanet* Today

In July 2000, after guiding Marimba through its first profitable quarter, Polese stepped aside from the top position in order to let John Olsen, an ebusiness veteran from Cadence Design Systems, take the helm. The company continued on its path to build new alliances, working deals with BeVocal, Novadigm, and Reuters. It expanded its reach into the enterprise world with the release of

98 | the dot.bomb survival guide

Timbale, its product for the control and deployment of server information and applications.

Like so many others, Marimba ended 2000 on a down note, posting a loss of 7 cents per share on fourth-quarter revenues of $11.3 million, up 12 percent from the previous year. Overall, Marimba ended the millennium with revenues of $44 million, a 40 percent jump from 1999. With the release of its fourth-quarter earnings, CEO John Olsen predicted that Marimba will prosper: "We've doubled our quota-bearing sales personnel since the second quarter. Additionally, we are currently refining Marimba's product roadmap to anticipate and respond to market needs. We believe that Marimba is positioned for a successful 2001."

Whether it can pull it off remains to be seen. At the beginning of 2001, Marimba's stock was down to 7⅝. But if past performance is any indicator of Marimba's ability to pull itself back up again, it probably will. It recently teamed up with 3Com Corporation to provide the software for its new "Audrey" Internet appliance. Will it again shift to take advantage of this rapidly expanding market that eTForecasts is predicting will grow to nearly 600 million users worldwide by 2005? We'll see. But things should get interesting. Here's what Marimba's CEO John Olsen said when asked about the company's future:

> Marimba's opportunity is getting larger as brick-and-mortar companies implement ebusiness strategies and struggle with increasingly complex IT environments. Going forward, Marimba continues to execute our strategic plan for renewed investment in the business. Additionally, we are currently refining our product roadmap to anticipate and respond to market needs. And, we are building a powerful executive team to take Marimba to the next level. We believe Marimba is positioned for a successful 2001.
>
> In terms of partnerships, Marimba is teaming with leading systems, network appliances, and ebusiness companies that will enable our customers to get to market faster, as well as, indirect partners, including systems integrators and OEMs. We continue to have a strong customer base from various industries, including software and services, ASPs, health care, financial services, telecommunications, and

retail. Looking forward, we will continue to invest in a very bright future for Marimba, with emphasis on sales reach expansion, partnerships, and rebranding the company and new product offerings.

today's fads or tomorrow's revolutions: what can we learn from push?

There is a striking coincidence between the early claims of push and what's going on in the wireless market today. But it's not limited to wireless. If you go back in time and read what was being written about portals, B2B exchanges, the application service provider software model, free anything (ISPs, computers, email, etc.), and broadband entertainment, you'll hear echoes of the same promises, the same hype.

But hype doesn't necessarily lead to failure, unless hype blinds us to what's going on in the marketplace. The decline of push, especially of *PointCast*, has a lot more to do with some severe miscalculations made by a company too caught up in its own hype to see what was going on. On the other hand, Marimba and BackWeb have been able to survive by taking a look at the marketplace and constantly readjusting themselves, never resting on their successes (or overhyped valuations), and living in a state of constant prototyping and innovation.

Let's look at the lessons from push and examine how to tell a short-lived fad from a true revolution:

1. *Fads assume that just because it can be done, people want it.* A fad starts with a previously unknown technology and tries to create a need. A revolutionary technology meets a previously unknown need.
2. *Fads don't know who the real audience is . . . or who the real decision makers are.* A fad is a technology in search of an audience. A revolutionary technology benefits those who need it most.
3. *Fads don't know where the money's going to come from . . . today or tomorrow.* A fad narrowly focuses on a present-day revenue-producing trend. A revolution does, too, and then creates new markets.
4. *Fads don't add up.* Good business makes sense. Viable businesses

100 | the dot.bomb survival guide

have real products, customers, and revenues. In contrast, fads don't add up.

5. *Fads rely on justification to keep going.* If you have to keep convincing yourself, it's probably a fad. Revolutions multiply resources exponentially. If you have to keep justifying your "revolution," it probably isn't one.
6. *Fads think they can exist in a closed world.* Fads are exclusive. Revolutions are inclusive.

How can you avoid the pitfalls that fads fall into?

1. *Be nimble.* Don't be a slug. Don't be afraid of change. Keep your eyes open.
2. *Fads breed megalomania. Carve out a niche.* Fads breed True Believers and Fanatics. Revolutions breed long-term customers.
3. *Make sure that your stuff works before releasing it to the public.* Once somebody uninstalls, it's tough to get them to install your software again.
4. *It's not always about the money (unless, of course, you're the one that has it).* Participating in a business revolution means, above all, building an actual business. Opportunists chasing a fad are in it to get rich, not to build something that's going to live on in the future. Changing the world by building a real business means looking beyond today's stock price to the future with a mission in mind.

> We are changing the world. We're creating an infrastructure that will make it much more possible for businesses to deliver powerful service in a cost-effective way. But separate from that, we are a company with ethics. We are a company that deals fairly with people, with other companies, where values like execution and follow-through, instead of concept and hype, define what we are. That's something people need more and more in this day and age, in this environment, in this industry—the values that feed us at the core as human beings, connections with other human beings, a sense of belonging. And I think in this environment we are not seeing a whole lot of it. But in years to come, I think we will see more people caring about that.

And I think there will be a backlash against all the greed. I think people are going to get just fed up and realize it is not fulfilling. I look around me, and I have so many friends who started companies who are worth $50 million and more, and they are depressed. They think that they've made it, and they take 6 months off and they realize they're more depressed than ever. Because this wasn't really what ultimately it turned out that life was all about. I look around me and I see unhappy billionaires, and I see them coming back again and again to start another company. And what really attracts them is connecting with other people. It is the team. It's creating something. It's having a mission. That's what turns people on. That's what life is about." [Kim Polese, "The Wall Street Journal Millennium (A Special Report): Money & Markets—Talking About Tomorrow—Kim Polese: A tech entrepreneur discusses creativity, values, and the gold rush mentality." December 31, 1999.]

the perils (and promises) of software products and services sold over the Internet

While most coverage about the revolution wrought by the Internet has centered on ecommerce and content-driven sites, the Internet spawned a whole huge category of businesses devoted to delivering virtual products and services over the Web. These companies don't necessarily sell physical *things* (though, as we'll see later on, sometimes their models depend on pieces of physical technology interfacing with the Internet). Instead, the products these companies base their businesses on usually revolve around software (renting it or selling it), interfacing the analog world with cyberspace (through specialized devices), or developing new technologies to deliver information on the Internet.

How they make money (or, in the case of several companies in this chapter, *don't* make money) varies. Looking at the world of content, some decided to adopt advertising-supported models: You get the software or hardware for free, they sell ads that show up in the device or program. Others have developed products that are essentially gateways to ad-supported content or paid services: You might get the software or device for free, but the intention is to hook you up to the Web to sell you things or capture information about you.

104 | the dot.bomb survival guide

Some revenue models, particularly the application service provider (ASP) model, rely on ongoing rental relationships, turning what were previously one-time-sale products into constant revenue streams (hopefully!). Still other companies developed new technologies, released as open standards, hoping they could later capitalize on the emerging marketplace by selling development or integration tools for those technologies. Other companies that developed technologies hoped to license their technologies to content providers or developers, ensuring a constant stream of cash that increased exponentially as the standards gained acceptance.

Lots of big dreams. Lots of finely crafted strategies. Lots of can't-go-wrong business plans. Unfortunately, lots of failures, too.

Like a lot of dot.bombs, the reasons for failure aren't always as cut-and-dried as we'd like them to be. There's not always one reason ("market forces," for example, aren't usually a reason . . . they're a symptom). And success or failure can't always be traced back to a fatally flawed product, management team, or the unwillingness of customers to adopt technologies. All these things play a part. But while reasons are complex, there's usually an overriding reason, the proverbial straw that breaks the camel's back. This chapter ferrets them out.

There are several main reasons why so many companies that sell products and services for and over the Net have imploded:

1. *They lacked a viable revenue model.* Revenue models for product/service companies are as varied as they are in the content sector. Some have opted to tap into the firehose of advertising revenue by carrying embedded advertising. The software is free, but it usually contains an area or two displaying banners. Other companies have provide free software or hardware in an effort to drive users to their main website . . . again, aggregating eyeballs in an effort to support themselves through ad sales. Still other companies have gone the old-fashioned route, attempting to sell their products directly. Finally, other companies became application service providers, renting their software to anyone who could connect to it online.

2. *Their technology or service became obsolete as a result of a competitor's action or change in technology.* Sometimes, companies

the perils (and promises) of software products . . . | 105

were leapfrogged by unforeseen changes in technology (or the signs were foreseeable but the companies ignored them) and were driven out of business when cheaper, faster, better alternatives came down the pike.

3. *Technical glitches . . . the product never worked.* Some companies simply tried to sell products that didn't work. While many, many companies participated in the beta culture of software on the Web (see sidebar "The Beta Galaxy"), some raised vast sums of money simply by promising to deliver a product that never materialized.

4. *The technology failed to be adopted as a standard.* For companies forging ahead into the unexplored territories of bleeding-edge technology, making money depended on their innovation being rewarded through mass acceptance of their technology as a standard. If this had happened, a company could have then become wealthy in leveraging its expertise to sell development tools and advice to other companies who wanted to utilize its technology (Macromedia's *Flash* and Adobe's *Acrobat* are two examples). For those companies whose product became a standard, the gravy train rolled in. For the others whose competitors pushed them out of the market . . . bye, bye!

5. *The company flamed out before customers adopted its technology.* Even though technology has been adopted very rapidly on the Internet, the pace of the adoption of previously unknown technologies has slowed since the crazy early days when anything seemed to go. If a company couldn't make enough money or bring in enough capital to survive until it had built up a critical mass of users, it didn't matter how great its technology was . . . it was history.

6. *Potential customers avoided it due to a perceived lack of trust, reliability, or the product and/or service's failure to meet a real or perceived need.* Finally, some companies died because their potential customers were reluctant to buy their products or use their services. Reasons for this varied, but many times (see reason 5) customers held back due to fear of the technology, the difficulty in modifying their systems to utilize the technology, or simply because the product and/or service didn't fit a real need.

106 | the dot.bomb survival guide

Of course, some of these companies died simply because of mismanagement or bad planning. We don't need to discuss those reasons here. Instead, we'll learn how the unique problems of delivering products and services on the Net led to the demise of some companies, why others thrived, and what lessons companies in these sectors should learn to continue to thrive into the future.

products in the digital age

What is different about computer products or services sold through the Internet? How does the Internet open new possibilities? The answers to these questions lie in understanding what happens when we move from physical products to virtual products.

Physical, tangible products have to exist in the analog realm with all of its attendant messy limitations. Physical objects (including shrinkwrapped software) have to be stored in a warehouse and moved through complicated distribution systems. They have to be displayed on shelves and purchased by a customer who actually makes the trip to the store to buy the product. If a store runs out of a product, it has to order more and wait for it to arrive. If a customer breaks a product, wants another one, or needs an upgrade, he or she has to physically take it in for repair, go purchase another, or bring in the product and wait for the upgrade.

These limitations are as true for software as they are for cars. The physical world limits distribution and cash flow based on inventory. Even for software that's stored on a company's internal servers and accessed by its employees over a LAN, someone has to actually come in, install the software, set it up, and fix it when it breaks. All the time, speed, and flexibility are limited by the physical presence of the program on the customer's hard drive.

Going the other way, performing transactions with a customer used to be limited by the ability to set up a channel from the customer to the company. If a customer wanted to be able to collect data and send it to a remote location or receive data remotely, that customer would have to interact with expensive, proprietary systems and networks. And while these types of systems of data interchange were expensive necessities in some businesses, the idea of doing something like this

the perils (and promises) of software products . . . | 107

with a consumer was out of the question. Before the Internet, direct computer contact with customers was virtually impossible.

innovation at Internet speed

Another innovation that affected the way products (particularly software) were developed and sold online was the rise of the "public beta." Popularized during the mid to late nineties, the drive to dominate the market through innovation, combined with ready access to a global marketplace, allowed software vendors to both release and test software at the same time by providing public test versions. "Beta tests" had always been a part of software development, happening at the phase where most of the product's features were coded in and the program generally worked without destroying anyone's computer. Prior to the Internet, beta tests were usually private affairs, with software distributed to handpicked groups of users (usually chosen from the customer base or internal constituencies) and they were tested in private until they were deemed ready for release. Software releases were more infrequent, usually occurring only after a long period of privacy and quality control.

During the Browser Wars, when Microsoft and Netscape duked it out to become the dominant browser on the Web (thereby locking in their own set of standards and assuring mass traffic to their preset homepages), betas went public. Innovation was quickly rushed out the door in an effort to be the first in the marketplace to implement features, from 3D to push to new HTML implementations. During this fight, various measurement organizations kept tabs on who was "winning" by publishing stats on what browsers were being used most frequently to access the most popular websites. Headlines were grabbed by those who emerged with features first, regardless of whether or not those features actually worked correctly. After all, these were technology demos—betas—and companies couldn't be held responsible for any errors or problems that occurred. All that mattered was who offered what first.

This compression of the software life cycle was one of the key factors leading to the dominant popular wisdom of "Internet time."

While estimates of what one year of Internet time "equaled" in real time varied from 3 months to 6 months to 9 months, one thing was clear: On the Internet, things happened faster. To keep up, you had to do things fast, regardless of what was happening financially or in the marketplace. To be first to market with a new piece of software or a new service meant being the dominant player.

Nobody knew what was going to work yet—the theory was that you had to innovate as fast as possible, throw it out there, and hope it stuck. If your software wasn't the first out of the gate, somebody else would create the next killer app (whatever that might be) and become the next Netscape . . . even if that somebody was Microsoft. It didn't matter if there was actually a clearly demonstrated need or even a market: Internet time waited for no one.

The Beta Galaxy—Death of an Empire

Neil Kleinman is a professor at the University of Baltimore and codirector of the School of Communications Design. With doctorates in English literature and law, he is an expert in intellectual property, technology, and the economics of publishing. Here's his take on the "beta culture," that strange new way of developing technology born of the Web. . . .

A long time ago, far, far away, in a universe parallel to this one, techies ruled. They never saw a technology they didn't like. A strange technology was even better. "That's cool," they'd say and play with it. (They called it "Pixelon," a streaming media technology.) A weird business plan was worth its weight in gold. (Who wouldn't want to have groceries or pet food delivered to his or her front door?) The untried and untested was too good to be true. (Of course, we all want to use Linux or wireless or broadband.) The unworkable was a marvelous challenge. The rulers of this galaxy wanted only one thing—to be the first to make it work. Who needs an instruction manual? they smiled. They were, in all things, happy to be confused. What's more cool, after all, than a confusion that we can figure out for ourselves?

Such was the Beta Galaxy. The laboratory for an idea was the marketplace, not the research laboratory. Testing was done on the fly. A usability study? A marketing plan? Who had time? Mistakes, after all, could be corrected later—in version 2, version

3, or 4. The user was a partner, the happy coinventor who was more than content to help improve the product.

That was then. This is now. The new technology and all its New Economy products were carried into the cosmos, illuminated by a million points of light, what we call the "mainstream mass market." Where else could they travel, burdened as they were, with investments of $1.2 billion (Webvan), a 6-month marketing budget of $1.2 million (Boo.com), or expensive Internet addresses priced at $5 million and more (Linux)? The early market had at best only 15 percent of potential buyers while the mainstream market promised so much more—more than 68 percent of the market. You figure it out. It's a big universe, and the mainstream market revealed plenty of consumers who might, at a minimum, buy "something."

The techies from the Beta Galaxy thought that everyone they'd meet would be like them, that every consumer wanted the unpredictable, the confusing, the untried and untested, that everyone liked to be challenged every time he or she opened a box full of technologies. But that wasn't so. When the techies landed in the world of the consumer and breathed its air, like aliens, they died.

The lesson: An economy based upon Beta Culture can't survive in a consumer marketplace because it is not that easy to change consumer behavior. If we've learned anything in the last few years, consumers are pretty straightforward. They want:

- A predictable product with standardized, interchangeable parts
- A service infrastructure that makes it easy to repair what doesn't work
- Lots of competition to show that a product is something that everyone wants
- A turnkey operation that's easy to use and one that comes with a friendly manual
- Some real evidence that a product or service will improve what they're already doing . . . that they will become faster, more efficient, more playful, more beautiful, or, simply, happier

Like most revolutions, the dot.com revolution was staffed by the bright and the young. Sadly, the marketplace was owned by the middle-aged and the established—baby boomers, who were nothing if not weary, careful, and lazy. Some time ago, they had put their old jalopy up on blocks, and they didn't care to look under the hood anymore.

110 | the dot.bomb survival guide

virtual reality makes a play

That's what happened in the world of VRML, one of the first big attempts to define the Next Big Thing on the Web that never took off as a public success.

From the beginning, the whole field of virtual reality practically glowed with a halo of hype that promised more than it could possibly deliver. Defined in the popular imagination of early computer visionaries by William Gibson's seminal cyberpunk novel *Neuromancer*, whose characters lived in a 3D world of data Gibson dubbed "Cyberspace," virtual reality *was* the future as far as the technoelite were concerned.

Before *Neuromancer*, virtual reality had existed only in the lofty realms of computer theorists who had access to high-powered computers that had the ability to crunch enough numbers to render 3D worlds on the screen. It entered into the popular imagination hyped by technoshaman Jaron Lanier, a dreadlocked visionary with a wild look and an amazing capacity to spin compelling philosophical raps on its benefits, and popularized in the pages of early cyberculture magazines such as *Mondo2000* and, later, *Wired*.

It was a compelling vision. In the future, these visionaries said, users wouldn't be bound by the computer screen, clicking away with mice, or (as was more common in the early nineties) interacting with their machines by typing obscure DOS or UNIX commands. Instead, data would be represented with 3D objects, and users would interact with that data with "data gloves" that allowed one to point, move, and fly around in this virtual space. Instead of computer screens showing us a mere window to this world, one could don head-mounted displays that provided 360-degree views. It would truly be a virtual *reality*, one that the computer users of the future would live and communicate in.

Unfortunately, to interact in cyberspace, one had to have a much more powerful computer than most folks could afford. And without an Internet, there was no infrastructure to connect people. At first, the dream of shared 3D realities connected across the world was only a dream. Then the Internet came along.

With the popularization of the World Wide Web in the early nineties, combined with the commercialization of the Net as it was

the perils (and promises) of software products . . . | 111

sold off to commercial carriers and the availability of faster modems and dialup Internet software, a platform existed for the first time that could make the vision come true. Unfortunately, the software didn't exist to bring these 3D worlds alive on the screen. That's where VRML came in.

The brainchild of Marc Pesce, an MIT dropout and veteran of the virtual-reality world from stints at startup Ono-Sendai (named for one of the companies in *Neuromancer*) and early experiments at Apple Computer, the Virtual Reality Markup Language was developed to bring virtual reality to the Net. It combined a syntax similar to HTML that allowed 3D worlds to be created with simple text commands with what seemed like low-bandwidth overhead for fast transmission. It seemed to be the perfect Net-delivered solution. When Pesce presented VRML at the first international World Wide Web conference, the crowd went wild. This was the Next Big Thing everyone had been waiting for.

Netscape and Sun Microsystems quickly became interested and began to develop their own implementation of VRML. But they wanted to be included in the VRML Architecture Group (VAG) to help set the standards. They weren't allowed in, and by the end of 1995, VAG was gone. Sun, Netscape, and Silicon Graphics announced their proposal for VRML called "Cosmo," which combined the 3D graphics of VRML with the interactivity of Java. Soon after, Microsoft announced its entry into the market with its own standard called Active VRML. The race was on.

Shortly after, SGI developed a separate unit called "Cosmo Software" dedicated to developing 3D interfaces to the Web and expanding the VR marketplace. Overnight, it seemed, 3D browser "plugins" and virtual-reality browsers began to crop up. Companies like Activeworlds.com, Inc., created virtual world portal sites where members could meet as virtual "avatars" and chat in 3D.

But the hype began to catch up to virtual reality. While the media touted it as the Next Big Thing and Web users downloaded software at a furious rate, people soon began to realize that virtual reality was far from a "reality." VRML had higher overhead than was promised, often causing users to wait as long as a half an hour on their 28.8 modems for a complex image to load. The images, once rendered, were often blocky—far removed from any sort of reality except Saturday morning cartoons. Even after they waited long hours for the files to download, many users were disappointed when their less-than-top-of-the-line computers choked and crashed (Figure 4-1).

Figure 4-1. A VRML Scene Rendered by MacLookat

By 1998 the VRML marketplace wasn't looking like it was going anywhere. While it had spawned many companies like Pulse Entertainment, SuperScape, and WildTangent, none of them looked like the next Netscape. In July 1998 Silicon Graphics shut its doors on its Cosmo Software unit, reassigning its 100 employees to other parts of the company after a deal with Sony fell through. Microsoft scrapped its plans for a high-end 3D browser called "Chrome" when interest waned after it was revealed that Chrome would require high-end computers owned by only a small portion of the marketplace. Later, Apple killed a project called "HotSauce" that was attempting to create a 3D interface for Web browsing and information retrieval.

The days of VRML as *the* technology that would change how the Web was viewed were gone. While it made perfect sense from the standpoint of the engineers (and inspired a lot of fantastic hype), regular folks never quite got it. The early 3D pioneers who are still around have modified their business models, turning away from trying to convert the Web into a 3D cyberspace and concentrating instead on using their 3D technology for onsite product demonstrations, architectural walkthroughs, and interactive characters. Activeworlds, while it still operates several online 3D communities, went public in May 2000, and it has expanded into developing virtual shopping malls and licensing its technology to others who want to add 3D to their site. But the market hasn't been kind to Activeworlds; constant losses have depressed its stock price since it went public at $4.25 to a current price of under a dollar (a price that threatens its NASDAQ listing). WildTangent has found success selling its 3D "visualizers" to music lovers. Plus, new entrants such as Pennsylvania-based 2CE with its CubicEye browser are trying to revitalize the 3D Web market for a new audience with faster connections and more powerful computers.

Ironically, while the market for 3D Web companies has declined, many game companies have had success combining the Internet with 3D gaming in multiplayer environments. In 2000, 52 percent of teens reported that they had played an action/fantasy game online, according to Jupiter MediaMetrix. Most of those games like *Quake Arena, Unreal Tournament, HalfLife,* and *EverQuest,* take place in 3D worlds and have huge followings (Figure 4-2).

Figure 4-2. *EverQuest* . . . We've Come a Long Way from Early VRML.

Why didn't VRML take off? First, it was ahead of its time. While the technology worked in the lab with high-speed computers and high-speed connections, home users couldn't make it work the way they expected it to. That expectation, too, is another reason that the technology had a hard time. The promise of what it could do—everything from immersive fantasy worlds to teledildonic "virtual sex"—was far removed from its reality of simple geometric shapes and flat colors.

But what may have really killed VRML and virtual reality (or at least limited its growth to more specialized applications) was that it was a product in search of a need. While theoreticians and visionaries may have seen a grand future in a world where we could "fly" through data, interacting via "avatars" in cyberspace, the real reality was that consumers didn't find virtual reality as compelling as the vision. While most people were just getting used to clicking a mouse and navigating through windows (and *Windows*), the VRML crowd wanted users to learn how to dig for information and control their computers in a whole new way, one many didn't want or care to learn. People didn't want to live in 3D but to use it as a tool to gather information that can be conveyed only in three dimensions. Like many technologies that initially seem capable of changing the world, 3D has become not a revolution that overturns the old ways, but a new tool in a user's experience toolbox.

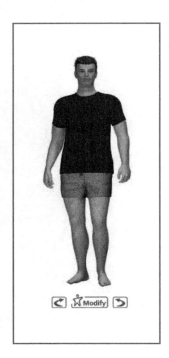

What's the future look like for 3D on the Web? Perhaps like MyVirtualModel, a company that makes software apparel websites that let users try clothes on a virtual model that looks like them. In use at LandsEnd's and JCPenney's websites, MyVirtualModel really does give users a good feeling for what clothes look like on them. The future of virtual reality, it turns out, might be more about reality than we thought (Figure 4-3).

Figure 4-3. MyVirtualModel . . . Your Humble Author in His Virtual Underwear

the real and the virtual: MusicMaker.com

Another place where the real world hasn't meshed very well with the virtual world is in the realm of the Net-to-CD industry. The story of the companies with these concepts that have bombed can explain a lot about what happens when a world starts to become accustomed to the move from atoms to bits.

MusicMaker.com was founded in 1996 with an idea that seemed ready-made for the Internet—why not allow users to log on, pick the music they wanted, and then receive a CD they had mixed? It fit right into the "mass customization" promise of the Web, in which consumers of the future would be able to create products they wanted rather than settling for products the manufacturers wanted them to buy. An idea practically impossible before the Web, MusicMaker seemed like a sure thing to investors.

While MusicMaker's catalog was limited to songs from the EMI music catalog, its $9.95 and higher price tag was initially popular with consumers. In 1999 MusicMaker posted $1 million in sales with more than 70 employees. By the quarter ending March 2000, MusicMaker realized revenues of more than $3 million.

The stock market initially loved the idea, too. When MusicMaker went public in July 1999, its stock rocketed to $239 opening day, eventually peaking at $281 per share. But losses were high, and the costs of goods sold far outstripped revenues. Even with $3.1 million in sales, the company had incurred over $8 million in costs. Then things really started going south.

In the quarter ending September 2000, MusicMaker's sales had dipped below $1 million for the first time in a year. Its stock price had slipped below $10. In addition, MusicMaker had failed to secure deals with the other big companies such as Universal, Sony, BMG, and Warner Music.

But the lack of deals wasn't its real problem: Napster was. Just coming into the popular consciousness about that time, Napster provided anyone with access to its client to share music with a worldwide audience. Instead of having to borrow friends' CDs or seek out pirated music on obscure websites, music lovers around the Internet could now just log on, type in the name of their favorite band, and download until their hard drives choked from the megabytes of MP3s.

116 | the dot.bomb survival guide

People didn't need custom CDs anymore—they could burn their own. According to PC Data, a market research firm that tracks technology sales, sales of CD burners more than doubled between the end of November 2000 and the end of the year. Why pay MusicMaker to do something you could do in the privacy of your own home for a lot less money?

By January 2001 MusicMaker's board of directors faced the music and decided to liquidate the company's assets in an effort to return some value to shareholders. The site was shut down and the announcement of MusicMaker's demise was sent out, citing Napster as the primary reason for MusicMaker's death.

beware the effects of bandwidth: EZGamer.com

If MusicMaker was killed by Napster, EZGamer was probably killed by bandwidth. Another company that made CDs from digital assets, EZGamer gambled that game fanatics would rather pay for convenience than wait for long downloads.

Volatile Media, owner of EZGamer, EZCD (a site similar to MusicMaker but with a more indie bent), and EZMP3, a music download site, focused exclusively on translating virtual digital media into tangible, "real" CDs for both games and music. They cut deals with everyone from American Express to BMG to game developers such as Eidos, GT Interactive, Microsoft, and Gathering of Developers. In a marriage that seemed perfect for its audience, EZGamer teamed up with hot game site GameSpot.com to allow users to compile discs of game demos (up to 650 megabytes worth of cyber-booty), saving tens of hours of download time. In fact, the 24-hour shipping time was faster than most folks over modems could download the same number of game demos.

Unfortunately, the bargain of time for money didn't work out. On August 22, 2000, with little fanfare in the media and scant information on their sites, EZCD and EZGamer shut down. Other than a note about ceasing retail operations, the sites went away without a trace.

What killed EZGamer and its sister sites? Like MusicMaker, the explosion of cheap home CD burners and media had a lot to do with it. When the cost of blank CDs goes from $10 to $0.10 in a few years, and

the perils (and promises) of software products . . . | 117

the cost of some CD burners nears $100, the value proposition of paying someone to create a CD for you seems a little difficult to swallow.

But high-speed access also had an impact. Volatile Media counted on people not having the patience to wait for a long download. Unfortunately, while long download times were fairly common in 1999 and early 2000, by February 2001, Nielsen NetRatings was reporting that 12 million people (around one-fifth of the U.S. Web population) had access to high-speed lines via ISDN, DSL, or cable . . . a 150 percent increase over the previous year. At the same time, the demographic of those with broadband access—men between 25 and 34—matched the demographic of those buying CD burners. And twice the number of people—24 million—had access to high-speed connections at work, according to Jupiter MediaMetrix. By 2005, the Strategis Group expects the majority of U.S. home users to connect via broadband connections.

Could MusicMaker and EZGamer have foreseen the changes in technology that led to their demise? In the case of MusicMaker, it's a tough call—few, if any, analysts saw the meteoric rise of P2P (peer-to-peer) file sharing that has rocked all corners of the music industry and helped drive CD-burner sales. On the other hand, EZGamer and its sister brands should have seen the writing on the wall. Since the beginning of the Web, users have been pushing for faster, cheaper access, and the marketplace has responded by providing it. Even as far back as 1995 DSL (then in its ADSL incarnation) was starting to roll out as a consumer alternative to analog modems, and Comcast was soon to debut its @Home broadband cable service.

In the digital age, all directions lead downstream to bits. If something can be digitized, it probably will be. And, once removed from the physical limitations of the analog realm, digital media will continue to move to consumers at ever-increasing speeds. Right now in 2001 as video tapes are beginning to be eclipsed by DVDs, a new MP4-based format called "DivX" has started to gain popularity online, allowing users to "rip" DVDs into downloadable files. Of course, those files are in the hundreds of megabytes and inaccessible to all but those with the fastest connections. For now. Five years ago, the thought of releasing on the Web a game demo of 100+ megabytes would have been absurd—nobody would have been able to download it. Today, the demo for Blizzard Entertainment's game *Diablo II*

118 | the dot.bomb survival guide

tips the virtual scales at a whopping 127 megabytes . . . and has been downloaded over 150,000 times at Download.com.

from here to cyberspace

Transforming data into physical objects seems to be a losing cause. But what about capturing data from the physical world and sending it to the Internet? And what about transferring data from the Net for mobile use?

By now, everyone knows someone who has a mobile computing device, whether a Palm Pilot, Handspring Visor, or *Windows* CE palmtop. Over 4.8 million mobile computing devices were sold in the United States in 1999, sales that Cahners In-Stat predicts will grow to 16.7 million by 2004. While many of these devices do not have real-time data access (except for the pricey Palm VII and palmtops equipped with aftermarket wireless modems), many more people are coming online with their mobile phones: A growing number of the 40 percent of Americans with mobile phones are being offered Internet access along with their regular service. In Europe, where mobile phone penetration is higher—at least 56 percent according to the Research Centre of Bornholm—41 percent of mobile users have some sort of Internet access on their phones, with 20 percent using wireless access protocol (WAP) services. In August 2000, Europeans sent over 1 billion short text messages (SMSs), a number that continues to rise.

Beyond cell phones and PDAs, several attempts have been made to create devices that allow users to interact with the real world by recording, marking time, or scanning barcodes and then uploading the information they gather to the Internet. Other companies have tried to make a go of it with devices that download information from the Internet (or information supplied by the company) to devices that users can carry around and use in their real life. Providing everything from books to maps to music, these devices allow users to carry a little piece of the Net with them wherever they go, without having to deal with the expense of wireless data access.

Some of these experiments have succeeded extremely well. Vindago, a service that allows users to download city guides into their PDAs, has enjoyed extraordinary growth since its introduction (Figure 4-4). Currently providing guides to 20 cities (with more on the way), Vindago brought in 250,000 users in 2000, more than 10 times the number of people who signed up for wireless Web access during the same period. AvantGo, another service for PDA users, lets subscribers define channels of news and information content that are "clipped" and downloaded to their PDAs as they sleep. The company posted 526 percent growth in the fourth quarter of 2000, as compared to the same time the previous year, allowing them to predict profitability two quarters earlier than they had originally thought . . . without any additional funding.

Figure 4-4. Vindago

Providing data to carry around in PDAs seems to be working pretty well for AvantGo and Vindago. Unfortunately, experiments with specialized devices that either allow users to interact with the analog world or receive wireless city-guide info haven't fared so well.

Scout Electromedia was born in 1999 and funded by Flatiron Partners, Idealab!, Chase Capital Partners, and Techfund capital to the tune of $22 million. Its concept was relatively simple: Create a device that consumers could use to wirelessly receive city-guide information. Charge users $99 for the device, deliver information overnight via pager networks when bandwith rates are low, and support the service through ads, not subscription fees.

"Scout Electromedia's goal is to design products for the 260 million people in the United States who don't use PDAs," said CEO

Geoff Pitfeild in the press release announcing its launch. "When we began the company we set out to create simple and useful wireless products that consumers really want."

The idea was to do an end-run around the more expensive Palm devices by going to the mass markets with a device that was cheap and easy to use. The egg-shaped device named "Modo" was a vision of simplicity, sporting a small (105-X 140 pixel) LCD screen, a single control button, and two thumbwheels (Figure 4-5). Ads were displayed as banners along the bottom of the screen; selecting a banner expanded the ad to fill the screen.

Figure 4-5. Modo, Courtesy of Ideo (www.ideo.com)

The company also forged relationships with retailers such as Virgin Megastores, DKNY, Rolo, ABS, and Fred Segal, as well as Village Voice Media. PageNet was to be the wireless network supplier. Devices would be sold at Virgin Megastores and online at modo.net.

Besides delivering entertainment content and ads, Modo was designed to deliver content that would drive customers to retailers in the form of coupons and other incentives. When the coupon was "redeemed" at the store by plugging it into a special cradle, the customer would receive a discount, and the retailer would get information about its customer. It seemed like an idea that couldn't fail.

It did. In fact, Modo was stillborn. Just 2 months after its initial launch in New York, L.A., and San Francisco (and 2 weeks before its scheduled launch party), Modo shut its doors, laying off 84 employees with just a few hours' notice. Its parting words stated that "despite strong consumer response to Modo, there was insufficient funding to support ongoing operations prior to the company's reaching profitability." It still held its party though, using it to say "bon voyage" rather than "welcome."

Yet another victim of Internet time and "market conditions." Actually Modo was a victim of too much spending too fast, and of a parent company that was sinking quick. According to *Silicon Alley News*, sources inside the company revealed that ad-firm Wieden + Kennedy had spent $20 million—half—of its startup capital, though other sources close to the company say the number was far less than that . . . the truth (of course) is probably somewhere in between. Scout Electromedia had also retained uber-design-firm Ideo (innovative designers of the TiVo, Polaroid PopShots, and 3Com PalmV PDA) . . . not a cheap partner by any stretch of the imagination.

But customer interest was probably at the heart of Modo's problems. While Scout touted "strong consumer response," ex-employees told the *Silicon Alley News* "the hip-clinging device never really caught on with the mass market."

Modo's pricing and revenue model caused it to be caught in the Catch 22 trap of ad-supported services. The company couldn't support itself on sales of the devices . . . the $99 cost couldn't support the whole company. It never got a lot of users. And advertisers wouldn't buy media on a device that had no audience, drying up that revenue stream. Throw in the fact that parent Idealab! was currently reeling under several high-profile failures (such as Eve.com), and you've got a disaster waiting to happen. No light at the end of the tunnel. No launch party. No money. No company.

Another company that had trouble leaping the digital to analog divide was Xenote, a San Mateo company that produced a keychain-sized device called the "Tag" (Figure 4-6). The iTag allowed radio listeners to bookmark songs by pointing it at the radio and pushing a button. Listeners could then go home, plug the serial cable into their PC, connect to Xenote's website, and find out the name of the song they were listening to.

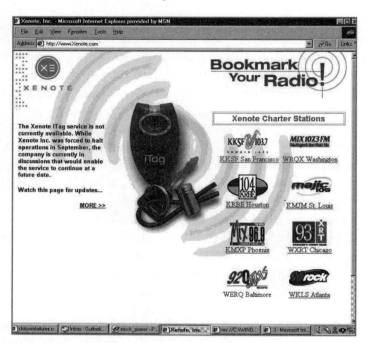

Figure 4-6. Xenote.com

No longer would you have to wonder what band played that catchy new tune you'd been listening to. No more sitting around listening to the radio until the DJ got around to naming the songs. And if you wanted to buy what you heard, a quick click and the CD would be yours.

The initial testing audience loved it. In testing groups in Houston and San Francisco, participants increased their radio listening time once they had the device. Surprisingly, 20 percent of the users had "tagged" ads so that they could check out the companies advertised.

Radio stations loved the concept, too. Before it shut down in September 2000, Xenote had signed deals with over 60 radio stations in its test markets. The device gave it the ability to attract advertisers in an increasingly competitive market as well as participate in back-channel deals through ecommerce. In addition, the devices provided instant feedback to the stations on its listeners' habits and music preferences—information that's gold to the stations.

In the end, even though Xenote had given away 15,000 of its iTags (which cost the company $5 each to manufacture), it couldn't get enough interest from investors to continue marketing and making the devices. Unlucky enough to have just come into its own after the April 2000 stock market crash, Xenote couldn't find an investor who wanted to dive into the murky realms of advertising-supported models. The fact that the company had to deal with real-world devices just made the risk harder to swallow.

Even with two well-publicized failures, the device market still continues along with some pretty heavy players and some early successes. Sony has come out with the eMarker, a $19.99 device that does pretty much the same thing as Xenote, only with one radio station and better style. Sony plans on partnering with music stores to get a commission on CD sales driven by the device.

Symbol Technologies briefly tested its CS 2000 Consumer Memory Scanner with both PlanetRx and startup FastFrog. The small, egg-shaped device allows consumers to scan barcodes on products and then upload the product information to the Web. PlanetRx used the CS 2000 to streamline customer orders: Customers scanned the products they needed and put the scanner in its cradle; their order was then completed automatically. FastFrog tested a service that kids could use to create online "wish lists" by scanning goods in participating mall retailers.

But why have some attempts to link data to real life worked while others have failed? Brand and resources are two obvious reasons. While Xenote was a small player with limited funding that was able to reach only two markets with a free device that cost $5 to produce, Sony is, well . . . Sony. It has got plenty of resources to put behind the eMarker, resources that can sustain it until it's proven that it isn't going to work or until it begins to become profitable. The price may prove to be the sticky point: Is it really worth 20 bucks to someone to be able to identify a song he or she heard?

Modo's demise is more complicated. There's clearly a need and desire for city-guide information in the marketplace. Vindago has proven that there's a viable economic model for providing such information, and a lot of the research around the wireless industry has validated the market desire for information and guides. In fact, one of the recurring themes found in our global wireless research (see Chapter 3) is that people really and truly *want* location-based information. They *want* guides. They *want* digital companions.

124 | the dot.bomb survival guide

And they're willing to pay for them. Japan's telco, NTTDoCoMo, reported in February 2001 that half of the users of their I-Mode wireless service are paying for content. Subscribers sign on for an average of 2.2 content services delivered through their cell phones, content that includes many location-based services including ticketing, maps, and restaurant guides.

There's also clearly a need for simpler devices to access mobile information. The Boston Consulting Group reported in a November 2000 study that one out of four mobile users stopped trying to use mobile commerce services after several attempts. Citing high costs, slow speeds, awkward navigation, difficult data entry, and unreliable services, consumers turned away from the services before they could complete their transactions. However, the study also reported that fully 82 percent of mobile users expected their mobile devices to become their own personal travel assistants by 2003.

And that fact may be the key . . . people expect their mobile devices to be their guides, their companions. As prices go down and adoptions of PDAs and cell phones go up (Cahners In-Stat expects Palmtop sales to hit nearly 16 million by 2004, and the U.S. cell-phone population has been widely projected to be above 60 percent in the same time period), the necessity for small, single-use devices will probably go down. Even now, how many people have to spend their lives juggling a PDA, cell phone, and pager. Probably too many. As devices become more general purpose—PDAs that work as cell phones or cell phones integrating PDA functionality—there will be less of a need for specialized devices such as Modo. In fact, Modo's $99 price tag is only $50 cheaper than Palm's m100 handheld or Handspring's basic Visor model. Both cost about 150 bucks, and can download software, play games, manage schedules, and keep telephone lists. Modo couldn't do any of that.

In fact, devices like Modo may be able to survive in the future only as advertising-supported freebies. But with personal computing becoming more ubiquitous as our dataspheres expand through personal area networking (PAN) using Bluetooth (or other wireless technologies) to allow us to swap data between our PDAs, cell phones, and desktop machines, the idea of carrying yet another device whose functionality can be replicated in software on any of these devices may seem laughably old fashioned. Vindago will survive because it is completely virtual, downloadable into devices we already have, and transportable across multiple access technologies. Devices like Modo, bound by their own limitations, are stop-gap technologies at best, bridges crossing the chasm until a better, more general solution comes along.

ASPs: virtual products (virtual profits?)

While many companies were delivering their own software products over the Web in a way that differed little from the old shrink-wrap method of one-box-one-license, others were thinking about how to use the unique qualities of the Internet to deliver software products in a new way. Enter the application service provider (ASP) model.

Developed as a way to use the Net to provide centralized access to software from anywhere, the ASP model has proven to be one of the most enduring. Instead of spending the vast sums of money to install and maintain software on internal LAN-based servers, companies can basically "rent" their software as they need it. Let someone else maintain it, install new upgrades, and deal with all the hassles that come with owning software. The ASP has made the prospect of using software less expensive and easier for a whole range of businesses. For the companies serving the applications, software transformed itself from a product into a service, with a long-term revenue stream from users who had to continue to pay to play.

Over time, the definition of ASP has continued to grow, encompassing a whole range of companies that "rent" software to a wide range of businesses. Wireless application service providers (such as Aether Systems) allow companies to deploy wireless applications via cell phones and PDAs without having to worry about maintaining the software themselves. Other ASPs provide rented software to B2B exchanges, ecommerce sites, and content providers. It's a compelling model and one that's been copied, modified, and reborn numerous times. In fact, as we'll see throughout this book, the ASP model is so compelling that many a dot.bomb in its dying days has tried to resurrect itself by licensing the technology that it failed to make profitable to other companies trying to make a go of it in the same space.

126 | the dot.bomb survival guide

Desktop.com was one of these companies. Launched in September 1999 by ex-Yahoo! millionaire Katie Burke and her partner Larry Drebes, Desktop.com was designed to provide applications to the masses by offering a virtual "desktop" that looked and felt like a typical *Windows* desktop. Members of the site would be able to use various applications hosted by Desktop.com that looked and felt like the stuff they were used to on their own PCs. Mail, calendar, word processing, email, and other applications would be held in a virtual "hard drive" (complete with 10 megabytes of storage) that could be called up by anyone with access to a Web browser.

The concept was powerful: In this world of mobile professionals who could find themselves in any place at any time, why should they be tied down to the machine that they had on their desk? Why not keep their information securely on the Web and use it where they happened to be? The Internet had become nearly ubiquitous in business at this point. The concept made perfect sense.

Investors seemed to think so. Venture capital firms Kohlberg Kravis Roberts & Co., Sequoia Capital, and Accel Partners all chipped in $29 million before launch. The company operated in secret for a long time, with none of its 38 employees giving the outside world any inkling of what it was up to. As Netscape had imagined a few years earlier, it felt that its system had the potential to unseat Microsoft, freeing users from their operating systems via a universal interface.

If it was going to succeed, the company knew that it had to do two things: get developers to create applications to run in what was essentially a new OS and get users to migrate from their desktop PCs to Desktop.com. Those goals were going to take some serious marketing to achieve, and Desktop.com knew it. According to SmartMoney.com, the company initially planned to spend $10 million of its initial capital (bolstered by some millions contributed from its founders who sold their first company, RocketMail, to Yahoo! in 1997 for $89 million) in order to drive traffic and build critical mass.

It wasn't the first into this space though. Jump Networks had launched a Web-based calendar service, as had startup AnyDay.com, which offered full suites of personal information management tools including calendars, address books, to-do lists, and reminder services.

the perils (and promises) of software products . . . | 127

Both promised to synchronize with PDAs, providing one-stop/access-anywhere solutions for keeping track of all your personal data.

Desktop.com wanted to go one better, though—it didn't just want you to keep your calendar on the Web; it wanted you to do all your computing on the Web. To do that required having applications. To get applications, it had to get developers, a task that its site said would be relegated to a developer relations manager who would "encourage software developers to build applications for the company's service . . . and [evangelize] the company's platform to the industry and development community." A tall order.

How did Desktop.com plan to pay for all this? Advertising, of course. Like many other Internet-only companies garnering big VC money in 1999, it seemed like the way to go. While users logged in to use their calendars, write memos, or send email, sponsored banners and buttons would help drive them to advertisers' sites and services.

By November 2000 the plan seemed to be in trouble, as the expected user base never materialized. Desktop.com announced that it was planning on shifting to a business-to-business-based ASP model, providing its software as a front end to other application service providers who wanted to aggregate all their solutions into one common interface provided by Desktop.com. In an interview with online ASP magazine *ASPStreet.com*, CEO Katie Burke defended the shift not as an abandonment of its previous model but as a way to take advantage of opportunities in the marketplace.

"We could pursue a model that would be getting end users on their own desktop," she told *ASPStreet* editorial director Todd Carter, "but we thought the bigger opportunity was for letting other people build their own desktops. You could say the other model didn't work, but you could also say that we didn't follow the other model to fruition. Because we didn't. We say this opportunity comes at a time when there's a lot of market change. And we decided that there are businesses interested in our technology; we should pursue that."

Of course, that "market change" she mentioned was the rapidly declining Wall Street interest in advertising-supported "pure plays" brought about by the April 2000 crash. In fact, at the time that the "shift" in Desktop.com's model occurred, the B2B market was seen

128 | the dot.bomb survival guide

as the one to put money into, and the ASP model was particularly hot. The ASP market had shown some signs of instability (such as the death of RedGorilla.com), but generally the sector was still viewed by analysts as one of the most promising. ASP-giant USInternetworking had seen its stock drop, but it continued (and still continues) to show revenue gains. Other dot.coms had changed their business model to take advantage of the interest in ASPs. Desktop.com seemed to be making a good move. It had missed the window to go public as a B2C play, and if it ever wanted to hit the big money, it had to create a model that the markets liked.

Unfortunately it was too late. On December 14, 2000, the company saw the writing on the wall, as markets plunged even lower and the prospects of finding funding for Desktop.com's shift to an ASP evaporated. Rather than lose all the investors' money (including the founders'), by changing to a model that required users to pay for a previously free service, the board of directors shut down the company, reportedly returning about half of the venture funding to the investors.

The ASP marketplace continues to grow and shift with the fortunes of the stock market. USInternetworking, arguably the grand-daddy of all ASPs, has seen its stock plummet in value since April 2000, but it has continued to post increased revenues, reporting over 200 percent growth in 2000 and investment from a variety of industry heavy-hitters. The number of companies counting themselves members of the ASP market is huge; ASPStreet.com has listings for over 10,000 companies in its *ASP Directory* as of February 2001.

While somewhat more cautious than they were in 1999 or early 2000, analysts are still hot on the future of the ASP. IDC Research predicted in its *ASPs in 2001—10 Market Predictions* report that the ASP industry would top $1 billion in 2001. Other analysts have been more ebullient: Dataquest predicted in August 2000 that the ASP market would be worth $25.3 billion by 2004. Scott McNealy, CEO of Sun Microsystems, and Larry Ellison of Oracle have continued to sing the praises of the thin-client "network computer" designed to access the Web and run applications remotely. Even Microsoft has embraced the model with its new .Net strategy that emphasizes the "run anywhere" philosophy inherent to the ASP model.

the perils (and promises) of software products . . . | 129

Undoubtedly ASPs will survive, but what happened with Desktop.com provides a microcosm of the challenges the ASP market will face as it tries to avoid dot.bombing-out in the coming years.

For Desktop.com to work and achieve critical mass, it had to get *used*. And *really* used by the people who signed on to it—they'd have to keep their calendars, to-do lists, address books, everything on the site. Even though many companies like Desktop.com eventually incorporated PDA synchronization features, making the leap from desktop to Web still required users to make major changes in the way they thought of computing. Truly embracing a service like Desktop.com meant abandoning the PC- and LAN-based solutions millions of workers have become used to. Also, putting all of their data on a remote server required trusting that company to keep out of their information stored on that server . . . not easy to believe as privacy concerns increase among Web users. Finally, using a remotely hosted service like Desktop.com required a connection to the Internet . . . not always possible for people on a plane or in their car.

Of course, synchronizing all this data with your PDA could potentially alleviate this issue, but the fact still remains that many people have client-server-based address books and calendar applications that work just fine, thank you. The benefits of moving to a remotely hosted solution don't outweigh the psychological costs of dealing with the hassles. When you face a decision to migrate to Desktop.com or not, it is just a lot easier to use your desktop machine or get a laptop if you have to be on the road.

The "online desktop" market didn't die with Destkop.com, but it's undergoing rapid change. Other companies with similar models to Desktop.com that are still in business (like MyWebOS.com) have seen the writing on the wall and have adjusted their models to primarily provide infrastructure as an ASP rather than try to make money in the wild and wooly consumer marketplace.

But the problems that Desktop.com had mirror the problems that many ASPs (and thin-client/network computer vendors) are encountering as they try to get the corporate world to shift to a remotely hosted, leased-access model. Privacy, security, and reliability are huge issues. In addition, making the shift to remotely hosted software means a major shift in culture and personnel. The IT department, secure as the keepers of the code, are at once both the ones to

130 | the dot.bomb survival guide

lose the most in this setup as well as the target audiences . . . a tough sell in some cases.

Eventually, the ASP model will take over. It just makes too much financial sense for a lot of companies to lease rather than own software. But as in the case of the B2B exchange model, ASPs may be loved more by CEOs, CFOs, and COOs than they are by the folks in the trenches who have to use them all the time.

To thrive, ASPs are going to have to move judiciously to keep from flaming out before profitability. Or they'll have to look for models that allow for flexibility. Jamcracker, a startup ASP that's drawn in more than $100 million in VC money, follows this path by aggregating services of other ASPs, allowing it to quickly change its model and offerings to suit an increasingly volatile marketplace.

Efficiency and cost-effectiveness may win out in the end, but getting there is going to require changing human behavior, and that can take a while.

respect the cost of change . . . and think different

Getting people to accept a new product and service is inherently more difficult than getting them to try a new Web page for their news or buy something from an online store. A product is a tool, something that people use in order to achieve a purpose. Whether or not that product is sold in shrinkwrap, on the Web, or packaged as a rented "service," making the commitment to purchase a product requires making a commitment to change behavior. Most people don't use two tools to accomplish the same tasks: How many folks do you know who use two different word processors, two separate accounting systems (OK, yes, there *are* reasons for that, but we're talking about legal uses here), or two different email programs? It doesn't make sense: If you're using a tool to create documents and to store and process information, you're going to want to keep that information in one format with one program.

Now there are people who use two different Web browsers. Why? Because even though Microsoft has essentially won the Browser War, each browser has its own quirks that sometimes requires switching

the perils (and promises) of software products . . . | 131

to the other. Additionally, browsers are information display programs, not information processing programs. Most people don't have to worry about storing processed information from one that isn't compatible with another. And both products are free. The cost of maintaining two browsers on a machine is minimal. Why not have both just in case?

In order for a product to be successful, its benefits must outweigh its psychological and financial costs. In the case of the many "free" programs out there (such as the myriad instant messaging clients), the "cost" is calculated by the number of people that someone can contact with the program. If all your friends use AOL's instant messaging service, then you are probably not going to use Microsoft's, unless the two programs can talk to each other. Then the decision becomes one of brand recognition and trust.

This cost-benefit calculus also applies to the real-world objects that interact with data from the Internet. As the functions become more common and commodified, when any cell phone can pull in data as well as any other, when all PDAs essentially have the same function, the battle will then center around the ancillary rather than the core features and benefits. Right now this is true in the PC world where innovation must be limited in order to maintain compatibility. PCs must compete in a more commodified space, luring users with special deals, ease of use, or better peripherals.

We're moving toward standardization in products. We have to. As more and more electronic gadgets are linked together via new technologies such as Bluetooth and home networking products, it'll be essential that those products be able to talk to each other. As the Internet moves away from the desktop to become a ubiquitous presence, when TCP/IP becomes the blood through which all data flow, resisting commodification will be essential for the survival of products.

The wrong way for product creators and manufacturers to do this is through price. As many ecommerce sites discovered, competing on price locks the competitors into a downward spiral of declining profitability and declining innovation. The Internet has an amazing power to commodify everything it touches: One store is as "far away" as any other, features are laid bare for the world to see, and everything is experienced through the mediation of the screen. Competitors in the product arenas of the future will have to compete on service and other intangibles, product "features" that can't easily be copied or coopted.

The ASP industry (and other industries that seek to turn software products into services) must understand these lessons too. Simply providing remote access to software for the lowest price won't be enough. With over 10,000 ASPs currently vying for market share, differentiation through unique features will be key. And while today those unique features can be exclusive deals with software vendors, that kind of exclusivity probably won't last forever. The longer-term solution will be building organizations that provide ancillary services tied to the "products" that add additional value in a way that a competitor can't.

Making the decision to switch to a new product (and remain loyal to that product) asks a lot from your potential customers. While your product may seem like a fantastic idea to you, if that product's benefits don't outweigh the cost of the commitment necessary for your customers to use that product, it won't take off. Online-only email services such as Hotmail are able to survive in the face of client-based email competition because they don't ask the user to give up all of his or her email functionality to the online service . . . just the part that they want to be online. In fact, these services really don't compete with desktop clients at all. The desktop-based PC email client can be used to keep work-related email, and the online email client can be used for personal correspondence. Essentially, they actually serve two different audiences in the same person: the private self and the corporate self.

That lesson may represent the final one to take away from this chapter: Products that succeed are ones that understand their audiences—what motivates them, what benefits they need that they aren't currently receiving, and what they're willing to pay (psychologically and monetarily) for what they need. Opportunities are everywhere if we look outside of our own experience and to our potential customers.

The risks of building new products are great, but the rewards are potentially huge. The companies that will succeed are the ones that understand their customers and can differentiate themselves based on that knowledge, taking into account the unique complexities and benefits of the Internet.

burnout: short-term thinking = short-term companies

While there are a lot of companies profiled in this book that failed because their management did not understand the marketplace, bad timing, poorly conceived products, unworkable funding deals, overspending on advertising, or business models that just didn't work, there are also a lot of companies who died simply because they burned through their cash too quickly. They weren't victims of complex economic forces or behind-the-scenes plotting. They didn't die because their models hadn't accounted for all the complexities of the new marketplace. The fundamental business model they had subscribed to wasn't wrong. If it had been, the others who survived in the sector would have perished too. No, many companies died simply because they thought the party would last forever . . . or at least last a lot longer than it did. They had lived not in the real world but in the white-hot light of "Internet time," risking a lot of other people's money for the big score that came on paper but blew away with the whims of the stock market.

One thing is now clear: Short-term thinking leads to short-term companies.

In retrospect, it's easy to blame many of them for thinking that everything was different. The commercial Internet had achieved 30 percent penetration in just 4 years, faster than any other major technology the world had ever seen. The popular media and the analyst community whipped the marketplace into frenzy with speculation extrapolated from a few years of data. If the Web was going to be as big as everyone thought and grow as quickly as popular wisdom held, then it seemed reasonable that those firms that could gain a toehold early on by raising the money could dominate the marketplace through brand recognition, locked-up exclusive deals, and sheer size. It made perfect sense that a company's survival depended on being bigger, faster, and louder than its competitors.

Unfortunately, things didn't work out that way.

how the concept of public markets changed

While the inner workings of the stock market have always been in constant motion, the reasons for going public with a technology company (or any other company) used to be pretty cut-and-dried. Companies went public because they needed money to build out their infrastructure, wanted to expand into new marketplaces or technologies, required capital to make major leaps in research and development, or to provide an exit strategy or liquidity for the owners. Once a company went public, the financial industry and public investors could use a series of well-honed tools and criteria for determining the value of the company and what they would pay for a share. After all the criteria were checked and the models modeled, they bought in. Or not.

But the decision to invest was based on time-honored principles. Was the company making money? Did it have a product that somebody wanted? Was it growing at a reasonable rate? What kind of cash reserves or assets on hand did it have? How did its earnings stand up when compared to other companies in its sector? What were its competitors doing? Did it have a lock on technology through patents? How did its prospects look 10 years out?

Of course not everyone followed these rules. There has always been speculation in hot marketplaces from personal computers in the eighties to biotech to oil to telecommunications in the nineties. For most of those industries many of the old rules *seemed* to apply. Make more than you spend. Make a product that somebody wants.

burnout: short-term thinking = short term companies | 135

Have a way to let them know about it and get them your products. Grow as fast as the industry will let you.

But, as discussed earlier, Netscape's IPO changed all that. Here was a company with little earnings, no major revenue stream, certainly no profits, that gave away its main product. By all traditional measures, it should have been a disaster, but it wasn't. The market loved Netscape, and all of a sudden the old rules didn't seem to apply. The New Economy was born.

In a way, the riches of the New Economy fueled a machine that ran itself. As the money flowed in, everyone who touched it became rich. The early investors and venture capitalists landed huge wads of cash when the companies they funded went public with huge valuations, bringing in many multiples of their original investments. The investment bankers, lawyers, and others who had their hands in the process got rich through commissions. Many of the analysts who were connected to the investment banking firms bringing dot.coms public had great incentives to keep hyping the companies that they were involved with, even though doing so was at one time considered a major breach of ethics. The industry media, hot for a story and basking in the sudden limelight of the popular press's attention, hyped each new shining star in glowing cover stories, all while sucking in millions that the new dot.coms spent advertising in these magazines. The popular press, always attracted to wealth, fame, and power was drawn in, inciting popular opinion with tales of instant wealth and opportunity. The public, seeing what was going on and not wanting to get left out, responded by turning to the stock market in record numbers. Words like *day trading* and *IPO* became part of dinner-table conversation.

There were fortunes to be made. The market rewarded big thinking, big dreams, big plans, and big risk. The fastest, the smartest, and the strongest were the ones that were going to survive. The timid could go home to their mommies.

money changes everything

The abundance of capital also changed the way companies thought of themselves and changed the way they thought they needed to operate. When cash seemed limitless, anything seemed possible.

136 | the dot.bomb survival guide

Money meant freedom. And it also meant tacit validation of what a company was doing. After all, if the financial world thought that revenue, profits, sales, and history didn't matter, why should a company operate under those seemingly Old Economy structures? This time, things were different.

This rejection of the old rules led to some incredibly short-sighted thinking. As stated earlier, growth rates and market projections had to be based on a very limited range of data, and plans were laid that counted on the market and the Internet growing at continued explosive rates. As a result, short-term thinking led to assumptions with fatal long-term consequences:

- *Profitability can come later.* The commandment was to be first and be big NOW. Profitability could come in the third, fourth, or even fifth year of operations. The goal was to dominate the marketplace through sheer size and count on continued investment and high stock valuations to keep things running until then.
- *We'll figure out who our customers are as we go.* This was standard operating procedure for a lot of dot.bomb ecommerce sites. Since nobody thought they knew who would be online, the idea was to test, measure, and refine as you went. Some companies committed an even bigger error—they thought they knew exactly who their customers were before they started, even without any real research to back them up. Most of them are gone.
- *Brand equals brand recognition. Brand recognition can come only from large, expensive advertising or PR campaigns.* As we'll explore in more depth in the next chapter, making a big splash with a big TV campaign might have led to an immediate boost in traffic for a short time, but it didn't necessarily lead to customers. Which brings us to. . . .
- *Eyeballs equal customers.* Many sites with big ad budgets did a great job of driving lots of traffic to their sites immediately after their ads ran, but once they blew that wad of cash getting the first crop of visitors to the site, many had a hard time getting them to come back or even remember who they were. In fact, one study by Active Research at the end of 1999 discovered that 25 percent of U.S. adults couldn't remember a single dot.com ad, and only 1 in 10 remembered a single spot. Not exactly a recipe for long-term success.

- *Valuation equals permanent wealth.* Other companies, jumping from the starting blocks with huge IPO valuations, assumed that money would always be available to them. While the initial surge of cash was able to fund expensive infrastructure and lavish ad campaigns, lock-out periods usually kept the rest of the value under wraps until it had started to decline. Plans laid when the company's stock is at $100 don't make as much sense when the stock's at $10 (or below).
- *Grow, grow, grow!* Once companies thought they had money to burn forever, many decided to act as though it would be around forever. They took advantage of their valuations to invest in growing themselves regardless of what their revenues told them was sustainable. The burn rate was justified because of a distant promise of possibility and ready access to capital.
- *Inefficiency doesn't matter.* When there always seems to be enough money to do anything you want, why bother with figuring out how best to use it? On the message boards of dot.bomb tracking sites like dotcomscoop.com and FuckedCompany.com, one of the most popular reactions to big layoffs or big closures is always "What the hell did all those people do?" Many companies covered up problems with process by just throwing more money and people at the problem. You can't keep that up when money's tight.
- *Extravagance is a right.* If there's a ton of money lying around, why not use it? While some dot.coms like Pixelon created a lot of noise (and got in trouble with their investors) by throwing lavish coming-out parties, many other companies treated themselves to opulent offices with $14,000 flat-screen video displays and $1,000 office chairs . . . *and* lavish coming-out parties.
- *Perks compensate for long hours and low pay.* By now, the perks enjoyed by many dot.commers at public companies are the stuff of legend. Game rooms, personal trainers, full-time concierges, company cars, company boats, and all the soda one could drink were standard at some companies desperate to hang on to employees in a tight labor market. If a firm was going to grow, it had to be at the expense of workers driven to 80-hour weeks with no sleep.
- *Assume that stock options will make employees happy forever.* At the time, "paying" employees with stock options seemed like the way to go. Only chumps went for cash that was worth only

138 | the dot.bomb survival guide

what it was worth the day you got it. Options in a growing company could be (and were for many) worth a fortune when the big payday came. Unfortunately, such schemes only worked when a company's stock was headed for an IPO and kept going up. As soon as the stock went down and employees' options were underwater (lost more than the current value of the stock), employee morale plummeted and defections rose. Talent needed to grow the company fled to the next big opportunity with little or no thought of loyalty to the loser they were leaving behind. Getting new top employees was impossible for companies in decline.

The companies that made these assumptions died. Their valuations plunged, many by several hundred percent before they went out of business. With the stock or venture money gone, they couldn't continue to pay for the employees they hired or the new distribution centers they'd built. As the value fell, just when they needed money the most, investors, smelling death, wouldn't give them any more cash. Employees who'd seen all their work come to nothing bailed out. Customers avoided the companies, fearful that their orders wouldn't get delivered or their subscription fees wouldn't get returned. Sites that depended on advertising had a harder and harder time getting people to place banners on the site, even at fire-sale prices. With no brand equity left (unless bad press counts toward brand recognition) and no assets to sell, most companies closed up shop and slipped away into the night.

But not all. As we'll see in this chapter, many companies have successfully weathered the storm of "market conditions" and have achieved profitability and continued success. They may have grown slower, but they grew smarter. And, in the end, all that matters in the world of business (ebusiness or not) is who is left standing.

ecommerce: long-term customers = profits

There's an old saying among merchants: "Retail is detail." This old saw turns out to be just as true on the Web as it is in the analog world. Ecommerce sites have to straddle both the digital and analog worlds successfully in order to stay in business. Not only do they

burnout: short-term thinking = short term companies | 139

have to invest in the development and infrastructure of their own site—no small feat when you're talking about building a site that can withstand the onslaught of millions of customers—but they also have to deal with the physical details of warehousing products, packing them, and shipping them successfully to their customers. Of course, they also have to spend money on actually getting customers: Customer acquisition costs and conversion ratios are the numbers that they must live (and die) by.

While ecommerce was initially seen as *the* business on the Web, making a buck on the Web by selling goods has turned out to be one of the more difficult businesses. According to WebMergers.com, of the 130 dot.coms that died in 2000, fully 75 percent of them were etailers. And while the size of these companies runs a pretty wide gamut from nonfunded startup to smaller seed-capital concerns like BBQ.com (which raised less than $2 million before succumbing) to huge losers like garden.com, many of the forces that worked to kill these companies were the same in kind if not always in scale.

Garden.com's rapid rise, spectacular burn rate, and meteoric fall made it one of the biggest losers among the dot.bomb etailers of 2000. Born in September 1995, garden.com sought to redefine the way that people bought lawn and garden supplies including tools, seeds, and plants. An independent concern stepping into a world previously dominated by old-line catalog companies like Burpee, garden.com combined stunning design with well-written content buyers' guides and a large selection of products.

Garden.com's site was beautiful. Rather than presenting its products using impenetrable jargon and pictures only a horticulturist could love (like many of the older seed companies), garden.com provided handy on-site guides that helped people who knew enough about gardening to know where they lived pick out and order a perfect prepackaged garden or pick the right tool.

However, this content and functionality came at a price. How much is unclear, though garden.com's SEC filings reveal that it lost $75.5 million before going out of business late in 2000. Some estimates are much higher. *Forbes* reported that garden.com blew through $455 million before imploding.

Visitors to the site found it compelling, and so did investors. On September 16, 1999, garden.com went public at $12 and saw its shares rise to $19.06 on the first day. This IPO raised $50 million, money that the site sorely needed as it continued its expansion.

The public's initial reaction was positive. In the fiscal year ending in June 2000, garden.com reported 187 percent growth and revenues of $15.5 million. The site had over 1.5 million members with more signing up every day. Yet these sales weren't enough to offset the company's prodigious burn rate. From the quarter ending September 1999 through the quarter ending September 2000, garden.com reported a total net income loss of $48.6 million . . . an average loss of more than $4 million per month. The site tried to staunch its wounds by laying off 40 percent of its workforce in 2000, but it wasn't enough (Figure 5-1).

Figure 5-1. Garden.com Announces That It's Not Taking Any More Orders

At the time of its demise, garden.com had only $390,000 cash on hand, not even enough to keep it running for a week at the rate it was going through cash building infrastructure, servicing orders, and spending on marketing (including a print "buying guide" magazine it published in March 1999). After announcing the company's closure in December 2000, CEO Clif Sharples revealed that garden.com's penchant for spending cash in the short term killed the company. In an interview with *DSN Retailing Today,* Sharples told reporter Debbie Howell that profitability was attainable ... once the company had reached $70 million in sales annually. It would have needed between $10 and $40 million right away to stay in business, money that it couldn't raise because of investors' skittishness to fund unprofitable ecommerce ventures.

Was $70 million even possible? Seventy million in revenues would have taken 450 percent growth, more than twice what the company was able to accomplish in its best year. At the rate it was burning cash, $40 million would have sustained it for only another 10 to 12 months ... probably not enough to increase sales by a factor of 4.

Clickmango.com: $4 million to 0 in 4 months

Starting with its launch April 2000, clickmango.com (Figure 5-2) was somewhat of a media darling. It boasted the support of popular *Absolutely Fabulous* actress Joanna Lumley ("Patsy" on the show) who appeared on the site as a shopping guide, reporter, and even as a character in a downloadable screensaver. The founders had created a buzz by reportedly raising $4.4 million in only 8 days from Atlas Venture and the venerable Rothschild family.

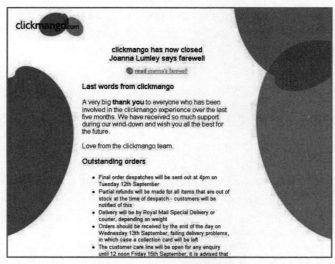

Figure 5-2. Clickmango Goodbye Page.

142 | the dot.bomb survival guide

The company ran into problems right away. Scared off by the U.S. dot.com market, additional potential investors avoided the site, and clickmango.com was unable to raise the $448,800 it said it needed to stay afloat. Amazingly, the site shut down in September 2000, a mere handful of months after its birth. Founder Toby Rowland told *The Industry Standard* that the site was doomed by "white hot competition" in the online health and beauty market. In fact, he saw dim prospects for the entire sector, declaring, "I don't see anyone surviving it."

It just couldn't sell enough to maintain the burn. Let's do the math. During its short life, clickmango.com burned an average of $733,333 per month of public operation. It had reported 750,000 page impressions per month at its peak. Assuming 3 impressions per visitor (a fairly reasonable assumption), that amounts to 250,000 visitors per month. In order to sustain its burn rate, clickmango would have had to sell $2.93 worth of goods to each and every visitor. But let's assume that a 100 percent conversion rate is unrealistic. At a very charitable visit-to-sale ratio of 25 percent, the site would have had 62,500 paying visitors per month. To reach the breakeven point, clickmango would have had to sell $11.73 worth of products to each customer just to break even.

In reality, the site reported modest sales of $12,000 per month. Going through the numbers again, that would amount to approximately 5 cents per customer, assuming 250,000 visitors. Even assuming a whopping 25 percent conversion ratio (62,500 visitors), that only amounts to about 19 cents of sales per visitor . . . way below the $11.73 it would need to make its numbers.

Short-term thinking. Short-term company.

Pets.com: traffic now, profits later

Like clickmango, Pets.com was another company that had a hard time spending less than it took in . . . a very hard time.

Launched in October 1998, Pets.com was out to revolutionize the way consumers bought pet food. Offering low prices on a huge line of goods, Pets.com seemed to make the idea of going to the grocery or pet store so, well, *twentieth century.*

It was a difficult, crowded marketplace. Gomez Advisors estimated that there were over 100 stores online selling pet supplies.

Pets.com had the cash though to make a go of it with more than $100 million in investment money. It also quickly had the brand; its sock puppet mascot became a cultural icon overnight, as the company spent $25 million in advertising. But even though it was able to bring in 570,000 customers, it was never able to make money.

By the end of 1999, Pets.com was burning through tremendous amounts of cash in an effort to dominate the marketplace . . . and that was its problem. In that year, Pets.com spent $55.3 million in an effort to sell goods that cost $13.4 million that brought in revenues of $5.8 million. Selling goods for less than it paid for them wasn't, in the end, a winning strategy. In November 2000, the board approved a liquidation plan that involved selling the company's assets (including the sock puppet mascot) in hopes of raising $9.75 million to repay its investors.

The company had burned through $147 million in 2 years by spending freely looking for the big score. Even at the end, its spending didn't slow. Pets.com paid 10 of its top executives bonuses totaling $1.35 million to stay until the end (Figure 5-3).

Figure 5-3. Pets.com? Nope . . . Now Brick-and-Mortar Retailer PETsMART.com Has the Domain

Based on analyst estimates of the online pet food market, Pets.com should have been a slam dunk. It wasn't. While the potential customers were there in theory, in practice, incredible brand

144 | the dot.bomb survival guide

recognition in the short term (who doesn't remember the sock puppet?) didn't equal long-term growth. Buying in to the Internet time fallacy, Pets.com believed that success meant grabbing market share today by building large volumes of immediate traffic.

What was the problem? People didn't come back. The experience of buying pet food online didn't add enough value (remember last chapter?) to entice people to change their ingrained spending habits. While it seemed to make more sense (in theory) to buy pet food online, most people, when Fido was hungry, would rather run to the grocery store than go through the hassle of purchasing online.

What would have saved Pets.com? Smarter spending that matched sales growth would have helped, with Pets.com expanding as its sales warranted. But the solution may run deeper. Pets.com should have emphasized the unique qualities that the Net brings to the transaction—scheduling, selection, etc.—and focused on models such as pet food "subscriptions" based on the pet's individual consumption or other value-added services. Let's face it: In the end, a bag of kibble is a bag of kibble. If a site doesn't make buying that bag of food easier, more fun, or better, most pet owners are just going to keep going to the grocery store.

MotherNature.com: artificial growth, natural death

MotherNature.com was another dot.bomb that closed its doors around the same time. Launched only 2 years earlier in 1998, MotherNature.com was a hugely unsuccessful attempt at mass marketing vitamin supplements and other health-food-store items online. Its story is another instructive example of ecommerce spending gone awry in an effort to build short-term gains.

Having gone public in 1999—just a year and a half after its birth—MotherNature.com was backed by some pretty heavy hitters. CMGI, Mortenthaler, and Besseman all owned about 8 percent of the multi-million-dollar venture. While the stock never hit the stratospheric heights some other dot.coms achieved, it did peak at $14.56, bringing in much needed cash.

Cash is exactly what it needed. The 1999 annual report announced that the company had enough cash to make it through the next year, but it would have a hard time surviving to the end of 2000 without more investment. That year, MotherNature.com had racked up a respectable $5.8 million in sales, but it had spent $59.1 million to get there. It claimed a 15 to 20 percent repeat customer conversion rate, pretty good for any store.

But that conversion rate wasn't enough. For the quarter ending in June 2000, MotherNature.com had racked up $3.4 million in sales. It had brought in 5.5 million visitors during that time with 107,000 orders. However, this represented a total conversion rate of only 1.9 percent with an average of 62 cents per visitor, not enough to stem the tide of red ink. Its reported gross profit margin was 29.4 percent—on par for packaged goods—but its total expenses equaled $10.3 million. To sell enough to break even, MotherNature.com would have had to sell nearly $2 worth of goods to every visitor.

It wasn't a likely prospect, but dot.coms at the time didn't think they had to worry about mundane details such as profits. In July 2000 CEO Michael Barach described the feeling of the day to *Business 2.0*: "For a couple of years the rules of gravity were suspended," he recalled. "No one worried about the bottom line." Eventually the rules of gravity kicked in. In November 2000 MotherNature.com announced its closure (Figure 5-4).

Figure 5-4. MotherNature.com Bows Out

146 | the dot.bomb survival guide

While etailers that sold direct through mail order have had a hard time of it, other firms that went into the home delivery market haven't fared much better. ShopLink.com went out in November 2000 as well, accompanied by innovative home grocery and delivery company Streamline.com.

But the biggest failure of all has to be Webvan, which shut down in July 2001 after burning through a reported $1 billion. In retrospect, it seemed inevitable: Webvan's burn rate was estimated to be over $100 million per quarter.

What did they spend all that money on? Most of it had to do with operations: While Webvan's customers selected their groceries from the site, Webvan's trucks had to deliver the goods to the customers' doors. This combination of online sales and offline delivery required Webvan to make huge capital investments in infrastructure, including 330,000 square foot distribution centers and a huge fleet of vehicles.

Webvan's customers loved the service because it freed them from the drudgery of shopping for groceries. The average customer order was $112 dollars, and the company reported that its gross margin per sale was 27 percent—good numbers for any grocer, online or off. The products Webvan carried helped to maintain those high profit margins; many were high-priced gourmet goods such as free-range chickens or specialty foods.

But these rosy numbers didn't tell the whole tale. While the average customer ordered $112 worth of groceries, the same average customer ordered only 1.8 times per quarter . . . hardly an indication that customers had made Webvan their primary grocery channel (unless Webvan customers were able to make their food stretch a lot farther than the average consumer). In a recent *Forbes* article, Prudential Securities analyst Mark Rowen estimated that Webvan wouldn't hit breakeven until the average order topped $400 . . . obviously something that didn't happen.

making it big in ecommerce by starting small

Are all ecommerce ventures doomed to fail? Looking only at the big bombs, it may seem so. The best lessons in ecommerce frugality and burn-rate control might come from one of the most under-appreciated successful dot.coms out there: FragranceNet.com.

Started in 1995 by CEO Jason Apfel with $50,000 borrowed from family, FragranceNet.com didn't begin life as a Web company. Apfel's idea was to sell fragrances through an 800 number, direct marketed through commercials on cable and radio. His company was called TeleScents—no ".com." But in January 1997 Apfel thought that he could get more attention for his company by creating a website to promote his 800 number. Reportedly spending a few thousand dollars on freelance Web designers and launching a simple static site, Apfel was amazed at the number of orders that began to pour in through the Web.

He decided to take his business online and was immediately helped by a $100,000 investment by Growth Capital Partners. Dipping into his small war chest, Apfel spent about $25,000 on a new website and renamed his company FragranceNet.com, Inc.

FragranceNet.com was designed to run on a shoestring, operating off of rented servers and outsourced hosting. Rather than invest in large warehouses and distribution centers, FragranceNet instead keeps very little inventory on hand, ordering from its suppliers when a customer's order comes in and shipping the order within a day or so after the goods come in and are packed for shipment.

While it may seem like a shoestring operation, FragranceNet.com offers its customers a lot of the perks and selection of far larger etailers. Customers can choose from over 3,000 items on the site, products discounted as much as 70 percent off the retail price. All orders are shipped for free, and FragranceNet.com includes a little gift in every box, a la Amazon.com. Even with all these perks, FragranceNet.com's costs amount to 5 percent or less of the price of each item it sells. In fact, its customer service is so good that FragranceNet.com was rated as one of the top 20 etailers in 2000 by BizRate.com, a rating that takes into account everything from ease of ordering to customer loyalty.

FragranceNet is just as frugal with its advertising and marketing as it is with its operations. In 1998 and 1998, it spent just 16 percent of revenues on marketing and advertising, a rate that increased to only 21 percent in 2000. FragranceNet.com claims that it spends only $7 to acquire a customer and boasts average

148 | the dot.bomb survival guide

orders of $50 . . . far above what its dot.bomb competitors Eve.com and clickmango.com were able to achieve. The company pays only for performance-based online advertising and eschews mass media.

Over the years, FragranceNet.com has been able to show slow but steady growth. In 1998, it posted $330,000 in sales, a number that nearly tripled to $986,000 in 1999 and quadrupled to $4.7 million in 2000, just as the company posted record profits. Yet throughout all this, FragranceNet.com remains relatively unknown and scorned by the market. Its stock currently trades on the Over the Counter Bulletin Board for under $1 per share, providing the company with a market capitalization of around $11 million. But the FragranceNet.com's small-business attitude and frugality may have been its salvation. Not having been graced with seemingly unlimited resources, FragranceNet.com has had to grow smart. As Jason Apfel told *eCompanyNow* in January 2001: "Not having money was really a blessing in disguise. If VCs handed you a lot of money and said 'spend it quickly, grow quickly,' you might be under a lot of pressure to do that."

The case of FragranceNet.com is important because it may represent the future of the post-dot.com-bubble Web. FragranceNet.com grew to its current size by living within its means, growing as it could, and not following every new etailing and marketing fad. As the Web matures and a few big players establish unshakable footholds, the idea that every new mom-and-pop store that comes down the pike could turn into a multibillion-dollar company will be seen for what it is—a ludicrous assumption built on faulty business models and single-moment, anything-goes investing. As FragranceNet shows, the old rules do apply, profit does matter, and anyone with a dream and a head for business can make a go of it . . . provided that he or she does it with intelligence and an eye toward the business.

In the analog world, very few nonmegalomaniacs opening a new supermarket, pet food store, or natural foods center think that they should become millionaires overnight or that the world will welcome them with open wallets just because they decided to sell stuff. The New New Economy may not be so new after all.

the Cadillac syndrome: UrbanBoxOffice.com

For content companies, those that make their living by selling advertising on their sites and providing content to other media partners, the issues haven't been about the physical challenges of selling products as much as about controlling personnel costs, building infrastructure to match their revenues, and selling advertising.

The doomed UrbanBoxOffice.com is a case study in what happens when spending brought on by lavish funding outpaces revenues. Founded late in 1999 and launched in January 2000 by Motown Records CEO George Jackson (who also produced the Wesley Snipes film *New Jack City*), UrbanBoxOffice seemed to have all the makings of a successful entertainment venture. Its urban content was tailor-made to a world crazy for hip-hop, and its founder had a long history of success in the world of entertainment. While its primary marketplace of young African Americans was underrepresented in the total Web population, hip hop had for years crossed over into the world of white suburbia, reaching a market with lots of disposable income and online access.

The concept immediately drew the interest of investors, and UrbanBoxOffice (UBO) was able to secure $33.5 million in funding from Chase Capital Partners, Flatiron Partners, and Quetzel/Chase Capital Partners. Using the money it raised, UBO grew quickly, hiring a staff of 300 and outfitting its offices in what a former employee named Nasoan Sheftel-Gomes described in a *Salon* postmortem as "right out MTV's *The Real World*, with big, open rooms, foldup furniture, and lots of overhead noise."

The concept was to grow big, fast, and loud, using the investment money to learn as it went along. As former employee Sheftel-Gomes recounted, "It didn't matter if you had Internet experience. One content producer admitted he hadn't used email before starting his job. But it didn't matter because the company's leadership, under the direction of urban entertainment mogul George Jackson, believed troops could be trained to be the Web gurus of tomorrow."

The company was barreling straight into the big-time. As the hot new dot.com in New York's Silicon Alley, it knew it had to make a big splash. And it did, throwing a launch party on Ellis Island that cost $100,000. As it built up its infrastructure, UrbanBoxOffice was reportedly burning $3 million in cash per month, a figure that makes sense considering it filed for Chapter 11 bankruptcy protection in November 2000.

The site wasn't suffering from a lack of interest from the media or from advertisers. *Seventeen Magazine*, Arizona Jeans, Emmis Broadcasting, and American Express all had signed on. The company had also worked to secure partnership deals with a variety of industry players, including Register.com, which was to provide domain name services to registered users of the site. Even though the urban market was fairly new and relatively unfamiliar to many companies, "getting advertisers interested [wasn't] a problem," according to CEO Frank Cooper.

What *was* a problem was having enough money to prop up failing technology and meet a ballooning payroll. At the time of its bankruptcy, UBO had payroll obligations of $1,359,461. But that wasn't all. The company also revealed that it owed another $250,000 for employee expenses, $175,000 for payments to 200 consultants, and $517,652 for employee vacation days.

UrbanBoxOffice had been able to secure a $1.8 million loan to meet its payroll, but had seen its bid for additional funding rejected by bailout-investor Saudi Prince Alwaleed bin Talal. To make matters worse, Eco Associates of Austin, Texas, had withdrawn a 2-week-old offer to lead the next round of badly needed funding for UrbanBoxOffice. "Unfortunately," Eco said in a statement released on November 2, 2000, "we do not have the resources to support a business that is losing approximately $3 million a month."

That statement signed the death warrant for UrbanBoxOffice and it laid off 200 of its 300 employees immediately. Adam Kidron, CEO at the time UrbanBoxOffice went bankrupt, blamed the company's death on Eco's pullout from a deal that the company had expected would bring in $35 to $50 million. But Nasoan Sheftel-Gomes disagreed: "UBO has not lacked the resources to realize its goal. And it has not lacked talent, although its employees may have been underutilized and mistreated. I peg its problems to the Cadillac Syndrome—you know, the guy who buys a Cadillac before he has a house or food."

the ripple effect

The go, go, go pace and the race to market that everyone seemed to be participating in during the growth phase of the Web was difficult not only for the dot.coms but for those building the sites for those companies. The rapid growth of the industry led to the meteoric rise of a few big players specializing in building dot.coms. Seemingly overnight, companies with odd names like Razorfish and Rare Medium as well as not-so-odd names like US Interactive grew to global concerns with thousands of employees and tens of millions of dollars in revenues. A few were able to parlay their early success into big cash by going public while others attracted major venture fund investments. Twenty-somethings who had started their companies in dingy, cramped offices within a year or so were becoming dot.com media stars and multimillionaires.

The growth came quickly, but with it came the consequences of short-term thinking and the belief that the party would never end. Often thwarted in their efforts to attract top talent, many Web services companies paid extraordinarily high salaries, offered amazing perks, or simply hired anyone (it seemed) who came through the door knowing what the Web was.

The fast growth meant that everyone was figuring it out as they went along. Processes and procedures so common in other industries had to be invented as companies grew at incredible speeds. While some hired veteran software engineers or corporate managers as they could, others sneered at old thinking and tried to invent their own rules.

For many of their clients, the results were spotty at best. For the new dot.com clients who were learning the ropes at the same time their vendors were, the fast-charged atmosphere and work-til-you-drop hours were just what they needed to get their projects launched on the schedules demanded by their investors and the market. For older companies, accustomed to detailed, sober plans, long sales cycles, and strict project management, many of the interactive companies they hired were a shock.

International Data Corp. (IDC) was the first to identify the fast-growing industry's early problems. In mid-1999, IDC issued a report on interactive agency client satisfaction. In IDC's research, they

152 | the dot.bomb survival guide

found that 35 percent of Internet project decision makers had fired their agencies before a project was complete, most because of concerns over project management. Corporate middle managers put in charge of Internet projects had nothing to go on when selecting an agency: IDC found that only 17 percent had formal agency review processes.

Most of the dot.coms didn't care, and the Web services firms didn't care much either. All the venture capital flowing into new Web ventures flowed directly through the company into the waiting hands of the companies they had hired to build their new sites.

All over the world, Web services companies thrived. Companies like Razorfish, begun in New York in 1995 by two digital-artist entrepreneurs, moved quickly from local projects to mega-site-building extravaganzas for companies like IBM. On the west coast, US Interactive, a firm started in 1991, moved from early-stage Web and CD-ROM projects to developing infrastructure for clients as diverse as Columbia House and the NFL. Another New York company, Rare Medium raised the money it needed to grow by merging with (and then selling off) a refrigeration company. Along the way it picked up clients such as Yahoo! and Microsoft.

These interactive services companies created an impression that they could do no wrong. Clueless corporate managers who didn't understand the Web (but had been put in charge of taking their companies online) pretty much signed blank checks and creative control over to these brash, young technogurus who seemed to know what they didn't. While print design companies usually had pretty strict guidelines for design and had to toe the company line when it came to concept, many interactive services companies seemed to be able to get away with murder. When Razorfish redesigned Time Warner's Netly News Site, it designed the site in a way that mirrored its own website.

But the market loved them, and when some went public it was huge. Razorfish saw its share price more than double on its first day out in April 1999. Internet services firm iXL jumped from $12 to $17.88 on opening day, and Scient went from $20 to $32.63 on day 1. But when US Interactive went public (in August 2000, *after* the crash), its price hovered barely above their $10 asking price at $10.63. It was a harbinger of things to come.

burnout: short-term thinking = short term companies | 153

While all of these companies continued to post huge earnings throughout 1999 and 2000, all except Razorfish continued to lose money. They couldn't stop spending. They had to build out, hire more people, open more offices, and move faster than their competitors. Since they were the ultimate recipients of so much of the dot.com capital floating in the marketplace, being the first in line to create a new company's site meant big money.

As in all things, the good times had to come to an end. And they did, big time. By the end of 2000 many of these firms saw their stock market valuations tank as the dot.coms they serviced became dot.bombs and their investors started to get nervous. According to Accenture, while the average market value to revenue multiple for publicly held interactive consulting firms was an astounding 23.8 in September 1999, that multiple had dropped to 4.7 by September 2000. The firms that weren't making enough money to cover the gap were in trouble. Even those that were making a profit saw that things could only get worse.

The problem was that while many Web firms had built up their companies rapidly expecting the growth to continue, it didn't. While the stock price was high, inefficiency in project management and employee allocation could be covered up or ignored. When the stock dipped way down and cash wasn't as plentiful, having as many as 40 percent of paid employees idle was not an uncommon occurrence.

At the end of 2000 and the beginning of 2001 the consequences of short-term thinking had come home to roost. In September 2000 US Interactive fired 124 workers when it became clear that revenues were going to be millions of dollars below the $29.5 million earned in the second quarter of the year. By January 2000, US Interactive filed for bankruptcy protection and accepted the resignation of its CEO Mohan Uttarwar. It closed its Los Angeles office and planned to relocate to Cupertino, California.

Razorfish reported difficulties at the beginning of 2001 as well. Its stock had plummeted to a dollar from $56 in the previous year. Analysts, alarmed at its burn rate of an estimated $20 million for the first quarter, became concerned that without an influx of cash the company would flame out. Razorfish responded, laying off 400 workers in February 2001 in an attempt to save $70 million. At about the same time, Rare Medium shook up its management, with

154 | the dot.bomb survival guide

two senior executives' taking over the responsibilities of the outgoing CFO but reporting that they wouldn't meet 2001 earnings estimates. However, the management change helped, causing the stock to go up 75 cents the day of the announcement.

How will this sector do into the future? These companies certainly will survive in some fashion, though there will undoubtedly be some consolidation as the marketplace shrinks. But these companies that got rich quick from fast-moving dot.coms are going to have to readjust to longer-term thinking and much longer sales cycles. Dot.coms that made decisions on hiring a Web firm in a manner of days are going to be replaced by larger, more established companies that can take weeks (if not months) to decide on a company. They're going to have to overcome the stigma of failure that surrounds them as the corpses of the dot.coms they helped birth continue to mount.

the art of the long view

All the dot.bombs discussed in this chapter have one common factor—they all burned cash faster than they should have. This seems like a remarkably simple-minded observation. At the time that they were making such a simple mistake, everyone from the media to the stock market was rewarding them for it.

Why? Well, why not? Conventional wisdom held that those firms that were first to market were the ones who would dominate it, that only the biggest could survive, that the stock market could stay where it was forever . . . and continue growing. Conventional wisdom said that if a firm wasn't growing at 40 percent or more, it was dying. Conventional wisdom held that you couldn't start a business without huge amounts of money.

Conventional wisdom was wrong. One look at the successful companies discussed in this chapter reveals the one thing they have in common: They don't believe the hype. Even though times were good, they grew at a rate that balanced earnings with growth to maintain a positive cash flow . . . or at least something close to it. They focused on the old, boring business principles of efficiency and cost control. They didn't try to buy brand overnight but instead built it slowly over time through the most cost-effective channels they

burnout: short-term thinking = short term companies | 155

could find. They didn't start their businesses because they wanted to become rich overnight, they started their businesses because they wanted to be in business . . . for the long term.

What can current and future dot.coms do to avoid the fate of the fast-burning, short-term dot.bombs in this chapter? Here are a few suggestions culled from the lessons learned by the failures (and successes) that have come before:

1. *A single datapoint does not make a trend.* In order to identify a trend and build a business on that trend, a firm must have a reasonable amount of data to work with. That data have to be old enough to cover the inevitable cycles of the marketplace. Companies that built their businesses expecting that the explosive growth of the early days of the Web was going to last forever forgot this. There had been no bad times yet, and so the set of data was incomplete. The ones that thrived took advantage of the growth but understood that it could dip at some point and so didn't overextend themselves.

2. *Think in scenarios, not plans.* Instead of building rigid plans based on a set of faulty assumptions, try building scenarios based on educated guesses as to all the possibilities that could happen based on the identifiable trends. This approach, popularized by Global Business Network's Peter Schwartz in *The Art of the Long View*, allows companies to develop a vision of the future that embraces uncertainty. In his book, Schwartz describes scenarios as "a tool for ordering one's perceptions about alternative future environments . . . stories . . . built around carefully constructed 'plots' that make the significant elements of the world scene stand out boldly." Scenario thinking allows companies to construct what-if stories that take into account all the consequences of their plans: "What if the market goes to hell? How can we survive?" "What if we can't get more funding?" "What if people don't buy our products at the rate we thought they would?" Answering questions like these can lead to long-range means of acting that don't always assume a best-case (or worst-case) outcome.

3. *Be flexible.* Because conditions can change quickly in a world connected by instantaneous communication, it's vital that companies be able to quickly change direction. Think of flexible

156 | the dot.bomb survival guide

strategies such as outsourcing or leasing rather than hiring or buying. If the market dips, be able to shed resources. If it rises, be able to acquire new ones. Don't assume that you'll need everything you have forever.

4. *Grow with your resources.* Similarly, don't build it until you need it. Just-in-time delivery and inventory procedures have worked for years and are made even more workable by the shipping and delivery infrastructures that have been developed. But make sure you know who's on your side: As we saw with Furniture.com and Living.com in Chapter 3, if you can't track your inventory (virtual or not), you can't serve your customers. And if you can't serve your customers, you're screwed.

5. *It's not who's first, it's who lasts.* The first-to-market advantage only means something if a company survives longer than its competitors.

6. *Investment is a tool, not income.* Don't think that you can always get more investment. If your strategy requires constant infusions of cash to survive until profitability, there's something wrong with your model. Money that's not yours and can't be produced by the resources at hand isn't real. Think of investing as a tool to reach your ends, not as an end in itself.

7. *Think cash, not flash.* Yeah, they threw big parties that everyone remembers. But they're dead. Living fast, dying young, and leaving a beautiful corpse only works for rock stars . . . and only then for their estates. As the world turns back to fundamentals, all those pretty toys and lavish parties will be seen for what they are: liabilities.

8. *Get straight with the basics first.* Look, if the technology doesn't work and you're a technology company, you're in trouble. Get the basic stuff working before you make the big promises or try to land the big deals. Money can mask internal process problems and infrastructure glitches for only so long.

9. *If you can get it for free, get it.* There's no dishonor in getting something for free if you can . . . survival is paramount. Try barter if you're cash strapped, or see if you can tap the free resources in your community before you hire the high-priced consultants (HPCs). Trust your own instincts—if it seems like a bad idea, it probably is.

burnout: short-term thinking = short term companies | 157

10. *Negatives don't add up to positives.* Finally, you can't make money by selling products for less than it costs for you to buy them, pack them, and ship them. No matter how many times you lose money, it's never going to add up to positive cash flow. Price is important, but so is the product and the service that delivers it. There's no economy of scale for losses . . . they just keep adding up unless something big changes. Besides, what are those "loyal" customers going to think when your free shipping suddenly costs money? They'll just move on to the next sucker.

There's no doubt that startups are risky by definition. And there's also no question that big risks lead to big rewards. But taking on risk can come only after a thorough understanding of the marketplace and the immediate business situation at hand. Just as professional gamblers don't get rich throwing their cash around without good reason, successful entrepreneurs succeed only because of their understanding of how their venture can fit into a marketplace need . . . and how it can survive long enough to execute its exit strategy.

Growth in the long term can come only from customer retention. While gaining customers is obviously vital, *keeping* those customers is probably more important. To be profitable, a company must be able to recoup customer acquisition costs, something that takes time to happen.

In the world of technology, it's tempting to assume that rapid changes in technology will lead to rapid changes in what customers do or want. It usually doesn't. While technology changes quickly, people change *very* slowly. Only by smart growth with an eye to the future can a company of today avoid burning out before people change their behavior and become long-term, profit-generating customers.

hype bites back: marketing disasters . . . and success stories

In 1997, dot.com ads were relatively scarce in the public media. Sure, there were plenty of banner ads on the Web and in trade journals, but as far as the mass market went, the Web was still relatively below the public radar.

The world has changed a lot since then. In 1999, IDC found that ecommerce vendors spent an average of $8.6 million to market their sites both online and offline. Competitive Media Reporting declared that dot.com ad spending amounted to nearly $1 billion in the first 10 months of 1999 alone, and $400 million of that was spent on television alone. The wacky dot.com ad has become a staple of TV, with nearly every big Web etailer appearing nightly on television screens. Advertising for websites has gone from a curiosity to big business.

But what has all that money accomplished? Many of the dot.coms that spent millions over the past few years have gone bust. In fact, as we've seen so far throughout this book, many spent themselves into oblivion by concentrating their resources in advertising on television, on the radio, and in print. Media outlets and advertising agencies have grown fat on the money flowing out of the VCs and the public markets, into the companies they funded, and then out into

160 | the dot.bomb survival guide

the media via advertising. While many dot.coms bet the farm on advertising and drove millions of users to their sites, they still went bust. Why?

Perhaps one of the biggest reasons is the hype-gap—that is, the difference between the incessant spiels and the actual experience of buying online. While many companies such as Pets.com found initial success (measured in visitors) as a result of their expensive television campaigns, people who went to the site discovered that even though the sock puppet was cute, it was a lot easier to toss a bag of pet food into their carts at the grocery store than it was to fire up the computer, remember the URL, go to the site, click and click and click to make an order, then wait for delivery. While the customer was waiting for the UPS guy, Fido was still hungry.

Another issue was the creative approach taken in so many of these ads. The fact is, many of them did nothing to drive brand recognition, nor did they clearly state the benefits of the site in a way that regular folks could understand. While the spots may have been memorable for their sheer weirdness, when people were done laughing, nobody remembered what was being advertised. Advertising writers tempted the public with visions of being paid to use a public toilet, boasted the fact that the ad was the worst one to air during the Super Bowl, and dazzled the public with stunning visuals of vast herds of cats. But did people remember what was being advertised? In most cases, no. While some sites imploded under the weight of their advertising budgets, others thrived and are still continuing to post record gains even with spending millions on TV ads. Why has advertising worked for some and not others?

just the facts

In 1998, as the dot.com advertising tidal wave began to crest, spending was already up. The Intermarket Group reported that year that the top 100 ecommerce sites spent nearly $9 million each to market themselves. The top 3 spent even more than that—Amazon.com spent $133 million, Etrade spent $71.3 million, and CDNow spent $44.6 million on ads. Intermarket also found that most of that advertising spending was off of the Web. Of the top 100 online retailers,

86 percent advertised both online and offline, while 14 percent concentrated all their efforts toward online ads. For those that were spending money offline, 55 percent went to newspaper ads, 54 percent to magazines, and 35 percent to television and radio.

This mix made sense. As most of the research was showing at the time (and still shows), people find their way to sites usually by offline advertising or by word of mouth.

In 1999, the amount spent by dot.coms to promote themselves rose by 58 percent. As more and more money flowed in from the public markets and into the hands of dot.coms, it prompted more and more of them to spend their money on offline advertising—500 percent more in 1999 than in 1998.

Companies looking to build recognition spent a lot of money online, too. Between January 1999 and November 1999, online ad spending rose to $4.2 billion, 141 percent more than 1998's $1.92 billion. Compared to inflation-adjusted numbers for television in its fifth year ($3.7 billion) and cable in 1984 ($1.2 billion), the medium was taking off.

By August 1999, the list of the top 25 online advertisers looked like the "who's who" of the dot.com world: TRUSTe topped the list, followed by Microsoft, Amazon.com, America Online, Next Card, CDNow, Yahoo!, the Ad Council, Wingspan Bank, and SexTracker. Interestingly enough, a year and a half later (December 2001), the list of the top 10 online advertisers still included TRUSTe, Microsoft, Amazon.com, Yahoo!, Next Card, and America Online.

brand and the dot.com

When many in the ad biz talk about "brand" as a result of advertising, they're usually referring to brand recognition . . . whether or not consumers in the target audience recall that company when they're thinking about the products or services it may offer. Brand recognition is vital online. With several million websites on the planet, cutting through the clutter to get people to your site is the absolute first step in survival. Unlike the physical world where people can stumble across your store while driving down the highway or walking down the street, online retailers must depend on people making a concerted effort—typing a URL, clicking a link in an article, clicking a banner, or following a friend's recommendation in an email—to get to a website. There's no equivalent to the real-world drive-by.

So how does a company build brand recognition? In the simplest sense, building brand recognition means exposing your target audience to your message over and over again. This may mean concentrating ad dollars in a single medium like television (Pets.com actually did this pretty well—who doesn't remember the sock puppet?) or by spreading the budget over many different media to create a "blanket effect" where people run into a brand's identity everywhere they go: through mass-media advertising, through sponsorships, online, outdoor, and in retail environments—Coke and Pepsi use this multipronged approach well. Different media can drive the message home at different rates—somebody may have to see a billboard more frequently than a TV spot for it to make an impression—but the idea is to get out there, to be everywhere your potential customers are as much as possible.

Being mentioned in the media—online or offline—can have a huge impact on the brand recognition of a company. People tend to believe things they see in the news (at least more than they believe advertising), and messages communicated through the media via PR can help reinforce the idea that a brand is real and valuable. In the world of brand-recognition building, public relations can have just as big an effect (if not bigger) on whether or not a company is recognized.

Regardless of how it's done, the goal is still the same—get your name in front of people. Get them to remember it and to know why they might want to shop there. Building brand recognition for online companies has a direct, measurable effect on the bottom line. Ernst & Young found that 69 percent of consumers who purchased online did so because they were familiar with the company. And 75 percent of those same consumers reported that they already knew both the brand and the online merchant when they made their last purchase. People buy from who they know.

Jupiter MediaMetrix confirmed this finding in its report on what factors influenced consumer shopping behavior in 2000. The study found that site recognition and trust drove more than half (51 percent) of consumers to buy from a site. Prior experience with the site influenced that decision, too—37 percent had previously made a purchase from the site where they bought their Christmas presents.

hype bites back: marketing disasters . . . | 163

Brand recognition is obviously vital to the success of a site in a very "chicken-and-the-egg" way—people won't buy from sites they haven't bought from before, and if a site doesn't have customers, it can't afford advertising. Getting consumers over that hump requires building memorable brands that convey the trust that is built only through experience.

Unfortunately, dot.coms haven't done such a good job at building memorable brands. At the end of the 1999 holiday season—after advertisers had spent a record of nearly $1 billion in the fourth quarter on advertising—Active Research did a survey of 1,734 consumers. What it found was horrifying. Of the consumers it surveyed, 25 percent couldn't recall a single dot.com ad. Amazon.com's ads, perhaps the best known, were recalled only by 10 percent of the subjects in the study. Yahoo! and eToys, companies that had spent millions on lavish ad campaigns, were recalled by only 3 percent of the consumers. Typically, 15 to 30 percent recall on television advertising is considered "effective"—most dot.com ads were coming in at far below the effective level. While there was a lot of ad money spent, most of it seemed to be wasted.

So why weren't the dot.com advertisements working? They were splashy and often quite irreverent. From gerbils being shot from cannons to zookeepers who found themselves inserted into the rear-ends of elephants to hordes of singing geeks, there was no question that dot.com advertising certainly got the consumer to notice if for even a moment. But that was exactly the problem. The average consumer was baffled by the ads. What are those people singing about? Why is that C|*Net* company using a bunch of scary nerds in ill-fitting T-shirts to tell me about their product? Why is that guy hiding behind a plant? What do they sell? Why would I want to be their customer?

Attracting and retaining customers was exactly the point. Unless a company could convert its investment in promotions into an actual sale, the ad was wasted.

acquiring customers

Offline and online advertising are vital parts of the customer equation. Online research firm eMarketer (www.eMarketer.com) found

164 | the dot.bomb survival guide

that 21 percent of Web shoppers reached sites because of offline advertising (Table 6-1). Thus many dot.coms desperate for revenues gambled big bucks on advertising campaigns. That big spending had a price, and that price was in the cost of actually acquiring customers.

Table 6-1. What Drives Shoppers to Sites Where They Purchase?

Previous visit or bookmark	48%
Offline advertising	21%
Known brand offline	16%
Link from other site	8%
Online mall	5%
Search engine	2%

Source: eMarketer's eCommerce B2C Report, 2000.

Dot.com retailers were at a major disadvantage when it came to acquiring customers. According to the Boston Consulting Group, it costs an average of $42 to acquire a customer, compared to so-called bricks-and-clicks multichannel companies for whom it costs $22 to acquire a new customer. In some sectors these numbers were even worse: Jupiter MediaMetrix found that online toy merchants spent between $30 and $100 to acquire a new customer while Shop.org's *State of Online Retailing Report 3.0* found that pure-play retailers spent an average of $82 in 1999 to acquire a customer.

High customer acquisition costs weren't limited to retailers either. Sites that relied on traffic in order to sell advertising spent a lot of money to drive that traffic. Competitive Media Reporting (www.cmr.com) found that C|Net, AltaVista, and the now-defunct Go.com spent 20 cents of every dollar of revenue on advertising to drive traffic. MSN (the Microsoft Network) spent an astounding $1.62 for ads on every dollar earned. Thank goodness for high stock prices!

In the race to build brands and entice customers online, these high numbers were seen as simply the price of doing business. As long as the VC money flowed in, as long as the company could depend on a stock market ready and willing to fund its next ad campaign, it stayed in business. But as soon as things went downhill . . . boom!

To see how, let's imagine a fictitious dot.com called EtoySmartStore.com, in honor of several of the dearly departed. EtoySmartStore has a generous $20 million in venture money, but it is currently privately held. Eager to get started, this dot.com spends approximately $1 million on setting up a site, another $1.5 million on a small distribution center and back-end system, and another $500,000 on legal costs, overhead, office supplies, etc. It has a respectable $17 million left.

The company has 80 employees and expenses of $700,000 per month. The product it sells has a 20 percent gross margin on the toy it sells for $100, resulting in $20 of gross profit per sale. At that rate, it has to sell 35,000 of its smart toys per month in order to meet expenses. If you assume a customer acquisition cost of $82, that means that EtoySmartStore.com will have to spend $2,870,000 per month for customer acquisition (assuming that each customer buys only once). Even if 30 percent of the customers are repeat buyers (a fairly high repeat sale ratio), this little store on the Web will have to spend $2,009,000 per month to acquire enough customers to break even. All of this assumes perfect receivables, an ongoing cash flow, and no expansion. You can see how it'll be tough. It'll have enough money to last about 8½ months just to hold the line.

This little scenario doesn't take into account a lot of the pressures dot.coms were under. Besides the costs of marketing to acquire customers, they also were toying (pun intended) with free-shipping schemes and cut-throat pricing in an effort to draw customers to their stores, leading to mounting costs and a profitless death spiral. In addition, their investors were demanding growth of 40 percent or more per year, resulting in spending far beyond what was sustainable. As we saw in the last chapter, this kind of thinking led Pets.com to do things like spend $55.3 million in an effort to sell goods that cost $13.4 million, which brought in revenues of $5.8 million. The center can't hold under that kind of pressure.

the Super Bowl shuffle

Perhaps one of the best ways to get a handle on the madness that surrounded dot.com advertising is to look at what happened during the

166 | the dot.bomb survival guide

last few Super Bowls, that mad annual showcase of advertising. Since Apple set the standard in 1984 with its breakthrough "1984" ad, no other venue has held as much expectation, risk, and attention for advertisers as the annual football showdown. In its own way, the Super Bowl is a microcosm of America itself, a no-holds-barred epic battle where vast fortunes are won and lost and where to the victor go the spoils . . . and the loser slinks away into obscurity. A perfect venue for the first big shots of the dot.com TV wars.

The Super Bowl of 1999 was the first place these shots were taken when two dot.coms took to the field for the first time. On one end of the field was Monster.com, a successful online jobs site that had realized $48.5 million in revenues the previous year. It was easily able to come up with the approximately $2 million its 30-second spot would cost. On the other end of the field was Monster.com's upstart competitor, HotJobs.com. Founded by charismatic CEO Richard Johnson with a tiny war chest of $4 million or so, HotJobs decided to gamble on one 30-second spot featuring a bored security guard fantasizing about other careers. It was a gamble that paid off . . . big time.

The only two dot.coms in the lineup of Super Bowl XXXIII advertisers, both Monster.com and HotJobs.com got a lot of attention for their commercials. Monster.com saw its job searches surge to 2.2 million just 24 hours after the spot ran, up from 500,000 searches the week before . . . a 450 percent increase. It was a hit with 2,900 searches per minute and had over 8,000 résumés submitted to the site.

HotJobs.com's success went far beyond the huge boost in traffic it received with its ad. There had been some controversy over the content of its proposed ad—Fox had initially refused to air the original ad that featured a zookeeper disappearing up an elephant's nether regions—and that combined with the Horatio Alger appeal of the little guy betting it all on a single dream led to intense coverage of the site long after the ad ran. Between October and January 1999, HotJobs.com had 200 mentions on television and 400 mentions in print. The site (and its story) graced the front pages of *The New York Times, The Wall Street Journal,* and *USA Today*. With the Super Bowl of 1999, HotJobs had arrived. Its success sent shockwaves through the Web industry. If this one little piddly dot.com could make it big through such a bold move, surely the better-funded and bigger sites could use the same venue to drive instant brand recognition too. It was a feeling that fit perfectly with the times. HotJobs had a made a go of it in Internet time with bold action. The market was rewarding bold steps. The next Super Bowl would be the way to go.

So it was that the 2000 Super Bowl became the ultimate coming-out party for the highly funded, aggressive Web companies born in the heady days of 1999. For some, it also became their Waterloo.

Even before the game, the buzz about the dot.com commercials to debut on the Super Bowl was huge. Everyone was waiting to see what kind of wacky stunts and outrageous commercials could make it to the air. Consumers had just come through the dot.com frenzy of the 1999 Christmas shopping season, and the Super Bowl looked like the place to make the next big splash.

Of all the advertisers that paid an average of $2 million per ad, 47 percent were dot.coms. While Monster and HotJobs (now successful and with cash to burn) returned, the 2000 Super Bowl also included a number of unknowns, including Epidemic.com, Computers.com, and the relatively new Pets.com, flush with cash after Amazon.com had taken a $60 million stake in the company. All the big agencies were there, too: McCann-Erickson was to do HotJobs' ad, Chiat/Day had developed the Pets.com sock-puppet mascot as part of a $25 million campaign, Grey Advertising was behind Kforce.com, WebMD with Ogilvy & Mather, Etrade with Goodby, and AutoTrader with W.B. Doner.

Many of the ads were as wacky as everyone hoped for, covering the gamut from public bathrooms to the self-described "Worst Commercial" cooked up by Lifeminders.com after its agency had refused to come through at the last minute (Figures 6-1 and 6-2). It would made a big splash. It seemed like it worked. In a postgame survey, NPD Research found that 12 percent of the audience had visited the site of a dot.com that had advertised. Of those 12 percent, 58 percent had shopped on one of the ecommerce sites. A full 22 percent were even logged on during the game. However, when they looked at what ads people liked, the results weren't as good: Big-spender Pets.com was picked by only 3 percent of respondents as their favorite ad, tied with 7-Up's "Show Us Your Can" spot.

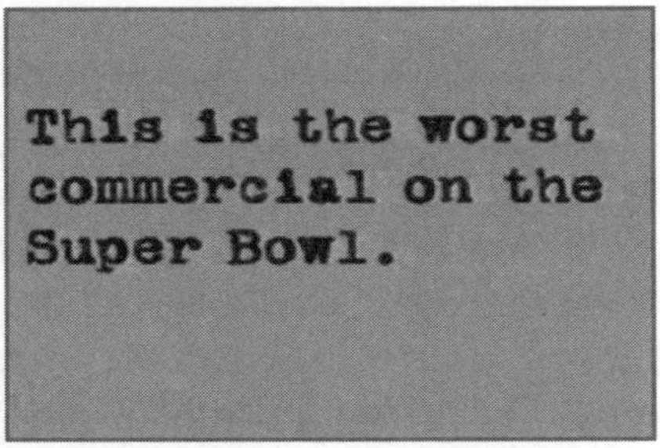

168 | the dot.bomb survival guide

Figure 6-1. Lifeminders.com's Self-Described "Worst Commercial"

Figure 6-2. Monster.com's Effective "When I Grow Up" Spot

Pets.com's score was telling. In a post-Bowl survey of ad effectiveness, D'Arcy Masius Benton & Bowles found that 17 percent of consumers could recall dot.com ads after the Super Bowl, but 57 percent could recall more with prompting. The numbers seemed to be in line with the 15 to 30 percent recall considered to be effective by most advertisers.

But when the survey examined specific ads, things didn't look as good. Only 4 percent could remember seeing the spots for Epidemic.com and OurBeginning.com, not surprising when both had done little or no advertising before or after the game. Lifeminders.com's "Worst Commercial of the Super Bowl" seemed to be fairly self-descriptive: Only 6 percent of consumers remembered the ad after the game was over.

None of the spots generated the response that the dot.coms had hoped for and expected after HotJobs' previous year's success. Many of the companies blamed their ad agencies, and a bloodbath of agency firings resulted. Monster.com fired Mullen in Wenham, Massachusetts, and retained a search firm to find a new agency. HotJobs.com dumped McCann-Erickson in Detroit, looking for a better "partner." Britannica fired Deutsch, and Kforce.com fired Grey Advertising in New York. Lifeminders.com had already fired its agency, but Epidemic.com halted all advertising, as did Computer.com (which said that it was in acquisition negotiations) and OurBeginnings.com, which halted all further advertising with Bennett & Co. in Orlando, Florida.

Super Bowl XXXV in 2001 looked a lot more like Super Bowl XXXIII. Instead of a 47 percent dot.com-to-other mix, only 7 percent of the advertisers in 2001's big game came from the Web. In fact, only three returned for another go at it: HotJobs, Monster, and Etrade all came back. In a mix that eerily mirrored the return to the traditional company seen in the rest of the world, 59 percent of the advertisers were brick-and-mortar stores (up from 41 percent the previous year), 17 percent were high-tech or telecom companies (up from 3 percent in 2000), and 17 percent were in financial services. All the ads sported Web addresses, but few were the pure dot.coms of yore.

Of all the dot.coms that have advertised during the Super Bowl, perhaps Epidemic.com is most emblematic. It folded about 6 months after its big Super Bowl debut. Epidemic.com spent nearly a quarter of its total funding—$7.6 million—on a $2 million 30-second Super Bowl spot to launch its concept to the world. Unfortunately, the obscure spot that featured the tag line "Get paid for something you already do" did little to explain the concept.

Epidemic.com's plan was to take advantage of the hot new Internet concept of "viral marketing." In a viral marketing scheme, awareness of a company would spread like a virus from one customer to another by word of mouth. Epidemic.com took the idea one step further. It wanted to use email as the carrier for its clients' advertising messages. Users would download a small email plug-in called an "epiNabler," which placed commercial messages for etail advertisers in every email that an Epidemic.com subscriber sent. Its site extolled the virtues of the scheme, declaring that epiNabler users would "be the first to tell [their] friends about the latest brands and coolest trends!" Users would be able to ingrati-

170 | the dot.bomb survival guide

ate themselves to their loved ones by "[getting their] friends and family excited about using the Internet!"

Unfortunately for Epidemic.com, most people saw the scheme for what it was—a way for them to spam their friends and family with commercial messages. Even though users would get paid a commission on every sale generated by their email ads (with the average user netting about $20), Epidemic.com's intrusive concept, which basically turned friends into spammers, never took off. At the end of the first quarter of 2000, it was selling only about 10,000 ad impressions per month, hardly enough to keep it going. On June 14, 2000, Epidemic.com shut down.

Of all the companies that have advertised on the Super Bowl, it seems fairly clear that sinking the kind of money that Epidemic.com did into a one-shot attempt at branding never really paid off. While some companies, like Pets.com, had the money to keep advertising, others, like Epidemic.com, didn't and saw their meager recognition disappear like the smoke after the halftime show.

big disasters beyond the Bowl

Two of the biggest advertising disasters didn't have the Super Bowl to blame for their deaths. The fact that eToys.com spent itself out of existence can't be blamed on not having a crack management team with stellar credentials. Launched on September 30, 1997, eToys was headed by Toby Lenk, a former vice president of strategic planning at Walt Disney. It was also able to boast the know-how and money of Idealab! entrepreneur Bill Gross (who was a veteran at selling to children) and included executives from Disney Online, Gymboree, Imaginarium, and Union Bank of California's Interactive Markets Group.

eToys combined a huge selection of toys with expert advice and a site that grouped products in various ways that helped parents get directly at the right toy for the right kid. The concept looked great, and on May 20, 1999, when eToys issued its IPO, it jumped from an asking price of $20 to close the day at $76.56, raising $166 million for the company.

Before and during the IPO, the company was fairly frugal with its spending, using only $5.33 million of its startup capital. But after the

IPO, the company began spending the big bucks, shelling out over $31 million between January and November 1999.

The company was losing money . . . lots of it. In the period ending March 1999, eToys posted a loss of $28.6 million. Even though its ads were running quite frequently and its sales of $134 million in 1999 were far above those of its nearest competitor, ToysRUs.com's $44 million, the ink continued to run red. In its third period ending in March 2000, the company posted a loss of $189.6 million, mostly from selling, general, and administrative expenses. It was also taking a beating on the sales end, showing a negative gross profit of $12.5 million.

The stock, which had at one time peaked at $90, plunged below a dollar at the end of 2000 when the company warned of low third-quarter sales that hadn't been bolstered by continued heavy advertising. In January it laid off 70 percent of its 1,000 workers in an effort to stop the heavy losses, but in February 2001, eToys laid off its 293 remaining employees and announced that it would shut down in April. On the day of the announcement, its stock plunged to 28 cents and went even lower in after-hours trading to 15 cents (Figure 6-3).

Figure 6-3. eToys UK Was the First to Go

172 | the dot.bomb survival guide

when brand recognition isn't enough

Pets.com was another etailer that went bust trying to acquire customers. As mentioned in Chapter 5, many of its problems were related to selling goods at below cost. But its advertising extravagance was a major factor, too. Jupiter estimates that Pets.com spent $240 per new customer in the first quarter of 2000. Considering that it spent nearly $147 million in less than 2 years, this figure isn't surprising. Even though its sock puppet mascot became such a cultural icon that the site was able to license the sale of the cute toy for sale on the Web and off, the millions it spent to develop it never translated into profits. Spending eventually met up with reality, and on November 7, 2000, Pets.com closed down, selling its assets to PETsMART.com.

In 1999 Pets.com's sales were $5.8 million, and it had received a big infusion of capital from Amazon.com, which bought 30 percent of the company for $60 million. In 2000 Pets.com leveraged its power to buy rival Petstore.com for $10 million in stock. It continued to spend on building a big brand and chased its tail looking for profits that never materialized. In the third quarter of 2000, Pets.com lost $21.7 million on revenues of $9.4 million. Its stock, which had never traded above $14, plunged to a dollar and dropped like a rock to 22 cents on the day it announced its closing.

What did eToys.com and Pets.com do wrong? They both had huge brand recognition. . . . eToys was one of the top etail sites of 2000. But because they didn't offer enough long-term value to their customers, they were never able to leverage their brand into sales and repeat customers: In the last 5 weeks of 2000, eToys had fewer visitors to its site than in the same period of 1999. And though it blamed the decline in online sales for its low numbers, rival ToysRUs.com saw its sales triple from the previous year during the same time period.

While Pets.com and eToys.com had brand recognition, they never really had a *brand*. Customers never really trusted them enough to come back and buy again and again. If they had, the companies would have survived. At the same time, in an all-or-nothing effort to keep bringing eyeballs to the sites and counting on the magic of conversion to bolster sales, the management continued to spend money on marketing as they always had, figuring that some of those people had to stick at some point.

ToysRUs demonstrates that it's not recognition as much as trust and repeat customers that win online. While ToysRUs had a rocky start and some rough times in the beginning with order fulfillment, it persevered, leveraging its brick-and-mortar assets. Eventually customers who had known the brand for years and who had been impressed by the site's continuing interest in them and investment in customer service, returned and kept on buying.

The two original dot.com Super Bowl stars, Monster.com and HotJobs.com, just keep on plugging away, regularly reporting profits and spending within their means. HotJobs has projected earnings of $145 to $150 million in 2001, even though it has had troubles as many of its dot.com customers went out of business. It beat analyst expectations in 2000 and continues to grow. Monster, too, continues to advertise regularly on network TV, but it also continues to grow by keeping costs down and earnings up. In the third quarter of 2000, Monster.com reported earnings of $23.4 million on revenues of $339.2 million. While it has tried wacky tactics like flying an orange blimp over San Francisco, it has also kept its advertising spending to a reasonable level in order to continue to make profits.

dot.com fatigue and the big shift

If you look at the companies that had trouble attracting (loyal) customers, it certainly wasn't because they weren't spending enough money. In the period from January to September 2000, Pets.com spent $26,380,900 on advertising, and eToys.com spent $11,909,800 . . . and went out of business. On the other hand, Amazon.com, which had the lion's share of all online purchases during the holiday season, spent a relatively modest $8,820,000 during the same period.

But Amazon's still around, and the others aren't. Why? Because even though those companies did have a fair amount of brand recognition, recognition wasn't enough. Their customer acquisition costs were extremely high, requiring them to spend more and more money to bring in more customers that didn't shop on a regular basis.

174 | the dot.bomb survival guide

The bigger question about some of the difficulties faced by dot.com advertisers and their ability to retain customers may be answered in part by the Active Research study mentioned earlier in the chapter. Amazon at least had an unaided recall rate of at least 10 percent for its holiday ads while eToys.com had an unaided recall rate of only 3 percent. At the same time, 25 percent of the consumers surveyed remembered seeing some kind of "dot.com" ad. And therein lies the problem. As the number of dot.com advertisers grew, so did the difficulty in telling them apart. Everyone, from the media to folks on the street, talked about "dot.coms," but they had trouble remembering a single one. To many, the Web itself became a "brand," a brand called "dot.com."

And it was a brand in trouble. As eToys and Pets.com demonstrated when news of their troubles surfaced, sales decline when people think a brand is in trouble. The whole Web has always presented barriers to sales for newbies, from issues of privacy to worries about credit card fraud. As the whole "brand" of the Internet began to decline and one dot.com merged in the public's consciousness into another, differentiation and lingering doubts about delivery timeliness, privacy, security, and trust became the key issues.

To this, Amazon.com's strategy of aggregating many different types of product offerings under one roof paid off. Because people had less trouble recalling Amazon.com than any other dot.com advertiser, they went there first. And because Amazon by this point had begun to sell just about everything under the sun (including toys), other retailers competing for mindshare had a big problem.

The trend of consumer confusion also played directly into the hands of the brick-and-mortar retailers coming online in vast numbers during the 1999 to 2000 period. Bringing with them their physical-world legacies and a trust born of the fact that they actually "existed" in the real world, multichannel retailers had a big advantage over the pure online properties.

For many online-only retailers, marketing played a constant game of catch-up, trying to shovel more and more people into a machine that had 65 percent of them abandoning their shopping carts before they forked over their hard-earned cash . . . all while continuing to spend money to grow the number of warehouses and distribution centers to serve customers that never materialized.

hype bites back: marketing disasters . . . | 175

According to Shop.org, dot.com stores spent 10 times what multi-channel retailers spent on marketing as a percentage of revenue. At the end of 1999 many realized that just getting customers to the store wasn't enough—they had to keep them coming back. Shop.org reports that the trend in dot.com advertising began to shift away from brand awareness to customer retention, but total order conversion rates remained low, rising from 1.5 percent to only 1.8 percent in 1999, and buyer conversion rates increased only 0.4 percent from 2.8 percent to 3.2 percent during the same period. The trend was up, but it was going to take a lot longer than many dot.coms had realized.

By the middle of 2000, dot.com advertisers had begun to pull back from expensive television campaigns and focus more on direct-response, sales-building online efforts. In the second quarter of 2000, the Boston Consulting Group found that 86 percent of online retailers had instituted spending cuts to staunch losses, with 28 percent of them no longer spending money on television advertisements.

Now, more than ever, the challenge for online-only retailers will be to stand out from the clutter, to break through the ever-increasing noise on the Web and differentiate themselves from the free-falling stores that consumers are avoiding. To be successful, they must establish credibility, build awareness about their specific benefits, and build trust in themselves and in the medium. Doing these things will require a renewed focus on customer service—something that the Boston Consulting Group reports dot.coms are doing—and rely on marketing measures that build loyalty and repeat purchases. They'll have to stand out in the crowd as something truly different and truly worthwhile, while cutting through the ever-increasing clutter of advertising.

spinning the Web

Guiding (or manipulating, depending on your point of view) public opinion to serve the interests of institutions has been a way of life since Edward Bernays founded the field of public relations back in the twenties. His early tactics were pretty over the top, even for now—organizing women to hold up their "torches of freedom" (cig-

176 | the dot.bomb survival guide

arettes) at suffrage marches (paid for by Lucky Strike) or urging homebuilders to build bookshelves in order to boost book sales. Bernays described his work as "engineering consent."

Over the years, public relations has cultivated a poor image, regarded as the venue of "flacks" who parroted the party lines of their clients without actually understanding what they were saying. Their only function, it seemed to many, was to call as many reporters as possible in order to get as many stories as possible to mention their clients. While in most cases this perception was totally false, it still often relegated public relations budgets and personnel to the lower rungs of the marketing ladder.

The dot.com explosion changed that perception dramatically as dot.coms discovered that getting ink in the press was often the most cost-effective way to promote themselves and the best way to build mindshare in their industries. The explosion in PR was so dramatic that by 1999 the National Labor Relations Board (NLRB) was listing public relations as one of the fastest-growing industries in the United States, a standing that the NLRB projected it would hold until 2005.

The late nineties marked a turning point for journalists and their use of the Web. While many journalists had barely heard of the Web or the Internet prior to 1995 or so, by 1998, 98 percent of journalists had some sort of Internet access, up from 91 percent the previous year (according to the *Fifth Media in Cyberspace Study*, Middleburg, 1999). Interest in technology and the Internet had begun to explode. In 1995 *The Wall Street Journal* carried only 31 stories that contained both the words "Internet" and "IPO." By 1998, that number had exploded to the hundreds.

Many of the early references to PR and the Web had to do with conducting PR *on* the Web, constructing corporate websites and accessing journalists via email. But as the nineties progressed and the dot.coms became the darlings of the Street and the media, PR became much more of a practice of influencing opinion *about* the Web and Internet-related companies.

The marriage made perfect sense. The Web was becoming an increasingly crowded space, and getting attention through traditional media outlets was (as we've seen) an increasingly expensive proposition. "They're not looking for ink," said John Fry, president of an executive search firm in an article on dot.com PR that appeared on the Public Relations Society of America (PRSA) website. "They're trying to get their name first and foremost in the reviews. They want to break through the clutter fast."

In the early days of the dot.com explosion, before Web companies were featured on the news every night and CEO technogods graced the covers of every magazine, most dot.coms concentrated their PR spending until the IPO was imminent. Then, as much as they could within "quiet-period" regulations, they began to turn up the heat, attempting to generate as much positive ink for their clients as possible. When the IPO hit, if the buzz was good, the company would see its value shoot through the roof as investors were egged on by the media, which was convinced of the company's value.

Throughout the heady days of 1999 and through 2000, PR, in effect, was the driving force behind the marketplace, the invisible hand that pulled the strings that influenced the media to endorse or damn a new venture. It had to be. Here were companies that had no history, no income, and often no products and that more often relied on business models that no one could understand. The mission of the company's PR team was to make sure that people understood the benefits of what the company was doing, how it differentiated itself from those that had come before, and why its new thing was going to be the big thing that changed the world.

The PR team had a big job ahead of it. Not only was there a whole new crop of media outlets and trade press that hadn't existed before the Web but there was also a whole new class of analysts, financial gurus, and pundits who rose up out of the woodwork with influential opinions that could make the difference between a billion-dollar company and a mere hundred-million-dollar one.

One of the gurus of the dot.com PR world was Pam Alexander, the head of Alexander Communications, a company that had worked PR magic for Novell, Sprint, Motorola, and Cisco Systems. Alexander's success came from her early realization that this new world required new tactics.

As she told *Fast Company* in a 1998 interview, "Ten years ago, our job was to manipulate people in the press. It wasn't that hard to do— there weren't that many of them. For every company, there were maybe 20 or 30 print and TV types you had to influence. If you had

178 | the dot.bomb survival guide

enough charisma and made relationships with them, it was fairly easy. Today you have to communicate with 300 people about every client. It's just not possible."

But she and others like her made it possible. By throwing lavish parties (on which, at the peak, Bay Area companies were spending as much as $1 million per month), by holding exclusive events in venues like Palm Beach, Las Vegas, and Vail, and by hosting an incessant round of analyst briefings, press breakfasts, and whirlwind roadshows, public relations companies were able to take unknown little companies and make them the talk of the Valley.

Startups and their VCs who saw this began to realize the value that a good PR firm could bring. In 1999 and early 2000, the demand for top firms like Middleberg & Associates (now Middleberg Euro), The Antenna Group, and Connors Communications far exceeded the supply. Like the VCs that prompted the need for immediate hype, PR firms began to actually interview clients before deciding whether to work for them, charging retainers of more than $25,000 per month in some cases, demanding proof of funding, and often taking equity in the companies they worked for. And as these firms that had gotten a head start on the space got more clients, they were able to parlay their increasingly widening spheres of influence into forces that could make or break companies.

With all the money pumping into new startups who then funneled a lot of it into PR horsepower, the mission became one of differentiation, and differentiation meant being louder and more "revolutionary" than the last startup. Reporters who used to spend days digging up an interesting technology story suddenly found their inboxes and voice mailboxes jammed with calls from PR pros, each more eager than the last to explain why his or her company was the one the reporter would be spilling the ink (or bits) on this week. "Buzz is everything," said Don Middleberg, guru of technology public relations.

Knowing that the press was becoming increasingly jaded to hyped-up press releases, some dot.coms turned to more extreme tactics to build buzz. Press releases by the thousands filled the wires: "Some of our clients were asking for three press releases per week, whether they had news or not," one dot.com PR VP told me. Blimps. Mascots. Huge events. At the StreamingMedia West show in 2000, one company staged a mock protest against itself outside the show hall in a bid for attention. The founders of now-defunct theMan.com had the company logo tattooed on their arms at a gala press event. (They're probably under the dermatologist's laser right about now . . . .)

Making dot.com PR work meant understanding and guiding the perception of the startup in the press as well as deftly changing how the press saw that company as market conditions changed. It wasn't about building an easily recognized logo or name brand through the traditional advertising methods of expose, test, modify, repeat . . . PR professionals took a particularly holistic view of the marketing problem, crafting strategies to take their companies from brash young startup to seasoned public company. (See sidebar "Nine Easy Ways to Kill a Startup through PR.")

Two masters of this game are William Ryan and Ed Niehaus, founders of the Niehaus Ryan Group, Inc., who parlayed their concept of "sustainable identity" to help make Yahoo! a household name. In an April 1998 interview in *Fast Company,* Ryan described how "before the IPO, we can't have the image of two crazy kids running around without shoes. It doesn't fly on Wall Street." Instead, they deemphasized the "whiz kids" they'd promoted before and emphasized Yahoo!'s crack management team. When Yahoo! issued its IPO, it was the biggest to hit the street up until that time.

 Nine Easy Ways to Kill a Startup through PR

Companies need to create two-way relationships with their customers.

By Tom Gable, founder and CEO of the Gable Groups (http://www.gablegroup.com), one of the top Internet public relations firms

Many new online ventures are rich in ideas, whizbang engineering features, and programming geniuses. But some 80 percent fail. Why? Maybe it's the PR. In 6 years of working with Internet companies, my colleagues and I have identified nine easy ways public relations and marketing communications can help kill a startup. Understanding these pitfalls can put a startup on the

180 | the dot.bomb survival guide

road to building a successful image and brand. The same concepts can be applied to traditional companies' moving into integrated online-offline marketing communications and public relations programs.

1. *Pandora's positioning.* The business and marketing plans are crammed with every buzzword on earth, yet the new venture isn't clearly differentiated. Jargon alert: If you talk about being first to move with robust, turnkey, best-of-breed, next-generation, leading, scalable, end-to-end solutions, journalists and VCs will laugh so hard they'll get a hernia (but won't cover or finance the venture).
2. *Babel branding.* Eighty percent of all new products or services fail, largely because they don't demonstrate and communicate why the new brand is better than the current one, and often they try to be all things to all people.
3. *Budget 22.* This is the PR equivalent of Catch 22. The CEO wants major global coverage on a neighborhood budget. The company loses sight of the fact that results are driven by agency time and creativity in carrying out the PR program on a consistent, continuous basis. Expectations must match the budget.
4. *Egomaniac expectations.* Budget 22 usually leads to demanding Fortune 500-type coverage (*Wall Street Journal, New York Times*, cover of *Time*) without looking at the reality of the company and its budget, products, services, and size. Breaking through depends on being able to prove that you are the harbinger of a new trend and a leader in your industry.
5. *Creative quagmires.* Companies kill creativity by having the wrong people do the writing. A close corollary is editing by committee. You don't ask lawyers to write software code or engineers to prepare legal briefs. So why involve them in positioning and the creative processes?
6. *Missing metrics.* The venture can't provide timely, relevant data to show progress in relation to the plan, the competition and the market, or its ability to scale. The media (and investors) demand ongoing proof of principle.
7. *Hysteria marketing.* The startup expects short-term miracles and changes directions faster than a hummingbird at a flower show. The result: diluted budget impact and internal confusion. Stick to an integrated, strategic program that ramps up in support of the business, marketing, and capital plans.

hype bites back: marketing disasters . . . | 181

8. *Dullness.* The startup lacks energy, passion, and personality. You have stuff, but so does everyone else. Become the messiah for your concept. "Flippers" (those looking to turn a quick buck rather than create something of lasting value) don't win people over.

9. *Old-economy thinking.* The startup is stuck in the top-down, one-way marketing model. Think interactively and environmentally. Go deep into your database; mine your data so that you know your customers. Connect with them. Find new opportunities to show that you are empathetic, sympathetic, and intuitive about their needs and beliefs. Create two-way relationships, and build environments for ongoing communications.

But the press wasn't always kind to New Economy companies, and a wrong move, spread over the pages of the national press, could have a huge impact on the valuation of a dot.com. After all, in a market that seemed to be making most of its decisions based on gut feelings, promises, and buzz, bad news traveled fast and had big consequences.

That's exactly what happened to advertising-network DoubleClick in 2000. On January 25, *USA Today* ran an article with the headline "Activists charge DoubleClick double cross" in which it charged that DoubleClick's purchase of database marketing firm Abacus Direct would allow it to link online information about customers with offline data in order to know a users' exact identity . . . something never before possible. The lengthy article pointed out the privacy issues inherent in the scheme, calling it "privacy invasion" and quoting experts who charged that the practice would "[mean] the vast majority of Web-connected Americans will likely lose their online anonymity."

DoubleClick immediately reacted by charging that what it was doing wasn't a privacy violation and that it wasn't much different than what other database marketing companies had been doing for years. DoubleClick also warned that any attempt to bring down the company would take down the Internet itself, a threat that didn't faze the Federal Trade Commission, which began an informal probe after thousands of consumer complaints. The press responded with more negative articles about DoubleClick.

182 | the dot.bomb survival guide

The bad press was doubly bad for DoubleClick. Its stock price fell 30 percent from its 52-week high. Michigan's attorney general began consumer protection legal proceedings as the privacy battle heated up. DoubleClick knew it was in trouble. They hired crisis-management experts Weber McGinn, who soon got DoubleClick to pull back from its plans and promise to take wide steps to protect consumer privacy and work with the government and other industry leaders to address the issue.

CEO Kevin O'Connor apologized to the world, something few dot.com CEOs had ever done before. "I made a mistake," he admitted in a press release, "by planning to merge names with anonymous user activity across Web sites in the absence of government and industry privacy standards."

The market ate it up. DoubleClick's stock rebounded (at least until the April crash), and the world soon forgave it . . . or at least seemed to forget the heat of the controversy. Score one for public relations.

Etrade found itself with an equally catastrophic problem in February 1999 when server problems brought the site down for three consecutive days. But what could have been a major disaster for the online trading firm turned out to be a customer trust-builder when the company used the press and the Web to immediately respond and restore customer confidence.

Rather than cover up the problem (tough to do when your site's problems are blocking thousands of people from their money), Etrade immediately posted a complaint email address on its homepage and notified the press about how it was going to fix the problem. It gave out thousands of free trades to customers in order to compensate them for their pain. The strategy proved successful as thousands of its customers stayed on to take advantage of the freebies.

The honesty paid off, and Etrade continues to be one of the Web's most successful online brokerages. As Dave Murray, the senior VP at its ad agency told the PRSA's magazine *Tactics*, "It isn't about what spin you put on the facts. . . . It's the facts that are important and we need to communicate them."

Good press can also have a way of coming back to haunt you, as Razorfish discovered. Rocked by class-action suits filed after its end-of-2000 earnings (which led to a rapid decline in its stock), it found out what could happen when hype bites back.

The lawsuits charged that Razorfish's management had knowingly misled investors by putting out press releases and issuing SEC filings that painted a much rosier picture of the company than its financial story told. Cited in the case were press releases issued by Razorfish on Business Wire on April 25, May 23, June 28, and June 30 that described how the company was "hitting on all cylinders now that [it has] successfully integrated [its] operations, insinuating that its rapid global expansion would allow it to rapidly expand its business by 'understand[ing] the nuances of local cultures, economies, and business practices.'"

In reality, Razorfish was having some financial difficulties, and in October it issued an earnings warning. After the class-action suits became public, Razorfish's stock sank like a stone. While it had been $3.09 on December 12, it dropped to $1.06 on December 21 when the allegations hit the press.

From a PR perspective, the story was even more interesting because the lawsuits quoted one of the best pieces of PR a company like Razorfish could have gotten . . . an article in September's issue of *Wired* that told the story of the thirty-something founders' rise to the top. In breathless detail, the article told of their successful meteoric rise, the trendy nightclub they owned, their showy vehicles, and even one of the founder's apartments, which had recently been covered in *Marie Claire*.

Analysts blasted the firm in the press when it refused to lay off employees in response to its declining earnings. The company eventually responded, vowing to lay off 400 employees in a plan to reduce its workforce by 22 percent in order to save the company $70 million.

spinning a crisis into a movement

Perhaps one of the best PR stories of late 2000 and early 2001 was the story of Napster. As soon as the service opened its doors (without a PR firm until 7 months later), it became one of the most popular Internet-based services for 18 to 24-year-olds and beyond. Of course, the fact that it allows people to trade music for free also helped, something pointed out by *Business 2.0* writer Jim Welte when he told *PRWeek*, "We all know the best PR trick in the world

184 | the dot.bomb survival guide

is to yell, 'Hey, we've got free shit over here!' If Wal-Mart decided to open its doors and give everything away, we'd write about that, too."

True, but the tactic has helped Napster (and its founder, 19-year-old Shawn Fanning) become a media darling even as the service searches desperately for a business model with its new corporate partner, Bertelsmann. In fact, the press gathered by Napster prompted *PRWeek* readers to vote the company first prize in *PRWeek*'s "best and worst" publicity for both the "best job by company/group in overcoming a difficult situation" and "best company/group publicity" categories for 2000.

Napster's PR firms (mPRm and Girlie Action) managed to orchestrate an amazing amount of grassroots goodwill for the company by playing up the youth of its founder, painting the record companies and the Recording Industry Association of America as bad guys, spoofing rock band Mettallica's assault against the service, and organizing nationwide tours of up-and-coming bands. But while its popularity soared through shrewd spin on its "underdog" image, eventually the revolution came to a screeching halt as the courts piled ever more restrictions on the company. Other services such as Gnutella and Morpheus have arisen to fill the gap left by the hobbled Napster. It was a killer ride while it lasted . . . .but, in the end, it's tough for technology to triumph over legislation.

avoiding the bite

If companies can learn one thing from the tales of marketing woes (and triumphs) in this chapter, it should be that misguided marketing and mishandled public relations can have a huge impact on the success or failure of a company. Overbuying ineffective advertising can drain a company's resources dry, and bad press can cause already-depressed stocks to plunge to unplumbed depths.

What can dot.coms do to survive and thrive in the current implosion? Here are a few suggestions based on lessons learned the hard way:

1. *Know thy customers . . . and where they are.*   Many of the wild spending sprees that spent so many dot.coms out of existence

could have been controlled if the companies had focused on understanding the Contact Zone, that place where companies and customers meet. Understanding all the venues in which your potential customer can come into contact with your brand gives your company the ability to accurately target your messages so that the right one gets to the right people. Mass media is fine if you have a mass-market product . . . that's where the customers are. But you have to be able to maintain expensive ad campaigns that are based on realistic numbers. Etrade, Monster.com, and Hotjobs have all done a lot of mass-market advertising . . . but they also have spent a lot of money to reach their other customers in the corporate world. Knowing how to split your resources correctly can come only from a true understanding of where your customers are.

2. *Build an actual brand that means more to your customers than a cute mascot.* Building a brand means building trust and loyalty . . . it's a lot more than brand recognition. Even though people know who you are, they won't necessarily spend their money on your site when another one offers superior customer service and a compelling brand experience.

3. *Deliver on your promises.* Similarly, don't overhype. If your technology actually will revolutionize whatever industry you're targeting by all means say so . . . but be willing to back it up with case studies or customer testimonials. If you promise a superior shopping experience, make sure that it actually is a great experience. Ask your customers what they think, and respond to their concerns. Don't assume that you always know best. In the end, it's your customers you have to make happy.

4. *Meet problems head on. Don't lie or deny.* Most of the major PR disasters outlined in this chapter could have been avoided had the company actually come out and addressed the problems head on. In our networked society, people talk at light-speed, and bad news travels faster than ever before. Newsgroups, chat rooms, and bulletin boards (as well as the ever-increasing numbers of consumer opinion sites) are all venues where people can and will talk about your company. If you tell lies or deny something that is an obvious problem, you can guarantee that somebody's going to find out and tell the world. As journalists troll the Web more and more looking

186 | the dot.bomb survival guide

for the big scoop, they're looking at these sites. And don't forget your employees have email too . . . and if they're pissed off, they'll probably use it to air your dirty laundry.

5. *Clearly define the features and benefits of your products and/or services . . . at least until you are sure that people know what you do. Then you can hit them with the more emotional brand-building messages.* While a lot of dot.com commercials made people sit up and take notice, the fact is that few people ever remembered the company that was being advertised. Wacky image ads or obscure hip references might make creative directors grin, but the Web is now populated by real people who don't live in the Alley or the Valley. Asking people to visit your website is a direct-response message at heart: If people don't have a reason to go to your site, they won't.

6. *Speak with a human voice.* As *The Cluetrain Manifesto* so succinctly points out, "The Internet is enabling conversations among human beings that were simply not possible in the era of mass media." Communication in the age of the Web really must be different. Corpspeak doesn't work anymore in a world where people are used to communicating constantly on a global scale. When they're on the Web, people have their marketing radar detectors turned on "high." Even if your company thinks that you can get away with speaking buzzword prattle to your customers, you can bet that your customers won't speak about you in the same way to their friends. If you're so imbued with buzzword culture that you aren't even sure how to sound like a real person anymore, check out The Gable Group's site Jargonfreeweb.com, and run your copy through its Jargonator.

7. *Pick your battles. Limited budgets should focus on niches.* Even though the Internet has brought mass amounts of people together all over the globe, they also tend to clump up in small communities based on mutual interest. The Web's just too big and our bookmark lists can become just too long to visit a huge range of sites. People are also overloaded with information and are tending to pull in their spheres of media more and more. While the mass media exists, if you've got the budget to advertise on it, go for it . . . but realize that you might be able to get better results not by looking at the big audience numbers but by looking at the *right*

audience numbers. As anyone who's ever used the automatically optimizing Flycast ad-serving system has discovered, you often get the best results in some of the least likely places.

8. *Focus on retention and conversion.* Finally, the old saw about birds in hand being worth more than the ones in the bush (yes, it's obscure, but you know what I mean), is true: Once you've got a customer, it's a lot less expensive to keep him or her than it is to get a new one. While tactics like free shipping and superlow prices might work while you can afford to use them, what's going to happen to those "loyal" customers once you can't afford to lose money on every sale? That's right . . . they'll go on to the next sucker who thinks he or she can buy loyalty. The Web commodifies everything, and one site is just as far away as any other. Your goal should be to use communications and customer experience to keep your customers on your site.

The hundreds of millions of dollars spent in a futile attempt to build dot.com brands that later went bust shows that building brand recognition isn't enough—successful companies actually have a product that people want. Hype works to get people to come to a site only once. Once they're there, they have to find enough value to keep coming back. Advertising agencies and media that got rich on ill-spent marketing dollars are now feeling the pinch as dot.bombs explode and survivors rethink their marketing strategies. But the ultimate beneficiaries of online ad dollars—the advertising-supported sites—are in even bigger trouble. We'll examine the problems of ad-supported sites in the next chapter.

the road to hell is advertising supported

When advertising first appeared on the Internet, it didn't exactly receive a warm welcome. By 1994, it hadn't yet become a commercial medium. Most of the Web was an odd mix of pages from research centers, universities, assorted enthusiasts, and a few corporations developing technology for the nascent medium. Websites (or "homepages," as they were quaintly referred to) were really just static brochures, crafted in rudimentary HTML and rarely containing more than a couple of pages of data and some pictures. While some visionaries discussed the future commercial value of the Web, nobody was really using it to make money yet. In fact, to the close-knit community of users at the time, the whole idea of "commercializing" the Web was seen as an evil to be avoided.

Enter Canter and Siegel.

In the early 1990s, Congress had authorized a "Green Card Lottery" system to help encourage more diverse immigration to the United States. Hopeful immigrants were able to send in a postcard containing their name and address, after which they would wait for their number to be called. It was a fair system, depending on the luck of the draw. But that didn't stop a lot of unscrupulous people from

190 | the dot.bomb survival guide

preying on the hopes of those seeking entry into the United States. They would charge big fees to those wanting to enter the lottery, insinuating that they had some special "in" or pull with the government.

Lawrence Canter and Martha Siegel were two Arizona-based lawyers who had left Florida several years earlier after becoming subjects of disciplinary action against their business. Once they had settled in Arizona, they set up shop in the immigration law community. Then they discovered the Internet.

In 1994, there really weren't any big "community" sites where people met and swapped messages. Instead, Usenet, a distributed message-board system containing thousands of "newsgroups" on just as many topics, was king. It was global, heavily trafficked, and could be used by anyone with Internet access and a newsreader client on his or her machine. In effect, it was a perfect place to advertise legal services around the world. With free access, a highly desirable demographic, and lots of eyeballs, Usenet circa 1994 was about to become the vehicle for the first experiment in Net ads.

On or around April 13, 1994, Canter and Siegel posted a message advertising their Green Card lottery registration services to thousands of Usenet newsgroups. And once posted, it flew freely around the world as fast as it could be propagated.

The response to their advertisement was overwhelmingly negative. People who were used to the idea of an Internet free from the evil influences of corporate America felt violated. It was *their* communities, *their* newsgroups, *their* Internet. Advertising had no place in it, especially advertising as crass as this spam.

Nearly as quickly as the message had gone out, complaints began to fill the inboxes of government officials and Internet service providers. The media jumped on the story, too, breathlessly recounting stories of the "Green Card Lottery Spam" and what it meant for the then-embryonic world of the Internet. The Net community was embroiled in controversy, with some of its more capitalistically minded members defending the move but with most condemning it.

The Net had lost its innocence. In the months that followed, Canter and Siegel would be relentlessly pursued by anti-spam activists and would write a book about their experience tastefully entitled *How to Make a Fortune on the Information Superhighway: Everyone's*

the road to hell is advertising supported | 191

Guerilla Guide to Marketing on the Internet and Other Online Services. Other spammers (such as the infamous Jeff Slaton) would follow Canter and Siegel's lead, filling the discussion groups on Usenet with ads for "Euphoria Tapes" and bogus A-bomb plans, fanning the flames and igniting a debate that would continue for years.

At that time there still was no such thing as Web advertising. However, at the same time that the Green Card scandal was rocking the world of the Net, *Wired* was making plans for launching its *HotWired* service, one of the first commercial online magazines. Unfortunately, it had no idea how to make any money from it. In a world where information was supposed to be free, who would pay?

The answer came from the print world—why not sell advertising space on the site? Small spaces could be carved out from the content designed to hold small GIF-based banners that advertisers would pay for. A revenue model was born. In October 1994, *HotWired* was launched carrying advertising banners from AT&T, MCI, Sprint, and Volvo. Some ads provided links to the advertisers' sites, and others led to amusing "microsites" on *HotWired*, which expanded on the theme of the ad and provided a gateway to the advertiser's site. Time Warner quickly followed suit, launching its *Pathfinder* site with sponsorships from AT&T. ZDNet also launched its own commercial site. NCSA's Mosaic "What's New" site (one of the most popular at the time) started trolling for commercial sponsorship, and TechWeb was launched by CMP publications. The Web advertising boom had started.

Most early commercial deals were pretty simple, with publishers charging advertisers a flat fee for space or other types of sponsorship. Ads were fairly distinct from content—it wasn't until iVillage launched in 1996 that the two really started to blur—and most ads were static with the advertiser "owning" that particular spot on the page. Online advertising really began to pick up in the next couple of years. Clear-malt beverage Zima and spaghetti sauce brand Ragu launched some of the first commercial packaged-goods sites aimed at consumers. Yahoo! began to start transforming itself into an advertising-supported service, attracting early advertisers by the strength of its (then) nascent brand and high levels of traffic. AT&T and Procter & Gamble both began committing increasing amounts of ad dollars to online initiatives.

192 | the dot.bomb survival guide

As the commercial Web grew, so too grew the companies that started to serve it. Advertising agencies, ad serving networks, and measurement companies all came together into what has now become a multibillion-dollar online advertising industry. At the same time, the advertising-supported model became the quickest barrier to entry for new Web entrepreneurs with a "big idea." It made perfect sense—build a site that attracts users because of its content, sell ads on that site, and rake in the big bucks. In a Web that was growing exponentially, most entrepreneurs (and VCs) that understood the advertising-based model could easily envision how it worked. In a complex, technologically driven, fast-moving new industry, the ad-supported model was the first one that investors could sink their teeth into. In a way, understanding the beginnings of the advertising-supported model and how it came into favor is the key to understanding much of the dot.com implosion.

how it works

The basics of the advertising-supported model are simple: Get as many people as possible to look at as many ads as possible. Since advertisers will pay for ad impressions (an ad viewed by somebody), the more people you have using your site, listening to your streaming radio program, viewing your videos, or using your piece of software, the more money you'll make.

Pricing for advertising is usually controlled by a number of factors. First, how many people will see the ad? Second, how good a match are those people to an advertiser's target audience? Third, what type of ad is it—simple banner, complex multimedia experience, or just a simple text link? Finally, where will that ad be placed—on the bottom of the page, in the center, or on the top? All these factors (and a lot more, including how it integrates with content, what other ads the person is buying, and the size of the deal add up to an amount of money that an advertiser has to pay to place that ad.

Ever since InfoSeek and Netscape decided to sell ads based on the number of impressions instead of flat sponsorships back in July 1995, advertising is usually sold on the cost-per-thousand (or CPM) model. An advertiser buys all or a portion of the eyeballs for that

the road to hell is advertising supported | 193

particular piece of site real estate, and he or she often shares that same place with banners from other advertisers. If an advertiser wants to "own" a particular spot on a site or have exclusive rights to a section, it usually has to pay a much higher price.

For advertisers and media properties, the CPM model seemed to make the most sense for a long time. Unlike many other media, the Web is ultimately measurable—every page view, every ad served, and every click on the ad can be measured. For the most part, banner ads were (and still are for many) considered a direct-marketing vehicle, designed to get a user to click through to the advertiser's site.

CPMs on the Web have a huge range, from mere pennies on some low-trafficked sites all the way up into the thousands for highly targeted properties such as some B2B portals. But while prices have varied widely, CPM prices have been in decline since the early days of Web advertising. While *HotWired* was able to garner CPMs as high as $150 in 1996, online ad measurement firm AdKnowledge calculates that the average full-banner CPM is currently around $32.

The CPM model was first challenged in April 1996 when Procter & Gamble demanded that Yahoo! allow it to pay only for ads that people clicked on. This pay-per-click (also known as *pay-for-performance*) model was controversial, as it suddenly put the site at the mercy of the creative pulling power of the advertiser. Instead of having a revenue stream that it could project, advertisers were becoming more and more dependent on the whims of a public who were becoming less and less likely to click on ads as time went by. While early advertisers on *HotWired* and other sites enjoyed clickthrough rates of several percent, once the novelty wore off, many advertisers have had to contend with clickthrough rates that average somewhere in the half-percent (or less) range.

In 1996, iVillage.com was able to accumulate more than $800,000 in advertising commitments by promising to merge editorial with marketing with complicated sponsorship deals. While the early sponsorship deals usually meant that an advertiser had exclusive rights to a banner position, these new complicated deals included links to editorial, banners throughout the site, and sometimes even creative input over content. These sponsorship deals (also pioneered by America Online), often cost well into the millions and served to bolster the early revenues of dot.com media companies.

194 | the dot.bomb survival guide

By the end of 1996, over $301 million had been spent on online advertising and 15.2 million people had come online. The Web had finally become big business. The advertising market exploded. According to the Internet Advertising Bureau, Internet advertising revenues rose to $906 billion by 1997, more than doubled to $1.9 billion by 1998, and quadrupled to $4.6 billion by the third quarter of 1999. By the third quarter of 2000, ad revenues topped $6 billion. Jupiter MediaMetrix predicted in mid-2000 that Internet advertising would top $28 billion by 2005.

Ads weren't just being sold on the Web. Entrepreneurs quickly began to see an opportunity to leverage the advertising community's seemingly insatiable need for eyeballs into other online media such as email, software, and streaming media. In April 1996 Juno Online launched a free ad-supported email service where users could get email accounts in exchange for having to watch ads. Other companies like PointCast followed with advertising-supported push technology schemes and other advertising-supported software.

The advertising model has been expanded as a way to support free content in a huge variety of venues. Ad-supported PCs were all the rage in 1999 when FreePC.com (an Idealab! company) offered to give free computers to users willing to view ads. Free Internet service providers also cropped up, giving users free access to the Internet in exchange for viewing ads. Many new wireless content companies plan on supporting themselves through the placement of advertising within their content, and there are plans in the works calling for consumers to actually receive free wireless Internet devices in exchange for having to watch ads. For cellphone users without Web access on their phone, voice portals such as Tellme.com offer Web content read aloud interspersed with audio advertisements.

The future, as it appeared in the late nineties, would be advertising supported. Consumers everywhere, hooked on free content and services, would be happy to put up with advertising in exchange for access. Wouldn't what had worked for commercial TV and radio for years work on the Web?

At least not to the extent that people had hoped. After the market decline of mid-2000, many advertising-supported sites went out of business, unable to get the traffic or the advertisers they needed to keep up with their spending. Once-promising advertising-supported

the road to hell is advertising supported | 195

content companies like Go.com, Kibu.com, quepasa.com, Pseudo.com, UrbanBoxOffice, iBelieve.com, and AtomicPop.com have bitten the dust. Other companies such as Pop.com folded before it could launch. Services such as sixdegrees.com have gone under for lack of revenues, and others like MyPlay.com have laid off large numbers of employees while forging their advertising models into something more profitable.

Why? Is the advertising-supported model dead or does it just need retooling? Is our basic concept of what online advertising's supposed to accomplish the Achilles' heel of the whole concept? What are some of the problems advertising-supported sites need to overcome to survive now and in the future?

problems with advertising-supported revenue models

Probably one of the biggest problems facing many advertising-supported Web properties is simply getting advertisers to spend money on their sites. According to the eMarketer eAdvertising report published at the end of 2000, the top 10 Web properties earned 76 percent of all the online ad dollars . . . and the top 50 properties took in 95 percent of the ad revenue (Table 7-1).

Table 7-1. Top 25 Properties of December 2000

Combined Home & Work		
Rank	Property	Unique Audience (000)
1.	AOL Websites	70,985
2.	Yahoo!	65,258
3.	MSN	54,677
4.	Excite@Home	34,622
5.	Microsoft	34,207
6.	Lycos Network	31,064
7.	Amazon	26,555
8.	Walt Disney Internet Group	25,102
9.	Time Warner	23,704
10.	CNET Networks	21,021

Rank	Property	Unique Audience (000)
11.	eBay	20,551
12.	About.com	19,881
13.	NBCi	19,540
14.	eUniverse Network	19,329
15.	Bradford & Reed Inc.	17,030
16.	AtlaVista	15,178
17.	Weather Channel	15,074
18.	LookSmart	14,651
19.	Ask Jeeves	13,793
20.	American Greetings	12,817
21.	Real Network	11,537
22.	The Go2Net Network	11,022
23.	Napster Inc.	10,805
24.	Viacom International	10,753
25.	InfoSpace	10,410

Source: Nielsen//NetRatings.

That's a huge chunk of the market, especially when two-thirds of major U.S. corporations are now advertising online, according to the Association of National Advertisers (ANA). The bigger companies with the bigger budgets are focusing most of their dollars on a relatively small number of sites, forcing the thousands of sites left behind to scramble for 5 percent of the money—$300,000,000 in advertising revenue. That may seem like a lot, until you consider that there are literally thousands of websites competing for a slice of the remaining 5 percent of that pie.

Even though the bigger sites are sucking up most of the revenue, there's still a glut of advertising inventory—the number of possible ads a site can sell—on the Web. When ad-tracking company Leading Web Advertisers (www.web-advertisers.com) studied 20 top properties between January and June 2000, it found that an average of 22 percent of the ad space was taken up by "house ads"—ads for properties the site itself owns (and doesn't derive any revenue from). In fact, it extrapolated its numbers to estimate that up to 80 percent of the advertising on top websites is unsold.

How did it make such outrageous assumptions? Actually, its methodology was pretty simple—it just looked at the ads on the top sites. On ESPN.com it found that 73 percent of the ads on the site were for other Disney-owned properties. On Netscape's Netcenter, 45 percent of the ads were for Netscape products. Go.com spent 30 percent of its space advertising itself or other parts of Disney. Conversely, some sites were nearly sold out. Yahoo! gave only 5 percent of its inventory over to house ads, and AltaVista's own ads made up 10 percent of all the ads it displayed. Even if these figures are off by 10 percent or more, it makes an important point—eyeballs aren't everything. Despite a site's ability to attract a lot of users, it can't make money unless it's selling the ads those people see. To add insult to injury, most of the online advertisers are other dot.coms. That used to be a good thing when dot.coms had all the money, but as more and more go out of business or curb their spending, online properties are starting to hurt.

But some of the issues rocking the industry attack the very core of the advertising-supported model. One of the biggest is how to measure success of online advertising. For a long time online advertising was popularly regarded as direct-response advertising—the only thing that counted was whether or not someone clicked through an ad. Unfortunately, as clickthough rates declined, advertisers became more and more concerned about the model and began to believe that if people weren't clicking, the ads weren't working . . . and not worth paying for. Even though more media properties and advertising networks have begun to push the branding value of online ads, advertisers are increasingly becoming attracted to pay-for-performance models, especially as revenues decline.

Is this a good idea? It really depends on what an advertiser wants to accomplish online. If the goal is to drive direct response that leads to direct sales, pay-per-click (or per-sale) advertising is by far the most efficient way to get there. With the case of FragranceNet in Chapter 5, frugal companies can use performance-based advertising to their advantage when money is tight.

In defense of the media, there's mounting evidence to support the claims that clickthroughs aren't as important as once thought. In a report published in November 2000, AdKnowledge found that simply viewing ads online can influence purchasing behavior and brand recognition. The biggest difference, however, is how long it took to

198 | the dot.bomb survival guide

convert that ad view into a sale. Forty percent of the people who saw an advertisement for a site but didn't click and later made a purchase did not make the purchase until 8 to 30 days after viewing the online ad. On the other hand, consumers who clicked through and purchased did so within 30 minutes of the click.

Understanding the concepts and controversies of online advertising makes it easier to wrap your head around what made some content publishers successful and what killed others off. But unlike some of the more complex business models that many ecommerce sites were built on, the online advertising model is pretty simple: Get enough people to view enough pages so that you can sell enough ads to pay the bills.

Sure, it's simple. Then why did so many ad-supported dot.coms die while others have risen into the top 50 and run away with the lion's share of the ad revenue? The answer comes down to a few basic factors:

1. *Economics.* If a company grows its infrastructure faster than its revenue stream and it can't get enough investment to tide it over, it's dead. Also, if consumer traffic patterns suddenly shift so that your audience declines and the company doesn't address the change quickly, it's in trouble.
2. *Audience.* Advertising is all about targeting the right audience. Advertisers want to know that their ads are going to be put in front of a lot of people who are potential buyers of their product or service. Not being able to draw the right audience is a problem, as is overspending to reach an audience that's too small.
3. *Technology.* While Web technology has finally standardized to the point where everyone with a browser has pretty much the same experience, cutting-edge technologies can present unique problems. Streaming media is one of the technologies that advertisers have had some problems with, as well as content that requires broadband connections.

portals: when expenses don't meet ad revenues

Portals—advertising-supported sites that aggregate content and often include search engines, ecommerce, free email, and auctions—

have been a fixture of the Web ever since Time Warner launched its Pathfinder service in 1994. They've competed openly for the most coveted real estate of all—users' homepage buttons, which are usually preset to the browser company's portal . . . a fact that's helped boost MSN into the ranks of the top websites.

Because of their wide reach, portals have been very attractive to advertisers. Approximately 34 percent of all online advertising spending goes to the main portal sites, according to eMarketer. Yet even with all this spending, the size of the sites means that there's an awful lot of advertising to sell. And, as discussed earlier in this chapter, many portals have significant amounts of advertising inventory that goes unsold. In addition, many users are starting to skip a lot of the content on the portals and going directly to other sites via search engines. Advertisers have noticed this, and revenue from content areas is starting to decline while search engine advertising is increasing. Search engines may be better at driving sales and traffic than banners on portals, especially as more advertisers strive for branding rather than clickthrough. Researchers at the NPD Group found that search engine listings are much more effective for brand advertising than simple banners are, three times better in fact. It also found that 55 percent of all purchases are referred from search listings versus 9 percent via banner ads.

The increasing importance of search engines has been a boon to portals—but search engines don't need a lot of content creators and editors. As a result, several major search engines have laid off workers after suffering severe financial setbacks, including InfoSpace, Excite@Home, and AltaVista.

Portals have also been hit by several other shifts in the marketplace. First, online advertising has been increasingly dominated by business-to-business advertising—not an audience served by the general-interest portal market. In May 2000 AdRelevance reported that the number of B2B advertisers had grown by 58 percent since the beginning of the year compared to 17 percent growth in other sectors. Rather than spread their dollars among sites that specialize in entertainment or general consumer information, B2B advertisers are much more likely to spend their money on business, finance, news, and technology sites.

In addition, there's been a general trend of advertisers moving their dollars away from portals and to more niche-oriented sites.

Forrester Research predicted in February 2000 that broad-based portals would see their share of the online ad market decline from 5 percent in 1999 to 1 percent in 2004. As advertisers shift from general portals to "vortals," or vertical-portals, they see the niche sites attracting 24 percent of all online advertising, up from 11 percent in 1999. Why? Because companies are looking for a better return on their advertising investment. The marketplace is starting to wake up to a lot of the facts discussed in the previous chapter: Once the money gets low, mass advertising loses its appeal. A report from Forrester confirmed this, pointing out that 62 percent of retailers saw ROI as their main advertising influencer, followed by demographics (58 percent) and traffic (48 percent).

Big surprise, right?

You'd think it would be obvious, but to companies swimming in a sea of cash, the idea that they couldn't continue to grow forever seemed crazy. As a result, many portals built up their staffs to incredibly high levels, employing hundreds of people as content providers, editors, salespeople, marketing people, and IT folks. While the market was strong, they were able to sustain the growth. As soon as it declined, they started to run into trouble. The economics didn't work anymore.

Go.com, Disney's portal site, was the first to go. It had been online since 1999, and it was formed from the assets of Infoseek and Starwave. Go.com floundered since its inception, seeking desperately to find a niche. In January 2000, Go.com changed focus to "entertainment and leisure" in an effort to distance itself from other portals, but it didn't work. February 4, 2000, Go.com announced that it was going bust, laying off 400 workers, taking a noncash writeoff of $790 million, and taking a hit of between $25 and $50 million in other expenses. That's one big boom for a dot.bomb.

Why did it happen? The answer has little to do with any fancy theories about portals, entertainment on the Web, or first-to-market advantage. Nope. Go.com's failure has a lot to do with simple economics.

Go.com's model had very little chance of survival from the beginning (Figure 7-1). Considering the amount of people Go.com employed to keep its operation running (at least 400), it would have had operating expenses of at least $60 million per year. To support

the road to hell is advertising supported | 201

an operation of this size (and assuming an average $30 CPM, Go.com would have had to sell over 2 billion impressions per year to break even. According to MediaMetrix figures from January 2001, all Disney properties combined were generating approximately 2.3 billion impressions per year. Leading Advertisers estimates that 30 percent of all those impressions were for unpaid "house ads," leaving a total of about 1.6 billion sold impressions . . . not enough to support Go.com's operations, even assuming a fairly high $30 CPM.

Figure 7-1. Go.com Goes Out of Business

The economics of an advertising-supported portal are tough. While there have been many layoffs in this sector, companies like Yahoo! have been able to survive the downturn in the same way that Amazon.com has ridden out the problems in the ecommerce sector—diversity and a big audience. They have multiple revenue streams that, in the case of Yahoo!, include ecommerce, auctions, and high-profile cross-media deals to build viewership and revenue.

At this point, jumping into the portal game would be pretty difficult—there's probably not going to be another rags-to-riches story

202 | the dot.bomb survival guide

like Yahoo! for a while. Portals are best left to extremely well funded organizations that can spend the money on marketing and effectively compete for market share. That could take some time. It took HBO 27 years to successfully make its way to the top of the cable heap. It could take a good fraction of that for an upstart to break into the ranks of the top sites at this point in the game.

niche sites with smaller audiences

Not every advertising-supported site with portal aspirations yearns to be the next MSN. Rather than own the entire Web audience, many just want a big chunk of their own specific audience. The two biggest problems that smaller, niche portals face is the clutter on the Web (estimated at 2.1 billion pages in July 2000 by Cyberveillance) and the amount of advertising money available, nearly 5 percent of all advertising revenue.

There are other, more difficult issues to quantify. Since these portals address smaller, niche audiences, the sites often have to battle it out for a share of the smaller budgets of companies that serve these niches. They're also designed to attract members of specific communities, communities that may not be as welcoming of commercial ventures as the general public.

It's these problems (coupled with out-of-control spending) that killed quepasa.com, an ambitious portal directed toward the Hispanic community that launched in 1998. Kicking off with a high-profile advertising campaign featuring Gloria Estefan, quepasa combined content with free email, auctions, chat rooms, and ecommerce to make a play at becoming *the* destination for Hispanics worldwide.

In 1998, quepasa seemed to be in a great position to capture a rapidly growing market. Jupiter MediaMetrix estimated that the Latin American market was set to explode. Statistically, there were millions of Hispanics online and few major commercial media outlets to serve them. So quepasa.com grew. It knew that profitability was a few years away, but it counted on a rapidly expanding marketplace to cover its losses: $6.4 million in 1998 and $29.3 million in 1999. It rapidly spent money on marketing and a growing infrastructure, heading for an IPO that would fund itself (it thought) until profitability arrived.

On June 24, 1999, quepasa.com went public with an offering price of $12, closing the day at a respectable $17.13. But investors got spooked when, by the end of the year, the site was losing tens of millions of dollars. The stock price began to fall, heading below $1 in April 2000. In December 2000, quepasa decided to throw in the towel and liquidate its assets after posting a third-quarter loss of $7.9 million (Figure 7-2).

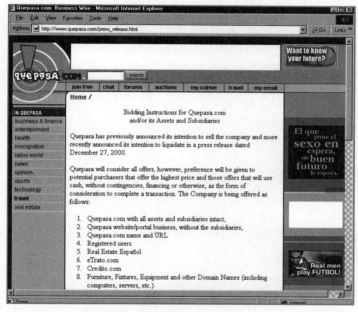

Figure 7-2. Quepasa No Mas

Why did quepasa.com fail? One of the obvious (and, by now, common) reasons was that it couldn't raise more money. Investors, shook up by the decline in the stock market, began to look askance at pure-plays that focused on niche markets.

But there may have been more problems related to its audience. A StarMedia report, released in April 2000, found that high-quality, localized content was key to cracking the marketplace. While many outside the Hispanic community tend to see it as monolithic, it isn't. Rather, it consists of many different subgroups with distinctive cultural heritages, and these smaller subcultures need to be communicated with in different ways. Quepasa.com made the mistake of treating every group in the market in a similar fashion . . . a move that probably hurt its readership (and therefore sellable traffic).

Ironically, quepasa's differentiating feature—its Spanish language content—may have also contributed to its decline. Research conducted by Puerto Rican research firm Research & Research in January 1996 found that online Hispanics actually favor English-language—not Spanish—sites. The study, commissioned by Spanish-language etailer Espanol.com, found that only 8 percent of Hispanics preferred Spanish sites over English ones. Of the people surveyed, 51 percent considered themselves bilingual, admitting that they would shop on sites of either language.

Finally, the "digital divide" may have doomed the site to slower-than-expected growth. Jupiter MediaMetrix reported in its study *Assessing the Digital Divide(s)* that the online Hispanic-American population would grow to only 3.8 million by the end of 2000 . . . not enough to support a portal spending $7 million a quarter.

Advertising-Supported Niches Can Survive

An Interview with Hurst Lin, U.S. General Manager and VP Business Development of SINA.com

Created in March 1999, SINA.com is a merger between two of the world's largest Chinese Websites—SINANET.com of Sunnyvale, California, and Stone Rich Sight Information Technology Company Ltd. (SRS) of Beijing. Since then, the company has become one of the leading Internet media and services companies for Chinese communities worldwide. Focusing on a global audience, SINA provides Chinese-language content, commerce, and community services to four localized websites targeting China, Hong Kong, Taiwan, and overseas Chinese in North America. While it doesn't exactly see itself as similar to dot.bombs like quepasa.com, it has built a successful business by concentrating on a specific ethnic community.

Why is it thriving when other ad-supported sites have had such a hard time? Here's what Hurst Lin, U.S. general manager and VP business development, said when asked about SINA's successful model.

Q: Please describe SINA—its audience, size of site, history, funding, revenues.

SINA is a leading Internet media and services company for Chinese communities worldwide, offering global Chinese-language content, commerce, and community services to four localized websites targeting China, Hong Kong, Taiwan, and overseas Chinese in North America. We reported consolidated net revenues of $7.6 million for the second quarter fiscal 2001 ended December 31, 2000. We enjoyed 1.5 billion page views for the month of December 2000, as audited by ABC Interactive, and had 16 million registered users at the end of the same month.

Q: While many dot.bombs fall, SINA has continued to thrive. Why? What makes your site special?

Unlike many of our competitors or peers, we have always focused on fiscal discipline, monetizing traffic, and shareholder value. As we announced in our last earnings call, our advertising revenues increased 218 percent over that of the prior year, and our net loss decreased 10 percent from the previous quarter. These numbers position us as the clear leader in the Chinese Internet space.

In addition, unlike many of our competitors who are focused only on one Chinese online market, SINA has a global presence, targeting Chinese communities worldwide, focusing on key markets such as China, Taiwan, Hong Kong, and the United States. This provides us with the local presence and international reach to deliver value on a global scale to our clients, partners, and users.

Q: What lessons have you learned that you wish you had known before you started the site?

The market that we had just experienced will not happen again any time soon; therefore, it's difficult to talk about what lessons we could have learned. The rules that worked during the bubble would not work in the more normal circumstances today, and likewise, anyone sticking to the normal rules of operations during the bubble would have missed the ride entirely.

> *Q: If you were going to give advice to someone starting a site like yours today, what advice would you give them?*
>
> Do not start a site like SINA today. The portal game is over in most major markets such as China, the United States, Europe, and Latin America today. The winners and long-term survivors are largely in place. The next stage of development in the portal space is the merging of online and offline media such as AOL-Time Warner.
>
> *Q: How have you made the advertising-supported model work for you? Is that where most of your revenue comes from? If not, what other channels have driven revenue for the site?*
>
> Over 80 percent of our revenue comes from advertising. The rest comes from software sales and ecommerce. SINA has long focused on "beyond the banner" advertising for our clients. We deliver everything including sponsorship/cobranding, direct marketing, special promotions, microsite development, and the latest online ad capabilities such as skyscraper ads and text-within-text ads.
>
> *Q: What does it take to create "community" on a site such as yours?*
>
> The creation of community on SINA is often driven by the critical mass in the audience of our site. With a large member base, it's easy for groups of thousands to congregate around any popular subjects. Fundamentally, most communities thrive on numbers. That more members beget more members is a well-studied "network effect" phenomenon. Therefore, it's very important for a community to get started on a large portal site such as SINA.

iBelieve.com was a casualty of a different market . . . the online Christian marketplace. Launched in January 2000 with $30 million in funding from Madison Dearborn Partners, iBelieve.com seemed poised to mine a previously untapped population. The founders estimated that there were 35 million Christians online . . . a fairly big chunk of the online population. Crosswalk.com (one of iBelieve's competitors) estimated that Christians spent a total of $25.6 million per year on products and charities. iBelieve.com jumped in with a bang, spending $10 million of its $30 million on a high-profile advertising campaign crafted by ad agency Hanon-McKendry. Featuring the tagline "Insert God Here," its ads blanketed Christian and mass media in print and on TV, radio, and the Internet.

Interest was initially pretty high: iBelieve signed up 550,000 members and had 2 million unique visitors. But it wasn't enough to sustain such a big investment. On October 23, 2000, iBelieve.com announced that it was going out of business, unable to find funding to continue (Figure 7-3). The founders had predicted profitability in 5 years, but at the rate it was spending money (nearly $30 million in 10 months), 2 million was a pitifully small number to support a venture of its size. For the sake of comparison, Yahoo! brought in 65 million visitors in January 2001.

Figure 7-3. No Resurrection for iBelieve.com

Even though it survived longer than iBelieve, Crosswalk.com might also be in trouble. Even though it signed an ad contract with Trinity College in February 2001 worth $600,000 over 2 years, it continues to hemorrhage money at a frightening rate—$7.2 million in the third quarter of 2000 alone. With the decline in the stock mar-

208 | the dot.bomb survival guide

ket taking Crosswalk.com's stock to around $1.40 (prompting Crosswalk.com to move to the NASDAQ Small Cap Market in June 2001), the Christian market as a whole may find itself without another portal soon.

Before you assume that the entire sector's in trouble, take a look at one site that's actually been doing pretty well.

multiple revenue streams = dot.com survival

While other portals in its space have died (or are on life support), Christianity.com has survived by remaining flexible. Rather than pray that advertising was going to see them through, Christianity.com has built a model that combines an advertising-supported content site with an application service provider backend in the form of Web hosting for churches and ministries. Christianity.com has built over 200 church sites, and it charges $29.95 for the sites that don't want to carry advertising from Christianity.com.

It has worked, and the company has continued to attract funding. While many dot.coms have crashed and burned due to lack of funding, at the beginning of 2001, Christianity.com landed another $15 million in venture funding, bringing its total funding to $34 million. It's not profitable yet, but its model has provided a way to survive the lean times. By spreading out the revenue stream to build communities locally (and get revenue through advertising and site hosting) while building critical mass on the main site, Christianity.com might be able to pull off a miracle yet.

on the bleeding edge

While text-based content sites have had their own share of problems, the broadband entertainment market has really been struggling to keep afloat. Bleeding-edge sites featuring streaming video, audio, animation, and films have teased investors and the public with visions of an infinite-channel future where TVs are obsolete and consumers watch whatever they want—whenever they want—online.

the road to hell is advertising supported | 209

Broadband content makes for really cool demos, under controlled conditions. Produced with a fast connection and a high-powered multimedia computer, rich media makes people sit back and go "Wow!" every time it's demonstrated. But the reality of making money with content that requires high download speeds and super-fast computers hasn't been quite as cool. One of the big problems has been access—getting high-speed connections into the home. DSL and digital cable have been growing stronger, but the reality is that as recently as May 2000, there were still 50 times as many users logging on from relatively slow modem connections than from high-speed pipes. Not only is much of the United States still waiting for the technology to be installed, but when it is, Jupiter MediaMetrix estimates that it usually costs twice what a low band connection costs . . . and many consumers don't understand the benefits.

In 2000, the audience for broadband was fairly small—only 9 percent of consumers had broadband access according to NetSmartAmerica (www.netsmartamerica.com). But for advertisers, that consumer group is an attractive audience, primarily male, around 34 years old, and fairly well off with average incomes of $59,700. The market is growing, as well. NetSmartAmerica estimates that 30 percent of all users will have broadband connections by 2003.

It seems like a demographic that advertisers should love, but they don't. One reason they don't is that broadband raises the bar for design creativity. While a banner ad might cost a few thousand to produce, broadband rich-media ads can cost tens of thousands of dollars to produce. In addition, a lot of the broadband sites have contained content that only a hipster could love. Cartoons like "QueerDuck" and "LilPimp" may have made a lot of blue-haired denizens of Silicon Alley snicker, but they've scared off advertisers.

"A tremendous amount of the content is of a bizarre nature," said Doug Jaeger, interactive creative director at Chiat/Day, in a recent *Wall Street Journal* article. "A lot of our advertisers don't want to sponsor that kind of program." Not even for free. According to *The Wall Street Journal,* Coca-Cola and Pepsi have turned down offers of free advertising on several of the more cutting-edge sites.

But there's more than wacky content holding back broadband content sites. Pseudo Programs, one of the first (and biggest) broadband sites, got its start in 1994 when Jupiter MediaMetrix founder Josh Harris jumped ship to start his own cutting-edge site. Combining streaming video and animation into different themed channels, Pseudo produced over 8,000 shows during its 6-year-life and raised over $18 million in venture funding.

Like a lot of advertising-supported sites, Pseudo struggled for a revenue model and suffered through a long string of management changes. The venture money had bought it its cool digs in Silicon Alley and helped it attract Larry Lux, founder of NationalGeographic.com. Under his command, Pseudo struggled with trying to find advertisers in the face of the mounting costs of running a site with high technology costs. The high-end computers, high-speed connections, and costs of storing all the digital media began to add up.

Lux gave up trying to make the model work and left in 1999. He was followed by CNN's David Bohrman who pared down the staff and tried to bring some efficiency into the freewheeling startup. His plan was to focus the content and relaunch the site as a 24-hour Webcast. Unfortunately, the site wasn't able to hold on long enough to make any money—by September 2000, Pseudo had decided to shut its door and liquidate its assets. It was later purchased for $2 million by the New York production company INTV (Figure 7-4).

Figure 7-4. Pseudo.com's Goodbye Page

Pop.com: too far ahead of the curve

Another broadband play, Pop.com, never even got off the ground. Funded for $50 million by Steven Spielberg, Ron Howard, and Paul

the road to hell is advertising supported | 211

Allen's Vulcan Ventures, Pop.com got a lot of ink because of its celebrity backers. But after coming together in October 1999 to serve films, video on demand, sports, and games, it closed its doors just 11 months later in September 2000.

Why did Pop.com go . . . well . . . pop? When it realized that it was in trouble, the owners tried to find a buyer for the site, but its $200 million valuation scared off any potential investors. Most of the management had little or no Internet experience and came from traditional media companies. Because they came from the TV and film world, they lacked an understanding of how the Web world worked, and a lot of content providers were spooked by Pop.com's insistence that it own 100 percent of any work shown on the site . . . something none of the other broadband sites required.

But the real end of Pop.com (and what made it decide to fold before even launching) was the very thing that attracted its investors to the business in the first place—the advertising-supported business model. After nearly a year of considering the economics of an advertising-supported model, the company threw in the towel. As CEO Ken Wong told *The Industry Standard*, "We believe this space is not yet a business. We're not clairvoyants, but we think it's going to take years."

He's probably right.

Is broadband content a dead end? Definitely not. It has a huge following, and anyone who has actually experienced it usually comes away with a feeling like "Yeah . . . this is what the Web should be like." Even though the cost for broadband access is twice that of a dialup connection, the demand is there. NetSmartAmerica found that 27 percent of Web users surveyed in 2000 would be willing to pay $40 per month for the privilege.

Up until now, most broadband content plays have focused on entertainment. However, a study released by Jupiter MediaMetrix in January 2001 may actually hold the key to the future of broadband on the Web. What Jupiter found was that 24 million people have broadband access now . . . from work. And that number is projected to more than double by 2005. What will business-related broadband content look like on the Web? It won't look like "QueerDuck." (OK. It might if you work in an office like mine.) Instead, it'll probably look something like BloombergTV, combin-

212 | the dot.bomb survival guide

ing huge amounts of information into a rapidly streaming display. B2B verticals may be able to take advantage of broadband connectivity in order to provide video news, 3D renderings of plans, and information-rich market displays. Eventually the consumer market will catch up. It's up to the remaining broadband sites to hold on until that day arrives.

free PCs . . . at a price

One of the more short-lived advertising-supported models has been the free PC—we'll give you a computer if you give us all your information and let us throw ads at you every time you use it. In the space of just a couple of years, the concept of advertising-supported hardware has gone from a "gee-whiz" media darling to a "we-could-have-seen-that-coming" has-been.

The concept originated with incubator Idealab! that developed a plan to give out free computers in exchange for consumer data and ad-views after the initial success of its NetZero free ISP service. In 1999, Bill Gross looked at NetZero's 300,000 subscribers and saw that many of them were using the service only when they were traveling or as a backup service if their own ISP was down. Seventy percent of those users had their own ISPs. If those users could be locked in full-time to the ad-supported ISP, the number of ad impressions on NetZero would skyrocket.

At the same time, PC prices had begun to drop like a rock, and Free-PC figured it could get a decent machine for around $600. It knew that the demand for Internet access was high and that price was a barrier for a lot of folks. If it could scale up the subscribers to the point where the numbers would allow it to support the whole scheme on advertising, it'd have a huge hit on its hands.

Initially it did, and the site was swamped. Other companies such as Gobi and DirectWeb followed suit, and startup Emachines got on the bandwagon by working deals with service providers that would provide huge rebates (effectively bringing the price to $0) in exchange for extended service contracts. But after the initial novelty wore off, people began to migrate back to free services and more expensive computers. In fact, by the end of 1999, low-end PC sales only amounted to 8 percent of the total PC market. People quickly realized the limitations of their "free" computers. Not only did they have to contend with irritating pop-up ads on their screens, but they also weren't able to play a lot of the high-end, graphically intensive games that were becoming popular at the time. Free didn't look like such a bargain.

By the end of 1999, Free-PC saw the writing on the wall and realized that it was never going to be able to make the costly economic model work. In November 1999, Free-PC merged with eMachines in a stock swap, deciding to concentrate on using Free-PC's ad-serving technology to extend the model to other companies.

Initially, the market didn't hate the idea, and Emachine's stock hovered around its $9 offering price. But as the PC market moved away from low-end computers, the company has continued to lose money (as much as $66.3 million in the second quarter of 2000), and its stock has plunged to under a dollar. Gobi changed its model to become a private label PC/ISP service, and DirectWeb closed up shop in February 2001.

While Free-PC took over a year to be felled by the economics of an advertising-supported model, the record for shortest-lived idea has to go to Virgin Entertainment Group's foray into the free Internet appliance world. In April 2000, Virgin offered to give away 10,000 VirginConnect WebPlayers. Users logging on to Virgin's site were asked to give up detailed demographic information, and, if they qualified, they were sent a spiffy little device that included a color flat-panel display, wireless keyboard (with integrated mouse), and a 56K modem. The device accessed the Net only through Virgin's portal, and it limited users to email and the Web. In exchange for all this hardware, users were expected to look at a never-ending stream of Virgin ads and targeted marketing emails based on their profiles.

Unfortunately, the device didn't quite live up to users' expectations (see sidebar "Free Ain't What It's Cracked Up to Be"). For people who had been used to high-speed Net access at work or powerful desktop machines, the experience of using the appliance didn't grab them. Just 6 months later, in November 2000, Virgin shut down the program and asked for the devices back, compensating users with $25 gift certificates for their troubles.

214 | the dot.bomb survival guide

Free Ain't What It's Cracked Up to Be
One User's Free Appliance Experience

If you weren't "lucky" enough to get on the free-device bandwagon, here's what Trevor Villet, an advertising account executive with Marriner Marketing Communications (and early adopter) said about his experiences with Virgin's device:

When I found out about the Virgin/IAN promotion offering a free Internet appliance device for the first 10,000 subscribers, I jumped. Heck, it would give me virtually free Internet access at home, and, more importantly, it would allow me to continue to be too cheap to buy a home computer. So, I signed up online and received an email a couple of weeks later congratulating me on being one of the lucky 10,000.

Two weeks later, I found a small box on my doorstep. I quickly opened it and ran upstairs to set it up in my office. I must say, it was as easy as they said. I just plugged it into my phone jack, set up my account, and off I went . . . slowly.

It wasn't the Virgin branding all over the place that bothered me. It wasn't the banner ads. In fact, their placement was relatively tasteful. What bothered me was the tiny screen I had to scroll all over—the fact that I had a tiny track ball at the top of my wireless keyboard and a click pad at the bottom so that I found my arms wrapped around the thing like I was hugging it—and ultimately the absolute snail's pace at which everything loaded. I was willing to accept that this thing wouldn't be as fast as my G3 and DSL connection at work, but come on. I would spend an hour trying to purchase a few groceries on WebHouse (yes, I was one of the few users of that service). One of the stipulations of using the machine was spending something like 10 hours a month on the machine. . . . I knew very quickly that if I decided to keep the thing, I would have no problem meeting those demands. And although they offered a standard email account, forget about downloading anything through their email account outside of text or a small jpeg.

A month later, I decided that this thing was not worth the trouble. I contacted Virgin and got instructions on how to send it back. They told me to box it up, and that they would send UPS within 4 weeks to pick it up—free of charge. Three months later, I got an email from the mailroom at work telling me that UPS had

the road to hell is advertising supported | 215

still not picked up the box and they "wanted it out of there." At that point, I figured something was up. Not a week later I got an email from Virgin telling me that . . . well, in essence, the entire idea was a flop and they were ending the IAN service. They once again told me they would follow up with instructions on how to prepare the machine for a UPS pickup that would occur within 2 weeks (is it possible that their automated email didn't realize that I had already done this?). It's now been 3 months since their latest email and I've heard nothing.

At work, I've got this cool office furniture that sits up really high. The IAN (in its UPS-friendly packaging) is a perfect footrest for a 5 foot, 7-inch, guy whose feet don't quite reach the floor.

The free ISP wave seems to have crested, too. While many users initially signed up for free accounts, the nonstop ads, slow connection speeds, and busy signals drove many back to pay providers. AltaVista and FirstUp have shut their operations down, and other advertising-supported ISPs have bent under the financial pressures of high churn rates and costly infrastructures. Innovator NetZero has moved to limit users' "free" time to 40 hours per month ($9.95 after), and Kmart's BlueLight.com free ISP service has retooled, limiting users to 25 hours per month. Interestingly enough, old-timer AT&T WorldNet has jumped into the fray by offering terms similar to NetZero's to lure away dissatisfied free-ISP customers.

It doesn't take a lot of complicated math to figure out why the free-device market has had such a tough time. With a per-customer acquisition cost near $1,000 ($600 for the PC plus the marketing to let them know about it) and ongoing ISP charges that don't decline with time, giving away Internet access and hardware is a tough—if not impossible—proposition.

riding the attention stream into the contact zone

Most of the advertising-supported companies that went out of business because of "market conditions" failed because they were paying attention to the wrong market. Instead of paying attention to the stock market (and depending on it to survive), they should

216 | the dot.bomb survival guide

have paid attention to their own markets: their audiences and their customers.

For a company to survive using an advertising-supported model, it first has to understand its audience: the size, the growth potential, their viewing and spending habits, how they act online, and what affects their behavior. Without an understanding of these factors, it's impossible to construct a model that will lead to profitability.

They also have to pay attention to their customers—the advertisers who will be spending money to get visibility for their products or services. Does the site have the content advertisers want? The traffic? The correct demographics? Can it offer packages that give the advertisers what they need to most effectively reach their customers? Are there enough advertisers with enough money to make the site cost effective? Wacky content is fine, as long as you have wacky advertisers who are willing to put their names next to it. Niche content is fine too, as long as there are enough people advertising to those niche audiences to pay for the site.

Do the models of online advertising really matter? Clickthroughs or pay for performance? Direct response or branding? These are some of the issues online advertisers and media properties are struggling with. But the real question is the scariest one of all—does online advertising actually *work*? Clearly it can build brand awareness. Sure, it can build sales. But is it really the right way for advertisers to accomplish what they've set out to do?

One of the biggest issues with online advertising is that it's the only form of advertising based on the premise that it is working only if the person experiencing it stops what he or she is doing and goes off to do something else. No other medium requires someone to stop and head off in another direction in order to respond to an ad. But the Web (for the most part) demands that the audience divert their attention stream.

The consumer's attention stream is linear, bound by time and space. Consumers have a hard time paying attention to more than one thing at a time. Even when looking at a website or a magazine page with multiple ads, their attention (if it's at all grabbed away from the content) goes to one ad, and only then to another—maybe.

That's why television and radio commercials and full-page print ads are so effective. They break into the attention stream and divert it, some by breaking into time (TV and radio spots) and some by breaking into space (print, outdoor, and, to some extent, Web ads). But, although they break into the attention stream to divert it, they don't require any immediate action to divert to an unintended destination. You don't have to call; you don't have go to the store and buy the new box of Super Snuggle Sugar Pop Toasties.

There have been a lot of problems for both the advertisers and the Web companies that depend on advertising revenue for survival. But that doesn't necessarily mean that online advertising "doesn't work." The definition of what works and what doesn't depends in part on a definition of outcomes. If driving direct traffic for a time-specific offer is the goal, then clickthroughs probably are the best measure of effectiveness. However, if the goal is to gain entrance into the attention stream and build brand, getting people to notice an ad, regardless of whether they click on it, should be the measure of success.

As clickthrough rates decline, the branding-versus-click debate is sure to rage even hotter than it is now. Advertising agencies and networks have a vested interest in selling the branding-click-throughs-don't-matter story. Advertisers want accountability. Those on both sides of this issue have ignored the fundamental point: It's not whether one is right but whether one is right based on the desired outcome.

What can those sites that depend on advertising do to survive the downturn? As many of the large and small sites that have survived on advertising have proven (look at the gaming industry to see examples of niche sites that can pull advertisers), an advertising-supported model can work, at least under some conditions:

1. *Sites must size themselves to the size of the audience.* Everybody can't be the next Yahoo! But a lot of sites can model themselves after Studio One Networks (www.studioone.com) which produces sponsored syndicated content for the Web. Studio One starts with the advertiser *first* and builds a site only after it has interested an advertiser in the content. They don't grow too big too fast—they grow as the market supports them.
2. *Be aware of the culture.* Many niche sites that cater to tightly knit ethnic and interest communities have run into trouble because they thought of their audience as a "market" first and a commu-

218 | the dot.bomb survival guide

nity second. Know what you're doing before you think you see an opportunity. Communities by definition are wary of outsiders. If you're not an insider and think you can build a site to attract a certain community, live in that community first before you try to sell to them.

3. *Don't get ahead of the technology curve . . . unless you've got the money to stick it out.* There's no question that broadband is going to revolutionize the Web . . . eventually. Until then, sites that rely on a relatively small share of the online demographic are going to have a tough time attracting advertisers. Of course, once the technology reaches a critical mass, they'll be perfectly positioned to be the leaders—that's what Yahoo! did. But hoping for market magic and VC gifts from on high isn't going to cut it anymore.

4. *Provide value to your customers.* As someone once said, nobody ever lost a customer for providing too much value. "Free" implies cheap and discourages loyalty. If you aren't differentiating yourself with stellar value or exclusive content, you're going to be killed by churn. Just as the Web commodifies the retail market, the culture of free also inherently decreases the value of the information (or services) conveyed for free. They become throwaways, junk to be easily discarded once something better comes along. If people had paid at least something for their PCs, they might not have seen them as low-powered pieces of junk. Instead, they might have seen them as low-powered pieces of junk they paid for and therefore are worth putting up with for some amount of time. There's a reason the online version of *The Wall Street Journal* has done so well—people are willing to pay for value. That doesn't mean that free can't work . . . it just has to work harder.

5. *Provide value to your advertisers.* As competition heats up and the ad market declines and begins to consolidate its spending into fewer properties, niche sites are going to have to survive on the value of the niches they hold. It's not necessarily the number of eyeballs you've got. It's the number of *right* eyeballs you've got. If you have the premiere site for industrial solvent marketing executives and only get a few thousand impressions a month, but those impressions are from most of the industrial solvent executives in the world, then you can charge just about any CPM you'd like. Just ask VerticalNet.

the road to hell is advertising supported | 219

6. *Churn happens.* If you're providing free content, there's going to be a lot of churn. Get used to it. Forecast based on the fact that your numbers today aren't necessarily going to be your numbers tomorrow. There's nothing tying people to your site . . . unless you follow point 4.

7. *Technology changes quickly. People change slowly.* Be aware that profitability may be a ways off . . . and plan for it. Getting people to change their behavior to rely on your site may take a while. Getting people to adopt expensive equipment and high-speed Net connections is probably going to take a while.

8. *Diversify.* Just as no prudent investor puts all his or her money on a single stock, don't put all your faith in the ability of advertising to drive enough revenue to your site to survive. And don't count on ecommerce. And don't count on auctions. Count on all of them together. And if you can develop alternative channels of revenue because of your knowledge of an industry or the technology you've developed, use them in a coordinated effort to build multiple ways of making money.

9. *Never forget that real people are going to use your site.* Flashy designs and fancy business plans aren't going to impress the casual average surfer who happens to stop by. They're not impressed. People are going to use your site or service only because it makes their life easier, richer, or more enjoyable. Speak with a human voice. Connect.

Making an advertising-supported business work is tough, and it requires smart thinking about managing capital, growth strategies, and content. But above all, knowing your audience (and growing with them) is key. Survival is about building a brand and an audience over the long term by providing enough value to keep people coming back.

funding the dream

The Internet revolution was fueled by money from VCs in search of the next big score. According to PricewaterhouseCoopers, almost $60 billion of venture money was funneled into Internet companies between 1995 and the third quarter of 2000. During this time VCs had gone from being seen as distinguished (if somewhat reclusive) businesspeople who operated behind the scenes of the companies they founded to something akin to rock stars, gracing the covers of business magazines and delivering keynote addresses at technology conferences where hopeful entrepreneurs with big ambitions listened in awe and dreamed about when *they* would get funded.

Between 1995 and 2000, according to research group Venture Economics, the number of venture capital firms in the United States doubled to 1,010, and the number of companies they financed totaled 5,380 by 2000. Just between 1998 and 1999, the number of venture-capital-backed deals tripled from 604 companies funded for a total of $3.4 billion to 1,798 companies in 1999 funded to the tune of nearly $20 billion. The New Economy was jumpstarted by this money, money designed to take new ideas and give them wings to fly to an IPO or a big acquisition. In 1999 PricewaterhouseCoopers found that the majority of deals were for early or seed funding—1,001 deals for a total of $8.925 billion.

While VCs have become the rock stars of the New Economy, few people understand their role and how the funding process works. Most of the public (and a lot of entrepreneurs) think that VCs are exceedingly rich guys (and they are mostly guys) who gamble their own money on gut-based decisions.

Not true. OK, not *entirely* true. To really understand how the whole process works (and how slippage in the process led to some of the biggest dot.bombs on the Web), it's important to start from the beginning—the beginning of a company looking for venture capital.

how it's supposed to work

Many companies started with a couple of founders and maybe a few friends who thought they had a "big idea." They'd often work their regular jobs during the day while building their dream company at night or on weekends until they'd scraped enough seed money together to quit their "day jobs" and go to it full time. Once they had made the leap, they needed money. They often sought seed money from wealthy individuals (so-called angel investors), family, and friends. These investors often didn't want any control, just a piece of the early action. But this money usually wasn't enough to do much more than let the founders quit their day jobs and get on with the real work of starting the company. Soon they would realize that if they wanted to grow, they needed some *real* money.

To get it, they'd write a business plan, describing in detail how the company was going to work, who was going to be in it, who the customers were, what the market looked like, how long it would take to become profitable, and (most importantly) how much they'd need to really get started. Then they'd start shopping the business plan around looking for startup capital.

Sometimes they'd try going to their banks for a loan, but most Internet startups were considered risky investments, and banks (if they gave them money at all) charged high interest rates to cover that risk. The hopeful company might have tried more private investors, but unless it was really well connected, this route usually didn't land it the money it needed either. Sometimes it would search for corporate partners—companies willing to lend money to the new venture in exchange for equity—but this route was fraught with problems. Or it would start shopping its business plan around to venture capitalists (Table 8-1).

While venture capitalists aren't usually rich guys investing their own money, they are rich guys investing *other* people's money. Drawing on contacts with pension fund managers, corporate investment managers, heads of mutual funds, other venture funds, or a network of high-net-worth individuals, venture capitalists got their money by pulling it together from all these sources into a venture fund, designed to provide a high rate of return for the investors in exchange for the high levels of risk entailed by venture investing.

Table 8-1. Sources of Venture Capital

Year	Corporations	Endowments and Foundations	Foreign Investors	Individuals and Families	Financial and Insurance	Pension Funds	Total
1990	$ 180	$ 330	$ 200	$ 300	$ 250	$1,390	$2,650
1991	60	360	170	180	80	630	1,490
1992	120	670	400	400	520	1,500	3,600
1993	330	420	170	290	410	2,300	3,940
1994	650	1,530	170	850	680	3,280	7,170
1995	340	1,610	310	1,330	1,580	3,040	8,220
1996	1,990	1,190	590	690	310	5,790	10,550
1997	3,740	2,490	620	1,870	940	5,920	15,590
1998	3,260	1,730	320	3,100	2,840	16,480	27,730
1999	6,920	9,680	2,770	10,140	5,990	10,600	46,100

Note: Figures in millions.
Source: National Venture Capital Association and Venture Economics.

At its heart, the game of venture investing is a game of risk management. VCs know that some of their investments are going to

224 | the dot.bomb survival guide

tank—they just don't know which ones. Terry Collison, one of the founders of Blue Rock Ventures, a Delaware-based VC fund focusing in startup capital, calls the process the "Rule of Ten:" "On day 1, every investment looks great . . . you never would have invested in them otherwise. But in 10 years, we count on three of the companies we fund being dead and three of them cash neutral with no hope of further growth . . . the living dead. Of the four that are left over, three will provide a significant return on investment through an IPO or acquisition. The last one will be your rocket ship, the company that hits it big."

In order to mitigate the risk, the venture fund has to have a good understanding of the company. So when a company with little funding shows up at the door of a seed-stage fund (or any venture fund), it's scrutinized with a fine-tooth comb in a process known as "due diligence." What's the management team look like? How strong is the business plan? Does it have any problems with legal hurdles, patents, or other factors? Does the company have any idea how it's going to market itself? If it passes these tests, a company usually receives some relatively small amount of money in exchange for a good chunk of equity in the company. The investors also take positions on the company's board of directors where they can provide guidance to move the company forward.

The risk for a venture fund usually increases in relation to how early a fund invests in a company. An early-stage fund (like Collison's) knows that the path to profits could be a long one—10 years—and insists on taking a larger chunk of equity than do the funds that come in later in the game.

Once the company's on its feet and starts pulling itself together, it may need money to enter the marketplace. That's where early-stage funds come in. Early-stage funds aren't the first, but they're pretty close to the beginning of the company. This investment may come from the seed company, or it may involve bringing in another partner. This is the money that will launch the site and begin the full-scale marketing.

As a company starts to grow (or starts needing more money to grow), it may begin looking for second-stage capital. Second-stage funding doesn't always require the company to be profitable, but it should require it to be on its way. If a company needs to grow even faster to expand into untapped markets or grab the market share that's going to take it to the top, it may go in search of third-stage capital. Once again, in exchange for more money, the founders give up more equity in the company. Finally, the company may be ready for an initial public offering.

Before the Internet, companies usually went public only because they had a significant need for capital in order to expand their already-profitable businesses. IPOs were also used to provide liquidity for the investors, owners, or founders of the company who wanted to be able to cash out. In addition, a public company could have an easier time merging with or acquiring other companies using its stock as currency in the deal instead of having to come up with cash. Also, a public company often had an easier time recruiting new employees once it had options to offer them.

Once the company went public, investors had an easier way out. They could sell their equity in the company on the public markets (often after a "lock-out" period that prevented them from selling in the first 2 years or so). They could sell their stock to another company through an acquisition or merger. Or they could sell their stock back to the owners. They'd then take the money they had earned and distribute it back to the original investors (or they could give the stock to the investors) to pay back the investments that had started the fund in the first place.

That's how it's *supposed* to work. When the Internet exploded, things got a little crazier.

investing on Internet time

Instead of starting with their own money, many entrepreneurs looked for venture money to fund their startups or hooked up with new networks of wealthy (but clueless) angel investors. In a frenzy to fund new companies, some venture funds began radically relaxing their previously thorough (and painful) due-diligence procedures and funded companies after the first meeting was over . . . which could take less than a half an hour. (*BusinessWeek* reported that San Mateo, California-based startup LogicTier, Inc., got its first funding commitment 20 minutes into a meeting with Kleiner Perkins in June

226 | the dot.bomb survival guide

2000.) "You couldn't wait to fund a company," was a common VC lament. "If you didn't, somebody else would."

Just as Internet time seemed to be radically compressing the time it took new technology to come to market, the funding frenzy of the late nineties changed the way companies went public. Rather than waiting years for a company to reach profitability (or something close to it), companies that were mere business plans 6 months earlier issued their IPO (Table 8-2). Rather than balk at companies that seemed to have no underpinnings, investors rushed in and snapped up shares as fast as they could get their hands on them, driving company valuations through the roof . . . only to come crashing down later on.

Table 8-2. The Top 10 First-Day IPOs

Rank	Company	Public Date	Offer Price	First-Day Close	Percentage Change	In 2001 (approximate)
1	VA Linus Systems, Inc.	Dec. 1999	$30	$239.25	698%	$ 5.00
2	theglobe.com, inc.	Nov. 1998	$ 9	$ 63.50	606%	$ 0.40
3	Foundry Networks, Inc.	Sep. 1999	$25	$156.25	525%	$49.00
4	webMethods, Inc.	Feb. 2000	$35	$212.63	508%	$14.00
5	FreeMarkets, Inc.	Dec. 1999	$48	$280	483%	$19.00
6	Cobalt Networks, Inc.	Nov. 1999	$22	$128.13	482%	Acquired by Sun Micro-systems for $1.3B
7	MarketWatch.com, Inc.	Jan. 1999	$17	$ 97.50	474%	$ 5.00
8	Akamai Technologies, Inc.	Oct. 1999	$26	$145.19	458%	$19.00
9	CacheFlow Inc.	Nov. 1999	$24	$126.38	427%	$ 6.00
10	Crayfish Co., Ltd.	Mar. 2000	$24.50	$126	414%	$12.00

Why did previously conservative (or at least risk-balanced) investors suddenly go nuts? Why were companies with a business plan and a dream getting tens of millions of dollars and then going public at huge valuations before they had really even gotten their businesses started?

Two words: Netscape and Yahoo!

What really kicked off the whole IPO revolution (and spurred so many venture capitalists into looking at the Internet) was the enormous amounts of money both Netscape and Yahoo! raised when they first appeared on the scene. On August 9, 1995, Netscape kicked off the IPO frenzy when its stock opened at $28 and closed the day at $58.25. All of a sudden, this company that few had heard of outside of the then-insular world of the Internet was worth around $2 billion dollars.

People started looking for the next big score. It came a little less than a year later. On April 12, 1996, Yahoo! made headlines when it leapt from $13 to $24.50 at the opening bell to close the day at $33. With an end-of-day market cap over $1 billion, David Filo and Jerry Yang, young Stanford Ph.D. candidates who had started the site to keep track of their bookmarks, went home multimillionaires.

For traditional investors used to old-fashioned indicators of company health like "earnings" and "profits" and "products" that were sold for money, these two IPOs were unfathomable. How could two companies started by (relative) kids be worth so much? The Internet was changing everything, they were told. It must be so—it made these people rich. Who's to say that the next nutty idea with no little or no revenues or profit wouldn't make the big time?

The frenzy began. The Internet was like crack to some investors. Returns were quick—instead of having to wait 3 or 5 or even 10 years to make big money from companies they funded, a rocketship IPO could bring in millions . . . even hundreds of millions . . . in a year. It was cheap—since putting up a website didn't involve all the traditional expensive barriers to entry like factories or costly distribution systems, a relatively small seed could grow into a very big money tree. It was easy—as soon as more and more investors started sensing there was money to be made, capital could be snatched up with a lot less legwork than before. The rules of the game had changed and it seemed as though anyone with enough chutzpah could make them work to his or her favor. (See sidebar "Entrepreneurs from the Outside.")

Entrepreneurs from the Outside: One Management Consultant's Experiences with the Dot.Com Boom

After 30 years in publishing, advertising, and promotional sales work in New York City, Paul Lee moved (or "escaped," depending on your point of view) to Annapolis, Maryland, to join another Madison Avenue transplant. They formed a marketing/management consulting firm focusing on hi-tech startups (and some established firms) needing help with business planning (plans), positioning, marketing, and media initiatives (in other words, whatever they need!). Here's the story (in his own words) of two of the startups he tried to help:

1. The Know-It-All

We took on an interesting startup in 1999 that had the potential of revolutionizing the B2B media scene, electronically . . . or so we all thought! And, it all went great . . . from the business plan development, research, writing, and so on. They had seed money to pay our fees, develop beta test(s) and create marketing materials. We were all cruising along with the project and getting along with each other with the exception of one of the "principals" who was a 28-year-old MBA, who made sure you knew it!

Although he was not a true "techie," he sure tried to make everyone believe he was. His position in the company-to-be was "CFO" since he had recently received his MBA from a prestigious Ivy League school. During the six months before we brought the founders into negotiations with a large VC fund, "Chad" (let's call him) started to put his nose into *everything*, claiming that it would be his responsibility to handle *XYZ* when the company was formed and open for business. He became a real pain-in-the-. . . .

The technical guys in the group were all pretty savvy with general business practices, but Chad always knew better. At every turn, he'd complain, fuss, fight, you name it. It was a long, slow process to get them ready for the real world, that is, asking for and getting $30 million from a NYC hi-tech venture fund company. Especially with only a beta-tested product, albeit a working model that seemed to function as designed.

My partner and I became suspicious about the relationship between Chad and another member of the founding fathers' team at a preliminary meeting in New York, before we met the "big guy"—the president who made the final decision to invest. There was something going on, we thought, but we couldn't quite put our finger on it.

We decided to confront Chad about "it". . . Well, welcome to WW III! He went on and on accusing us of undermining the entire project, turning one against another, etc., etc. Later on, with the due-diligence phase approaching, we asked everyone if there were any issues that we were unaware of that would jeopardize the deal. "No" was the short version-answer.

During due diligence, the president of the funding company called us into his office. "Did you guys know that Chad and 'Bill' had a side deal?" No, of course not, was our answer. . . . The side deal, as petty as it was, killed the deal. End of startup. All the principals went back to corporate America, but we did manage to salvage some of our fee.

2. The Greedy Techie

"We don't need a business plan; we've got the greatest killer application . . . " was what we heard for several months after we were hired to write marketing, media, and promotion plans for this B2B startup. They had been in "business" for about a year before we met them through a mutual business associate.

When we finally got to the point where the product had been fully beta tested and refined, we brought them to a VC company. They were very interested in the product (it did have great potential—it was a solid product with good functionality). All went well in the first few meetings, and the president and his (now wife) partner were very satisfied with the deal on the table as were the others involved. Except one . . . (let's call him "Bernie"). Bernie was admittedly the technical force behind the product although all the members carried Ph.D.'s and had extensive academic experience and input in the product as well.

Bernie would not accept the percentage offered to him. "I don't see why I should have to settle with 13 percent when I am responsible for the creation of the product. I want at least 30 percent or I'm out," said Bernie at the last meeting we had with the VC (and the company, for that matter). After the meeting concluded, we tried to persuade Bernie to accept the offer (a very substantial amount, which would have carried the company for 3 years). "You know, Bernie, 13 percent of something is a hell of a lot better than 30 percent of nothing," was our position and last words over drinks.

The company did get some private money elsewhere, but I have not seen or heard about them. I also heard that Bernie went back to the United Kingdom and is again teaching . . . hopefully not "business negotiations."

These experiences (and others) have since prompted Paul Lee to move on to other work. He recently joined a "new" mall media company as their marketing director. He remains involved with the interior design site he helped to found (www.DesignIntuit.com).

But the party built on the bigger-fool theory—the idea that there would always be somebody more foolish than you willing to buy your stock—couldn't last forever. By 1999 cracks had started to show in the pyramid as some previous high-flyers started to come down to earth. By April 2000 when the tech market crashed, the party was essentially over (Figure 8-1).

If you look at the top deals of 1999, it's clear that the Rule of Tens won't be working for funds that invested in these companies any time soon . . . unless they have some major aces up their sleeves. Three of the top 10 deals—Petstore.com (funded for $97 million), Petopia.com ($79 million), and JuniorNet ($70 million)—are dead as of early 2001. Three more—Third Age Media ($89 million), Looksmart ($60.5 million), and Healtheon ($46.1 million)—have seen their stocks plummet and have laid off workers. Only one—Equinix ($65 million)—hasn't yet laid off any appreciable percentage of its employees, but its stock is down to around $3 from a 52-week high of $16.50, and it lost $119.8 million in 2000.

Figure 8-1. A Frame from Flatiron Partners' Christmas 2000 (As the Ecard shows, some VCs aren't feeling too optimistic— look at the graph line behind the snowman!)

All told, the losses have been huge. In fact, the peak market capitalization loss for America Online, Yahoo!, and Amazon alone totals more than $300 billion, according to Lawrence Haverty, Jr., senior vice president at financial analyst firm State Street Research. In fact, Haverty reported to *The Industry Standard* in February 2001 that the loss for just those companies destroyed 214 times more than the savings-and-loan scandal in the late eighties.

funding the dream | 231

the incubators

While a lot of venture funds lost a lot of money on the Internet, the Internet incubators have been hit harder. While the idea of business "incubators" has been around for a while, it really didn't take off until the Web made it the model everyone wanted to copy.

Pioneered by Idealab! in 1995, incubators reversed the typical VC concept of raising money and waiting for the ideas to walk in the door. Instead, as Idealab! founder Bill Gross envisioned them, incubators would *start* with the ideas and then nurture them along into companies by providing them with seed money, advice, office space, computers, and contacts with VCs who could help them take off.

It's no surprise that so many new Internet companies started by incubators were headed by Ivy League MBAs . . . they were a business-school dream come true. In the near-frictionless business environment of the Web, new ventures could leap straight from the business plan to the stock market with few stops in between. With rapid development, new business could be tested immediately . . . sometimes within days. With the abundance of capital, these prototypes could be turned into working businesses . . . fast. With the eagerness of the stock market to fund these new ventures, big returns could be realized in a relative handful of months.

At first, incubators were all the rage. All over the United States and around the world, companies providing the smarts, the space, and the hardware to startups jumped into the marketplace. In fact, the incubator model even began to bleed over into all parts of the Internet economy as it started to become standard practice to ask for equity in the companies that the PR firms, ad agencies, and Web-building companies were helping to launch.

The crash in April also started the downward slide of the incubator industry. As public capital began to dry up, many high-flying incubators began to have burn-rate problems as they struggled to fund themselves and their portfolio companies. As their portfolio companies declined, so did the incubators, especially those that had gone public during the boom years. And as bad news began to scare off investors, many of the incubators had an increasingly difficult time raising money for new ventures. Finally, the markets began to look askance at the model as it became clear (and many revealed) that their model almost forced them into conflict-of-interest battles with their subsidiary companies.

In a February 19, 2001, article in *BusinessWeek*, Harvard Business School professor Morten T. Hansen painted a bleak picture of the industry, predicting that half of the 200 or so incubators in the United States will go under within 2 years. He may be right. But to understand the problems that incubators are having (and, by extension, to understand the problems the funding craze brought to the Internet), we'll have to dive into the stories of a few.

the Idealab! that started it all

Kicking off the incubator concept in 1995, Idealab! was immediately the talk of the Internet world. With funky offices, a nonstop barrage of ideas, and a charismatic founder, Idealab! soon found itself talked about in the pages of *Wired, Fortune, Inc.,* and newspapers around the world.

Figure 8-2. Idealab's Homepage . . . with Some of the Bombs Still Onboard

Idealab! created some of the biggest names—and biggest bombs—of the Web. eToys, CitySearch, NetZero, FreePC, Cooking.com, CarsDirect, and Goto.com were all Idealab! inventions (Figure 8-2).

The brains behind the ideas was Bill Gross, a serial entrepreneur who had first achieved success with Lotus Development and later hit it big with multimedia company Knowledge Adventure, which he sold for $100 million in 1997. In 1995 Gross had his first success with CitySearch (sold to Ticketmaster at a value of $260 million) and kicked the incubator into high gear.

In an early article appearing in *FastCompany* in 1997, Gross told his story of the experience that inspired Idealab!: "I would go over to DreamWorks, and Steven [Spielberg] would invite me to tag along. His assistant would drive him around the lot in a golf cart, whisking him from meeting to meeting," he told Eric Matson in December 1996. "It was just continuous creative power. He was playing with ideas all day long. I knew that's what I wanted to do next—create a playroom where I could work with ideas." In order to get the ideas started, he invited some big names over to play. Sherry Turkle from MIT and Bob Kavner from AT&T were just a couple of members of his advisory panel.

The model he developed was elegant in its simplicity. Each company he incubated would get $250,000 to start with. They'd then take that money and prototype a company that would attract more funding. Once the company had funding, Gross would help it along with advice, nurture its development, and then take it public in order to pay back the investors and reap a profit. And rather than go with untested ideas, Idealab! would work with models already on the Web . . . with an Idealab! twist to set it apart.

His model seemed to work. In May 1999 when eToys went public with a market capitalization of $7.9 billion, Idealab!'s $200,000 investment was worth $1.5 billion. When Goto.com went public in June, its capitalization peaked at around $5 billion.

But there were problems. He broke his own rules and lost $810,000 when Ideamarket went bust. In 1998, Idealab!'s reputation was scarred by a stock manipulation scandal. While some of the incubator's public companies did well initially, their values declined precipitously before he could sell out. In fact, the losses were so bad that *Slate*'s Rob Walker calculated that if an investor had put $10,000 into CitySearch, Goto.com, eToys, NetZero, or Tickets.com at the end of the first day the companies went public, they would have lost $33,700 when the values plunged later. Ouch.

234 | the dot.bomb survival guide

By early 2000, Idealab! needed money. That's when Gross committed what may be, in the end, his final error. In order to raise the $1 billion he wanted, he had to give guarantees to investors that if Idealab!'s future IPO didn't go so well, they'd get compensated with as much as 50 percent of the company. He raised the money but didn't go public . . . and the investors started to circle.

The year 2000 also witnessed a crippling spending spree by Idealab!. It spent $200 million of the $1 billion on CarsDirect.com . . . only to pull its IPO in December 2000. Twenty million went into Goto.com . . . and its stock is in rapid decline. Sixty million went to Homepage.com, which had problems making money and has since shifted to an ASP model, with uncertain results. Ten million went to fund entertainment site Z.com (with promises by comedian Chris Rock to provide content). Z.com died in February 2001. Idealab! put $16 million behind Modo, the ad-supported city-guide device from Scout Electromedia that went bust soon after the first units went out.

By August 2000, Idealab! had blown through $800 million dollars. By October, a declining market populated by investors avoiding risky Internet deals caused Idealab! to pull its IPO. In December 2000, Idealab! had only $50 million in cash and a burn rate of between $8 and $10 million per month. In January 2001, Idealab! began slimming down, laying off 10 percent of its staff in an effort to trim the burn rate.

Will Idealab! survive? It's hard to tell. It's had some goofy ideas—Blastoff.com died before it could send its rocket into outerspace . . . really! But Idealab! has also had some relative hits with DotTV (a domain name registry for the .tv domain) and Compete.com, a B2B concept for measuring consumer clickstreams through ISPs. It has reportedly cut its burn rate and is tightening its belt. It remains to be seen if the innovator of the incubator won't choke itself on it.

B2B and ICG

While Idealab! focused almost exclusively on B2C deals, Internet Capital Group focused on B2B companies. Founded in 1996, ICG went public on August 5, 1999, and ended the day at nearly double its opening price of $12 and a market cap of around $3 billion. The Pennsylvania-based incubator is host to some of the biggest names in business-to-business and infrastructure Internet companies: VerticalNet, BidCom, Arbinet, Clear Commerce, and Breakaway Solutions all have the incubator to thank for a good portion of their startup capital (Figure 8-3).

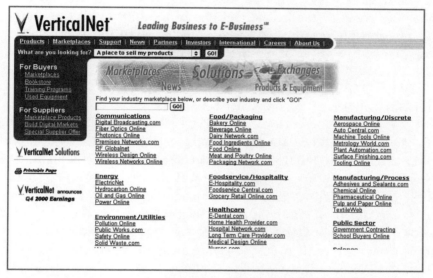

Figure 8-3.   VerticalNet: One of ICG's Biggest Successes

While the B2B market was hot in 1999 when ICG went public, things have started to cool down a little. In order to fund its portfolio of companies, ICG spent about $1 billion in just 9 months during 2000 . . . a burn rate of about $83 million per month.

The stock market hasn't been too kind to ICG either. As investors began to cool on the prospects of B2B commerce on the Web and ICG was forced to report losses of $264 million in the third quarter of 2000, its stock dropped $5.06 to $11.19 on November 9 of that year. It had been losing money before, but when the $264 million was compared to the $15 million in the third quarter of 1999, investors got nervous. ICG fired 35 percent of its staff in an effort to stem the tide of red ink, but prospects look grim—ICG reports that it will have to spend $100 million on its top 15 companies in 2001,

236 | the dot.bomb survival guide

and it has decided not to provide any funding for the remaining 45 companies in its portfolio. ICG thinks that the company will survive 2001 with $200 million in cash, spending between $125 million and $150 million in total. It has trimmed its burn rate significantly, and revenues are up.

As of February 2001, ICG was trading at around $3.50 per share, down from $24.44 on the day of its IPO. However, ICG's portfolio includes some of the heaviest hitters in the B2B market, a market that's probably best poised to take advantage of the Web over the long term. If it can hold on, the prospects look good.

CMGI: the big guns shoot blanks

In January 2000, *The Motley Fool* reported that CMGI CEO David Wetherell made the following bold prediction: "Eventually, the vast majority of users will access the Web for free. It's inevitable. The cost of bandwidth is going down, and the quality of advertising is going up, both the content of the ads and the way they now look on the computer screen. ISPs can generate enough revenue now from selling ads to justify giving away the connection." In particular, Wetherell was talking about CMGI's new free ISP, 1stUP.com.

Now fast-forward to November 2000: "Given the investments required to be successful in the marketplace, as well as the challenging dynamics within 1stUP's free, ad-supported businesses, . . . CMGI no longer believes it can achieve the scale on a stand-alone basis necessary to drive this business to profitability within an acceptable time frame."

In particular, CMGI's release referred to the fact that it was hitting the kill switch on 1stUP.com. Yep, hubris abounds from another incubator. But CMGI's not any ordinary incubator (in fact, it doesn't like the term). It's now a holding company for some of the Net's biggest brands. And it isn't doing so well (Table 8-3).

Yes, like the other incubators covered here, CMGI's decline is linked to the decline in the stock market. While the company pulled in $898.1 million in 2000, it also lost over a billion dollars—$1.364 billion—during the same period.

funding the dream | 237

Table 8-3. CMGI's Major Properties

Company	Status
AdForce	Closed, June 13, 2001
AltaVista.com	Losing money, not profitable
Engage	Loss $377 million in 2000, CMGI cut off additional funding
MyWay.com	Closed its portal; is changing strategy
NaviSite	Lost $58 million in 2000
Vicinity Corp.	Losing money
Yesmail.com	Sued as a "spammer" by Mail Abuse, Prevention Systems

One of CMGI's biggest problems is that 20 percent of its properties derive their revenue from advertising. As discussed in the last chapter, that can be a problem. It burned through $214.3 million in the third quarter of 2000. In early 2001, CMGI was forced to shut down its online email-based payment system, ExchangePath.

What's the future look like for this once-mighty incubator? No one, including CMGI, can tell: In February *Forbes* reported that the company says "it has no visibility beyond the current quarter and can't provide guidance on profitability, gross profit margin, burn rate, or revenue targets for the rest of the year." It had $1 billion in cash in early 2001, and it projected it would still have $600 million at the end of its fiscal year. But as the Internet goes, so goes CMGI . . . its portfolio closely matches a good portion of the public companies currently online.

Divine Interventures:
in need of some divine intervention?

Divine Interventures CEO Andrew "Flip" Filipowski hates it when people refer to his company as an incubator. "It sounds like a bunch

238 | the dot.bomb survival guide

of chickens running around with their heads cut off," is how he supposedly responded to the description of Divine Interventures. Ironically, it may be apt.

The seed for Chicago-based Divine Interventures was planted by Flip in 1999 after he sold Platinum Software to Computer Associates for a whopping $3.6 billion. Arriving to much fanfare in December 1999 (including a greeting from an excited Mayor Richard Daley), the forward-thinking company styled itself as an "Internet Zaibatsu" on the Silicon Prairie.

The public markets weren't as excited about Divine Interventures. When it went public in June 2000, it raised a mere $128 million (OK, mere for an Internet company) when it closed the day at $8.78 . . . 22 cents below its asking price. The bad IPO had been off to a rocky start anyway—Divine Interventures reportedly fired underwriter Credit Suisse First Boston after it advised against the offering, probably a very good piece of advice considering the trends in the market. Divine Interventures hired Robert Stephens to do the deal, but it had to refile after CEO Filipowski broke quiet-period rules by talking to the press.

At the time of its IPO, Divine Interventures had invested in 52 Web startups of all kinds, including Aluminum.com, iGive, Farms.com, and Perpetual Robotics. In all of 1999, the company had made just $1 million and had lost $9.4 million. In July it also declined to fund iGive for a second round, leading to layoffs. For its biggest portfolio companies, the market hasn't been too kind, leading to double-digit drops in Neoforma.com's and Sequoia Software's market values. The decline in the portfolio had brought the company's market capitalization down to $200 million.

Investors don't seem to be hanging on to Divine Interventures either. *Forbes* reported in February 2001 that institutional investors quickly dropped Divine Interventures' stock when its lockup periods expired. When Divine Interventures stock hovered around $1, Filipowski was asked if the drop in price bothered him. It didn't. "We'll be trading where we are now for the next 50 years," he told *Forbes*.

He wasn't one to let sleeping dogs (and stocks) lie. In February 2001, Divine Interventures renamed itself divine.com and relaunched as a software company in an effort to reinvigorate its model. Concentrating on "enterprise information portals," divine.com has pledged all of its $250 million remaining behind the new venture, planning on rolling up smaller companies with the cash. It's not funding any more startups. "It's cheaper to buy than to build," Filipowski told *The Industry Standard* in a Valentine's Day report.

Will it work? The market seems to think so: divine.com's stock jumped 12 percent after the announcement, and it has hovered around that mark since. In its switch, Divine Interventures has done what so many other struggling Web companies have done: go from tool user to tool seller.

incubators: a world of hurt?

As a whole, the incubator model has had a tough time across the board since the market began to decline in mid-2000. As companies based on the fortunes of the companies they build, they've been at the mercy of winds of change. Here are a few examples of incubators in trouble:

- In October 2000, VenturePlex, San Diego's first Internet incubator, shut down, selling its remaining assets (mainly computer files) to then-Managing Director Dante Fichera for $150,000. Vowing to restart the business as a "business refinery" focusing on more tried-and-true businesses such as telecom, biotech, and advanced technologies, the company currently resides mainly in Fichera's laptop.
- In January 2001, Anaheim, California-based Odetics laid off 25 percent of its staff when it couldn't find additional funding. It had reported a decline of 5.7 percent in revenue from the previous year.
- NRG Group, one of Canada's most celebrated incubators, laid off two-thirds of its staff and changed its strategy to move away from funding startups in January 2001. It had gone public in 2000 and had followed the Idealab! model by seeding its startups with $250,000 and hoping for the best. While a lot of the incubator founders have been dreamers, NRG cofounder Vicki Saunders

240 | the dot.bomb survival guide

probably takes the cake for the most incomprehensible New Economy psychobabble. When asked to describe herself in an article in the *National Journal* about the layoffs, Saunders said, "I am the visionary, and exist in the cloud of possibilities, and I'm intuitively strategic." Yeah, right.

- Incubator problems haven't been confined to North America, either. At the end of January 2001, United Kingdom–based THINKVENTURES lost approximately $40 million in funding when United States–based Providence Equity Partners pulled out of the fund. In Italy in February, ex-Olivetti executive Carol DeBenedetti (one of Italy's first Internet investors) pulled out of the incubator market in order to transform his Cirlab incubator into a straight VC fund. One source close to DeBenedetti told Reuters News Service that the owner had come to believe that "the incubator model didn't work."

the future of funding

According to Venture Economics, in 1999 the average 1-year return on a venture fund was 164 percent. In the first three quarters of 2000, that return had dropped to 43 percent. Not bad, but not what investors have come to expect. A chill has spread across the world of Internet venture funding, and it isn't expected to lift until the market heats up again . . . if at all.

At an investment conference in mid-February 2001, Martin Fridson of Merrill Lynch pronounced that, according to *News.com* reporter Rachel Konrad, "the Internet boom of the late 1990s and 2000 will go down in history as a silly fad similar to other trendy investment boondoggles." While not quite as bearish, other investors at the conference berated the shoddy accounting practices at dot.coms (used to hide losses and boost gains), as well as the investment bankers, day-traders, executives, and others that let the market slip to the point where it is now. Many predicted that companies of the future would have a much harder time getting funding and would have to get by with a lot less money than changed hands during the boom. (See sidebar "Promises Made to Pizza Kids.")

Promises Made to Pizza Kids, by Douglas Rushkoff

As the dot.com boom wound to a close, there was a lot of blame flying around. The author of *Media Virus, Playing the Future, Coercion,* and *The Ecstasy Club: A Novel,* cyberculture analyst, and occasional *Frontline* correspondent tells this original story of blame he witnessed.

I was asked to participate in a conference hosted by a respected Internet business consultancy firm, who chose what has become the default theme for a once-booming dot.com industry's events: what to do after the crash.

Perhaps predictably, the gathering degenerated into something of a blame game, with each panel and speaker choosing a new target for the assembled failed dot.com investors' collective wrath. The people attending this conference, like most Internet investors, were latecomers. They had learned of the network's existence a couple of years ago—after billions of dollars had already been made by earlier investors and speculators. Having finally earned a spot on the bandwagon only to watch it fall off a cliff, these ladies and gentlemen were ready to lynch the bandleader. If they could just figure out who that was.

By late afternoon, one panel had come to an agreement. The culprits are those pimply twenty-something kids who work in makeshift studios over their garages, eating pizza and drinking Coke late into the night. "It's those pizza kids who fooled the investors," an Internet strategist agreed. "They didn't care about your money at all. They just took it."

We all know by now who they were referring to: the "neckbeard" independent programmers of Silicon Valley. Those obsessive young Internet enthusiasts and inventors, who toiled late into the night just for the fun of it. Kids who had bizarre visions of the way people might enjoy networking and the energy to materialize these visions from concept to code. These same kids were delighted that some adults took interest in their activities and gleefully accepted money in exchange for a piece of their fledgling projects (they didn't even think of them as companies). They thought of it as a way to pay for a few more months of pizza, Coke, and video games to play while they worked. These were the same kids who, for the most part, failed to create sustainable revenue models for their self-interested benefactors.

The angry panelists had their blame equation reversed because it wasn't the pizza kids who fooled the investors—it was the investors who fooled the pizza kids!

First off, what self-respecting businessperson would bet his or her money on a hacker? A hacker's interest is in creating and expanding networks, not earning a fast buck. Hackers are almost never businesspeople themselves. They are visionaries and explorers.

One angry Internet strategist griped, "The pizza kids didn't care about your money at all." Of course not. They weren't in it for the money. They were in it for the thrill of discovery. And discovery, for its own sake, doesn't necessarily yield revenue.

But by greeting the investors in their over-the-garage offices and accepting their dollars, the pizza kids surrendered their spirit of adventure for a value system they just didn't understand. It killed the fun, and dampened their ingenuity. Ideas that couldn't be patented were no longer considered valuable. Extending the functionality of someone *else's* products was deemed insanity. Results could be measured only in terms of revenue. Everything else was "burn."

True, they didn't know how to think in terms of sustainable revenue—but this was never their job. In the old days, when giant corporations had thriving "research-and-development" departments, crazy inventors were shielded from the harsh reality of a technology's applicability in the marketplace. CEOs with a long-range view knew that if even 10 percent of their skunkworks and laboratory inventions could be brought to market someday, the R&D was well worth the effort.

The pizza kids, often living off day jobs as IT office workers or university computer instructors, served as the Internet's real R&D department. The people who developed email did not earn a profit—though many companies are now making money off using it. The hackers who created the Web and the first browsers distributed their work as freeware, and an awful lot of revenue has been earned subsequently thanks to these inventions. Unfortunately, the latecomer investment community had no real understanding of how technologies trickle up to profitability, and they turned to the pizza kids as if they were a commodity to be mined.

The pizza kids are not without blame. They believed the same hyped-up magazine articles that had fooled the investors—those stories of young dot.com millionaires who had cashed in their code for stock options and their over-the-garage offices for mansions in Redwood Hills. And they were so desperate for someone, anyone, to acknowledge their existence that they took the investors at their word.

Sorry, pizza kids. The investors didn't really care about your projects at all. They never even understood what it was you were trying to do.

Is the funding situation hopeless? Not if you look at which companies are being funded. While it's pretty clear that investors aren't too keen on pure Internet B2C companies, advertising-supported models, or wacky revenue models, they do seem to understand that the Internet isn't going away, that it's ingrained in society and will continue to be a force in business and home life for a long time to come. Rather than funding those hoping to get rich quick on untested entertainment concepts and undifferentiated retail concepts, the investors of today are focusing on more solid stuff. Recently, the following Internet companies received first- or second-round VC funding:

- *Infrastructure.* B2B company Metreo received $10 million and content management system provider got $8 million.
- *Peer-to-peer.* Centerpsan received $5 million in February 2001.
- *Fiber optics.* Sigma Networks landed a whopping $435 million in late February 2001.
- *Services.* Intellispace received $60 million in 2001.
- *B2B services.* Chapter 2 got $50 million in January 2001.
- *Telecommunications.* Xtera landed a second round of $110 million in January 2001.

What does the future of funding hold? Terry Collison, one of the founders of Blue Rock Capital, offers the best advice for that question. A well-respected VC with a handelbar moustache, a gleam in his eye, and a passion for entrepreneurship, Collison's experience in funding high-growth seed and early-stage companies has led him to some keen insights for anyone interested in starting up a new company:

Q: Has there been a dot.com "crash," or are we just seeing natural attrition of startups? In other words, is the number of failed dot.coms par for the course?

There has been an abnormal number of failures following an abnormal number of startups. You can't temporarily suspend the laws of physics. You can't temporarily suspend the laws of economics. The chickens are coming home to roost. There were a lot of get-rich-

244 | the dot.bomb survival guide

quick and get-rich-easy schemes out there. All that mattered was cash . . . as long as there were a lot of greater fools lined up to buy your IPO.

The rule of the day was get big fast. Get cash. Use cash. The start-ups thought that going for broke was the only thing that was going to differentiate them.

There was an overlay that affected sophisticated investors. The psychology abroad in the land said that the Old Economy business models would be changing over for ecommerce and hardware/infra-structure. It was a phase change. A paradigm shift. You didn't have to debate which one was going to win. The demand side will absorb the mistakes of the supply side. But this was a window of specific duration.

There *is* a New Economy. The portion of the investment commu-nity that perceived the long boom was right, and once the market opens up to accommodate startups without the baggage of the Old Economy, we'll be in a New Economy type of market with needs that will be defined in real time as things proceed.

But nobody can predict all those things in advance. The first wave effects the transition . . . that's what we've been through. The second wave is all the things you can do when you're operating in the new paradigm. Unsophisticated investors applied this thinking in an undifferentiated way to all things and failed to discriminate. They also failed in their investments.

There's no question that we're moving into a new economy. But it is taking time.

For the business-to-business market, the problem isn't the tech-nology. The real gatekeeper is the culture of the incumbents in those customer companies. We're still being governed at the top by the people who have the C: prompt burning into the top of their screens. They're not people who are yet fundamentally thinking about enabling technologies. The generation under *that* is the one that will move things forward.

Q: What kinds of companies would you like to see?

There's not a good connection between the university of hard knocks and the entrepreneurs. Most entrepreneurs are virgins. And as a result of that, they are motivated by all the right aspects of entrepreneurial fervor and zeal, but they don't have the benefit of having gotten stung. They may have run out of money before, but that's different than having spent a couple of years building a company through its second wave to a second round of funding when you actually have to hire people you don't know to fill the slots. A founder who's been through that transition really wakes up.

Q: What kind are you looking for?

We're looking for ways to get top-line bookings fast. I want a company to tell me, *here's* where we are in product development. *Here* are some customers we've lined up. We still think that companies need to have revenue to be fundable. It's important that they have a path laid out to get them there.

Our exit strategies have not changed—they range from sale to IPO. In the past, it was just the drive to IPO that got reported because it was very exciting.

Q: What is the big lesson (or lessons) that you feel the Internet industry should learn from failed dot.coms?

The first thing I'd do is get a show of hands to ferret out the guilty parties. I'd like people who haven't acted stupidly to have a chance to stand up.

"How many of you invested in a deal with the following characteristics: 'We've gotta be there . . . due diligence be damned! Look at those comparables!'"

(laughs)

If everybody had been in only one model, the failure rate would have been higher than it was. The failure rate on the Internet—applied to the traditional investing model—is not that screwy. I admire the investors that stuck to their knitting.

The frustrations we had were that the market environment was so screwed up that our portfolio companies would come to us and tell us that we were going to have to do a second round of funding . . . and we're having trouble. We have some real businesses! We have companies that have been doing right and having a difficult time, and in some cases the failure rate of those companies has gone up. And that's the fault of the screwed-up investment environment at the moment.

Right now, one of things driving the problems with funding is the stories of funds turning money back to investors. That's a problem. Money can't sit there. It has to go out the door. At a certain point, somewhere down the road that logjam has got to break up.

In the future, the most attractive companies will be ones that have seasoning, that have been through cutbacks and can clearly demonstrate that they are past the point of thinking cash flow doesn't matter. Companies seeking a seed round are going to have a harder time.

Q: How would you advise entrepreneurs now?

Get big fast is still a good precept: Get positioned securely fast. But big does not mean secure. Companies that tried to get big fast suffered when the market didn't support them—all they had was more funding to look for. Companies that have worked very hard to get themselves positioned to have good customers and real sales and real implementations. . . . Suddenly then you get to the point where the company is close to achieving cash flow neutrality. That's a very different kettle of fish. I'd much rather invest in a company in which the money is going to build, not just stay afloat.

are we learning anything yet?

On the surface, the story of the dot.com explosion and subsequent implosion is simple. A lot of people thought that the Internet had changed everything. They thought the old rules had changed. They saw an opportunity, got really greedy, and made a lot of bad decisions based on that greed. As their big plans went belly up because they hadn't figured out how to make money out of them (besides attracting additional funding), cracks started to show in their plans. The public caught on when their portfolios began to slide and refused to fund any more risky experiments. The market collapsed, entrepreneurs began to look for opportunities somewhere else, and the survivors struggle on. Boom! End of story.

But that simple story doesn't tell the deeper reasons for the dot.com implosion, nor does it offer any hope for those who want to survive. No, the deeper reasons have a lot more to do with the very nature of the Internet itself, what we can do with it, and what people want from it.

In the space of a few short years, the Internet has evolved from an object of curiosity to a fixture of American life. We've built an incredible infrastructure of high-speed pipes and powerful comput-

248 | the dot.bomb survival guide

ers, and today the Net offers a dazzling array of information and services that many people couldn't live without. In the United States, the Internet has become completely mainstream: At the beginning of 2001, the majority of U.S. citizens have Internet access. Around the world, numbers are growing, too. Sure, adoption is growing faster in some places than in others, but the global village is a reality, built one node in the Net at a time.

Looking at the surface of the dot.com implosion, things look pretty grim. There's been a lot of money lost—$300 billion in peak market capitalization just from AOL, Amazon, and Yahoo! Tens of billions of dollars flowed into venture capital firms from pension funds, corporations, endowments, and individuals and then was lost. Hundreds of companies have gone out of business, and more than 58,000 highly educated, highly skilled, and highly paid workers have been laid off at the time I write this. The U.S. economy, buoyed for several years by the ebullience in the stock market, has slowed down considerably and may slip into recession at any minute as people who lost money in the market lose their confidence, stop spending, and hunker down for the rough times ahead.

dot.bombs: lessons learned

How could all this happen? As we've seen throughout this book, many of the reasons are pretty simple from a business standpoint. The concept of ultracompressed "Internet time" that drove wild spending in an effort to build market share, mindshare, and first-mover advantage resulted in huge losses in a short period of time along with an unhealthy dependence on investment capital—not revenue—to sustain a lot of dot.coms.

There was a generally accepted view that the old rules of business didn't apply to the Internet. It was new. It was faster, quicker, cheaper . . . a frictionless way for businesses to instantly reach a global marketplace. Instead of having to deal with the ugly details of the Old Economy—factories, real estate, distribution, and stores—the ultraefficient New Economy was supposed to make the leap directly from company to customer. Who needed an intermediary when time and space had been conquered by technology?

And because the old rules didn't apply, the old ways for judging the value of a company didn't apply either. Companies that made profits, spent slowly, and grew on revenues were growing too slowly, being too conservative. The only winners were going to be those that could become the biggest the fastest, making the most noise and grabbing the most eyeballs. Who cared how much money it took to reach that top spot—the New Economy was going to wipe out the old one. A couple of hundred million spent now was a good investment when getting the top spot meant owning the global marketplace for your product or service.

In the New Economy, information wanted to be free. Never mind that the original meaning of "free" really referred to "freedom of expression," not "having no cost." But never mind: The advertising-supported, free-content model took off immediately. Why wouldn't it? Who wanted to pay for something as ephemeral as content? The only reason that Old Media had to charge for it was because the physical limitations of print required that someone foot the bill for all the paper, printing, and distribution. The Web wouldn't have any of those problems. Publishing to a global audience could be accomplished virtually for free (or so we thought) just by slapping up a website and putting the content out there for all to see. The money would come in from all the advertisers willing to pay to put their commercial messages in front of all the eyeballs on the site sucking up free content.

As far as products and services went, a lot of people assumed that a public in love with new technology would put up with an endless stream of beta releases and technology they didn't really have a need for. We could do it, so why not make it? In the New Economy, the barriers to creating, testing, and distributing products would be eliminated. Just post it to the Net and wait for people to download it! And since advertising seemed to work for everything else, if you slapped enough banners on it, a ready and willing advertising community would foot the bill.

Ecommerce seemed like the perfect driver for the New Economy. With access to customers in a global marketplace who could serve themselves 24 hours a day, 7 days a week (in their underwear if they wanted!), commerce would flow at the speed of light. And if we could eliminate stores, why not eliminate their money-sucking inven-

250 | the dot.bomb survival guide

tories, too? Companies could be virtual, linked by high-speed, inter-connected webs of information. Orders would flow through and be shipped directly. Sure, some companies took it upon themselves to build their own distribution centers, but that was just a way of aggre-gating control, and he who controlled the channel controlled the marketplace.

The Internet was going to change the world, and the opportunities were endless. The Long Boom was going to last forever. Companies servicing the New Economy built out as quickly as they could hire increasingly scarce employees. Financial and legal advisors retooled to service the ever-increasing flood of wealth and new deals. As the New Economy grew, so did the old: All that money had to go to something, and new wealth bought new cars, houses, exotic vaca-tions, and toys.

People are always attracted to wealth and power, and the elite of the New Economy had no shortage of either. The media responded through increasing their coverage of the boom, and new magazines, websites, newspapers, and even cable channels sprung up. All the while, the media rose to the top of the food chain as the public, increasingly excited about the money being generated by the New Economy, invested even more heavily in the stock market, which directed more money into New Economy companies, which spent a good portion of that money on advertising . . . going directly to the media, continuing the cycle. As a member of the media, I certainly don't think there was any sort of big conspiracy behind the hype; it was an exciting time with a lot of interesting stories to write about. But I also remember one of my *Business 2.0* writer friends calling me up one day desperately in search of story ideas. "They'll print as many stories as I can write for them," he explained to me. "They've got more advertising than content and need to fill up the space."

As we've seen in this book, a lot of these assumptions turned out to be false . . . or at least a long time away from being fully realized.

First, it turns out that the Net *isn't* a disintermediator . . . in fact, it makes the value of mediation abundantly clear. By being able to link sellers directly with buyers, the Web is able to strip out all the inefficiency that's arisen in the value chain. On the Web, value (or lack of value) is readily apparent. You know right away whether or not a company is actually adding value to the transaction or is merely tacking on extra charges for the privilege of dealing with it. The Web has delivered a good smack upside the heads of the travel and automobile industries, for example, when their customers suddenly discovered that they didn't need travel agents to type for them or salespeople to hide information from them. On the other hand, now that people can trade directly online, many are discovering the value of information and are willing to pay to have access to information that's going to give them the edge.

Next, the Web's also made clear the value of differentiation. Since everything on the Web is as "far away" as anything else, it has an amazing ability to turn everything it touches into a commodity. While several pet stores in one town used to be able to survive independently of each other because their locations gave them access to different markets, online, it's just as easy to go to one store as the next . . . as long as you know its location. What makes the difference are the intangibles that are difficult to commodify; service, information, and the experience of buying on a particular site are what set it apart from its competitors . . . and what draws customers back.

Price, it turns out, isn't always the deciding factor. In fact, competing on price is what killed many companies. While people do indicate that price is important in their decision, it's not the only factor. Companies that thought that they could buy customers by selling products below cost (or losing money on the sale through free shipping) often found themselves in a pricing death spiral that they couldn't pull out of. Instead of building customers that were loyal to them, they created customers who were loyal to their prices . . . and as soon as they couldn't afford to keep those prices down, their customers went somewhere else.

Making money through advertising isn't as easy as people thought, either. Getting and keeping viewers is tough, and providing them with the content that keeps them coming back can be expensive. And while online media properties were initially able to sell themselves based on the accountability of their clickthrough model, when clickthroughs started to decline, they found themselves having to backpedal on their promises of accountability, trying desperately to explain to their advertisers why now it was branding . . . not clickthroughs . . . that mattered. In the process the model was tarnished and revenues declined.

252 | the dot.bomb survival guide

Finally, it turns out that while technology changes quickly, people change very slowly. The Internet revolution is still underway, but it is going to take a lot longer than people thought it would take. While techies, visionaries, and early adopters have always been quick to see the value of new technology, it can take years for the general public to catch on to its value. In the business-to-business world, adoption of new technology can take just as long. Even if new tech makes perfect sense to the C-level management, they're not using it . . . their workers are. And even if their workers are doing things in slow, inefficient ways because they know no other way, getting them to switch may take some time. Companies that bet that the world would change overnight have lost. As Mark Walsh, chairman of VerticalNet told me, "The Internet doesn't change people. People change the Internet." And people take time to change.

surviving and thriving in the dot.com implosion

These are just the lessons we've learned coming out of the biggest beta test the world has ever seen. Now it's time to take what we've learned and move into the future.

Success has to rest on a solid business, one that grows in proportion to its income. This doesn't mean that it can't lose money—most startups do, no matter what the industry. But it means growing smart. And smart growth rests on three pillars: (1) understanding the customer, (2) understanding the technology, and (3) understanding how customers and technology come together.

First, the customer. Understanding your customers means understanding the Contact Zone, that virtual space where you and your customers meet. And your customers aren't just the people buying your stuff, using your services, or reading your content. Customers are anyone who comes into contact with your company.

While companies must be focused on what they do, your customers aren't that focused on your company. They lead lives of their own, lives that intersect your company in various places depending on their needs. It may be that they experience your company on the Web, and your website must be able to meet the specific needs they have when they're there. But they also may experience your company in older media, through your ads, press coverage, or through contact with your products.

Your customers also come into contact with your company through interaction with other people. Word of mouth has always been a powerful force, but with the connectivity afforded by the Internet, that force has increased exponentially. People are wired now, and they communicate constantly with friends, family, and coworkers. They share files, stories, and experiences. Bad service or bad products can't hide themselves in the haze of distance anymore. Once somebody has a bad experience, they're going to tell other people about it through email, chat rooms, discussion boards, consumer opinion sites, letters to the editor on sites that cover your industry. People have more access to more channels to be heard than in any other time in history. While we live in a global village, you have to remember that one of the characteristics of a small town is that everyone knows everyone else's business.

Your customers also have contact with your company through the information they gather. A lot more people research products online than buy online. People like to compare prices and product information. They're smart, info-savvy, and want to be shown, not sold. If you can't provide them with this, they'll go somewhere else.

Your customer service must communicate your value every time you answer the phone or get back with an email. Many ecommerce companies went out of business because they thought that the transaction ended with the "submit" button. It doesn't. That's just the beginning. If you're going to build a viable business, you have to have loyal customers who trust you, and the only way to build trust is through service.

As *The Cluetrain Manifesto* pointed out, email has made companies more porous now than ever before. While management may want only the official story to be told, the employees may be communicating their own version of the story to anyone they email . . . inside the company and out. There is no official story anymore. Information does want to be free. If you put a block on the information, there's always some way that your employees will find to route around it. Don't believe me? Go to Fuckedcompany.com some time and look at the postings from angry ex-employees and those about to be laid off. Those stories aren't coming from the investor relations department.

254 | the dot.bomb survival guide

Your vendors are in the Contact Zone, too. They talk. They swap stories of your company with other netizens. Antagonize one through unscrupulous practices and you can bet that the next time you're out looking for a "partner," they'll probably be waiting for you with their foot firmly planted behind the door. And don't forget that your vendor companies are populated by people, too . . . people whom you may want to be your customers some day.

Managing the Contact Zone means managing the experience in every place that your company touches your customers. Your brand isn't your logo; it's the sum total of all those experiences within the Contact Zone. You can't create a lasting brand by simply paying attention to one part of the zone. You need to understand your customers as completely as you can . . . and then work tirelessly to deliver them better products and services than your competitors can.

The total experience is the only thing that matters.

On the technology side, many companies forgot that what matters about technology is what it can accomplish for those who use it, not just what it can do. "Because-we-can" technology impresses only a small minority of the population who are interested in technology.

The killer apps on the Web aren't necessarily the most technologically sophisticated . . . they're the ones that provide the most value for the lowest psychological and financial cost to those that use them.

What are they? Email is probably *the* killer app on the Internet. It's what people do online more than anything else. Auctions are another killer app—especially eBay because it has reached the critical mass to provide the most value (potential customers) to its users. Ecommerce sites that sell commodities and then decommodify themselves through a combination of information and service also have done very well. While it's tough to get people to buy furniture or clothes online, books and CDs sell well because people know what they're getting. And the sites that do this best are the ones that provide the best service to their customers and the most information to assist the buying decision.

Never forget that online gaming has been a huge success. While the game industry lives under the radar of many looking at more "serious" businesses, the successes of games like *Everquest* (and other massively multiplayer environments) point to a very serious market . . . one that's only going to grow bigger as Gen Y (and subsequent generations) get older and increase their spending power.

Good search engines are another big technological success story. Why? Because people who go online are goal directed and are in search of information. Technology that can assist that process does well . . . provided that the rest of the business remains intact.

Applications that eliminate the value-suckers in our lives have continued to do well. The online travel, automobile, and financial services industries have prospered because they've eliminated barriers that used to suck value out of the transaction.

Finally, applications that allow contact with other people in new ways have done extremely well in terms of usage and adoption. Napster, ICQ, and other P2P and instant messaging systems are popular for the same reason email is: They connect people.

Which brings us to the third pillar of successful companies: understanding how people and technology come together.

Understanding this begins with the knowledge of what people truly want. They want to connect with other people. They want their lives to be easier and more stress free. They want to be entertained. They want more money. They want choices. They want more enjoyment and more autonomy in their lives. They want to be able to fulfill their own aspirations.

If you look at the technologies above that have done well, you'll see that many of them address these needs. Email, instant messaging, and peer-to-peer technologies connect people. Travel, financial, and automotive sites simplify through providing information and access. Search engines and sites that provide valuable information give people the information and the power they seek to make their lives easier. Games provide enjoyment. And ecommerce sites that sell goods and services for a fair price and provide excellent service make people's lives easier. People want the most value for the least cost . . . financial *and* psychological cost.

The story of the dot.com explosion and implosion is not the story of technology—it's the story of people. And people are complicated, complex, unpredictable, and motivated by their own needs . . . needs that you may or may not share.

Do you want your company to survive the implosion? Give people better products and services. Give them value. Connect them with each other. Speak to them in a human voice, and make their lives easier. Provide them with superior experiences that communicate why your company's different and better.

The New Economy is out of beta. It's time to get down to business . . . the business of people.

glossary

10Q: A document that a publicly traded company files on a quarterly basis that discloses the financial health of the company, including details about profit, loss, officers, and spending.

Angel: Typically, a high-net-worth individual who contributes money to a startup company in its earliest stages. Angels can also be family members, friends, and others who contribute startup money in exchange for equity. Many startups began with money from angels and later received larger amounts of money from venture capitalists.

ASP: An acronym for *application service provider*. A company that "rents" software to other companies, usually over the Internet. In an application service provider model, the ASP hosts the applications on its own servers, saving its customers the expense of installing and maintaining the software on their own equipment.

Assets: Something that is owned by a corporation and that has economic value. Assets can be converted to cash when needed.

B2B: An acronym for *business to business*. B2B sites concentrate on selling goods and services to other businesses, not individual consumers.

258 | glossary

B2B marketplace: On the Web, a site set up, usually concentrating on one type of business, where buyers and sellers can meet and transact. B2B marketplaces offer goods for sale via catalog, auction, or reverse auction.

B2C: An acronym for *business to consumer.* B2C sites sell goods and services directly to individual consumers.

B2G: An acronym for *business to government.* B2G sites sell goods and services to government entities.

Banner: An advertisement on a website, usually consisting of graphic or rich media content designed to get users to click on them. Once a user has clicked, the banner takes the user to the advertiser's website. Advertising banner sizes were standardized by the Internet Advertising Bureau into full banner (468 x 60 pixels), half banner (234 x 60 pixels), Microbar (88 x 31 pixels), Button (120 x 90 or 120 x 60 pixels), Vertical Banners (120 x 240 pixels), or Square Button (125 x 125 pixels) sizes.

Brand: Originally the graphic identity of a company as communicated by its advertisements or publications. The definition of brand has expanded to include the intangible feeling about a company held by its customers.

Brand experience: The sum total of all the feelings that customers have about a company. A brand experience occurs every place where a customer touches a company, regardless of medium.

Branding: The process of developing a brand identity for a company.

Brand recognition: A measure of whether a random group of consumers can recall a particular company's name, graphic identity, logo, or slogan.

Broadband: High-speed Internet connectivity. While there is no set definition of what constitutes a *broadband connection,* it is usually taken to mean any connection that is as fast as or faster than ISDN, which operates at 128,000 bits per second.

Burn rate: The amount of money a company spends within a particular time frame.

Capital expenditures: The money a company spends on its infrastructure—traditionally its property and equipment.

glossary | 259

Cash: The money that a company has on hand.

Cash flow: The amount of money a company takes in less the amount of money it pays within a particular time frame.

Chinese Soda model: A term first used by Garage.com's Guy Kawasaki to refer to an ill-conceived business plan that estimates its sales based on naïve assumptions about its target market. Chinese Soda business plans usually don't account for the difficulty or expense in manufacturing, promoting, or distributing their products and services. Most follow a formula that reads something like this: "There are X number of people in the world. My product will cost Y. The potential value of the market is X times Y. If I can sell to a small percentage of that market, I'll be rich!"

Clickthrough: The action a person takes to click on a banner in order to link to an advertiser's site. In the early days of online advertising, the measure of success for an online campaign was its clickthroughs: how many people responded to the advertisement. Over time this measure has come under scrutiny for not measuring the effectiveness of the ad on those that saw it but did not click.

Contact Zone: The virtual "place" in which companies and customers intersect. The Contact Zone includes all points of contact, regardless of medium: the Web, in print, on television, on the radio, within the retail environment, and so on.

Content: Words, pictures, music, animation, movies, games . . . the elements of a site meant to be consumed by viewing and not related to its back end functions.

CPA: An acronym for *cost per acquisition.* An advertising model in which the site running the ad is paid when a customer is acquired by the advertiser.

CPC: An acronym for *cost per click.* An advertising model in which a site running an ad is paid a set amount when a user clicks on a banner ad.

CPM: An acronym for *cost per thousand.* A term used in advertising to indicate what an advertiser must pay per thousand impressions of its ad.

260 | glossary

Deal: In venture capital parlance, a *deal* is an arrangement put together by the investors to fund a startup company.

Disintermediation: The theory that the Internet can "remove the middleman," linking buyers and sellers directly. In practice, the theory didn't hold up so well. It turns out that people *like* having distributors and retailers make choices for them.

Equity: The value in a company, calculated by subtracting total liabilities from total assets. *Equity* can also mean the amount of ownership interest in a corporation.

Exchange: On the Web, a place where buyers and sellers meet to transact business. See also *B2B*.

Expenses: Operating costs of a company that are not long-term capital investments.

Experience design: A new discipline that seeks to shape the experience that a customer (or potential customer) has with a brand. Experience design recognizes that the digital age has made all points of contact with a customer— no matter in what media—important in shaping that customer's experience with a company.

First-mover advantage: A concept that states that the company who is first into a particular industry or niche will have a distinct competitive advantage over all those who follow. During the dot.com boom, many startups spent large amounts of money very quickly in order to be first onto the Web with their particular concept. In the long run, the first-mover advantage turned out to be a lot less important than originally thought.

Flash: A vector-based animation format created by Macromedia. Fast loading and graphically rich, Flash was used on many sites that sought to distinguish themselves through impressive graphics and cool animations.

Fulfillment: The process of getting a company's products to its customers. Many ecommerce sites had problems setting up and executing effective fulfillment procedures.

Gross profit: The amount of money left over after the cost of goods sold is subtracted from the company's revenue.

Gross profit margin: A percentage resulting from the ratio of gross profit divided by the revenue of a company. This fraction tells investors what amount of every dollar brought in by a company results in gross profit.

Hits: A measure of the number of times a Web server displays a piece of information to a user. Since servers count every discrete element of a site (graphics, text, animation, etc.) served up as a *hit*, a hit count is a very inaccurate measurement of total site traffic.

Impressions: The number of times a particular object is seen by visitors to a website. Impressions can measure the number of pages viewed by users (*page impressions*) or the number of times a particular ad banner is seen (*ad impressions*). See also *unique visitors* and *hits*.

Income: The amount of money taken in by a company.

Incubator: A company or investment group that provides startup capital to new companies and then contributes guidance, infrastructure, and even offices in order to provide a safe growing environment while the startup gets going. Incubators typically take a percentage of equity in companies they help start.

Institutional investor: A company or group that invests large amounts of money in other companies. Typically, institutional investors are pension funds, insurance companies, mutual funds, endowments, and investment companies. Most of the money invested by venture capitalists came from (and comes from) institutional investors. See also *angel*.

IPO: An acronym for *initial public offering*. An event in which a company sells its stock to the public for the first time in the public markets. During the dot.com boom, many IPO stock prices rose many times their initial offering price, making getting in early on an IPO an attractive game for many professional and amateur investors.

ISP: An acronym for *Internet service provider*. A company that provides other companies and individuals with a connection to the Internet. Many ISPs also provide Web server hosting services as well.

Market capitalization: Usually refers to the amount of outstanding shares of a public company multiplied by the price per share. Often shortened to *market cap*.

Market share: The percentage of a particular industry that a company sells

262 | glossary

to. If a company is said to have *high market share*, it can be assumed that it is one of the dominant companies in its industry.

Mindshare: While impossible to calculate with any certainty, *mindshare* is usually used to refer to a company's brand recognition or presence in a particular industry. The goal of many public relations and marketing efforts is to gain mindshare in an effort to have customers and investors remember a company and (hopefully) buy its products or services.

Name-your-own-price model: A business model, first popularized by Priceline.com, in which customers would declare how much they wanted to pay for a particular item or service. Once they had declared their price, the company (or companies) providing the product or service would tell the customer whether their offer had been accepted. See also *reverse auction*.

Netslaves: A term used to refer to underpaid dot.com workers, first popularized by the book *Netslaves* by Bill Lessard and Steve Baldwin. Also a site by the same name (www.netslaves.com) that has documented the trials and tribulations of the dot.com worker.

P2P: An acronym for *peer to peer*. A technology with which individual computers share files or data with each other over the Internet. Peer-to-peer technology became popular with the Napster file-sharing service.

Palmtop: A small computer with limited functionality designed to be carried around in a pocket.

Pay-to-surf model: A business model popularized by AllAdvantage.com, which paid users to view ads while they used the Web. In the end, pay-to-surf models often proved to be too costly for their supporters when many more users signed up than the company could support. Also, automated programs that mimicked the behavior of users often were used to defraud pay-to-surf companies into making payments for advertisements not actually seen.

PDA: An acronym for *personal digital assistant*. A computerlike device used to keep personal schedules, notes, and contact information. Palm Pilots are probably the most popular PDAs.

Portal: A site that strives to become a user's first stop on the Web. Portals typically aggregate content from a large number of sources including news, stock prices, sports scores and personal entertainment such as horoscopes. A variant of the portal was the *vortal*, or *vertical portal*, a site designed to aggregate all the information on the Web pertaining to a particular industry.

Profit: The amount of money left over after a company has subtracted its expenses from its sales. For many companies in the early dot.com boom, "profit" wasn't considered important as they spent money building infrastructure and market share.

Push technology: A system in which information was delivered to a user by a content provider (*pushed*) rather than being retrieved by a user from a site (*pulled*). Early push technology companies such as PointCast strove to bring a more "broadcastlike" model to the Internet that didn't rely on users finding content.

Revenue: The total amount of money a company brings in for the products and services it sells.

Reverse auction: A system in which a buyer declares what he or she wishes to buy (sometimes also specifying a price range) while sellers compete by offering up the lowest price. This differs from the traditional auction model in which a product or service is offered up and buyers compete by offering the seller the highest price they will pay.

Rich media: Typically multimedia programming delivered over the Internet that contains sound, motion, and interactivity. To work flawlessly and provide the best user experience, much rich media requires the user to have high-speed connections, though these requirements can be reduced by streaming the rich media so that it plays as it downloads.

SEC: An acronym for the *Securities and Exchange Commission,* the government agency that regulates the securities industry. The main purpose of the SEC is to protect investors.

Shares outstanding: The amount of a company's stock held by the public.

Stock options: A document or an arrangement that gives its holder the right to buy a certain amount of a company's stock for a certain price (the *strike price*) during a limited time period. Many dot.com employees' compensation packages included stock options that were usually priced below the current market value of a company's stock. If the company's stock increased in price, an employee could make money by exercising his or her options, purchasing the stock at below-market price and then selling it at the current higher price, benefiting from the profit of the sale. In the early days of the dot.com boom

264 | glossary

when stock prices often increased by hundreds of percent, many people made a lot of money exercising their options. Unfortunately, as stock prices declined, the market prices for stocks often dipped below the price of the options, making the options effectively worthless unless the stock rebounded. Options that cost more to exercise than the current market price for a company's shares are said to be *under water.* Many employees who had accepted options in lieu of salary were hit hard when their company's stock price declined in value.

Streaming media: Motion graphics, video, and/or sound that plays on a user's machine as it is downloaded.

Unique visitors: The number of people viewing a site within a particular time frame. Usually the number of unique visitors is calculated by counting the individual IP addresses noted in a Web server's log, an inexact practice at best because it doesn't account for shared usage of a machine (such as in a home) or proxy servers that "hide" the number of users behind their firewalls.

VC: An acronym for *venture capitalist.* A person who provides money (usually assembled with funds from *institutional investors*) to startup companies (often called an *early-stage venture capitalist*) or established companies in hopes of gaining a high-yield return in a relatively short amount of time. While venture capitalists often provide guidance and other advice to the companies they fund, they are not interested in sticking with a company for the long term—VCs count on their exit strategy to recoup their investment by selling the company or taking it public through an *IPO.* Venture capitalists typically take on high risks with the hopes of a high return on investment.

Virtual community: A group of people who meet online and get to know each other within a particular time frame. Virtual communities are usually built around bulletin boards, discussion lists, and other communal forms of communication, but they can also arise around websites, multiplayer games, and chat rooms or facilities.

VRML: An acronym for *Virtual Reality Markup Language.* An early standard for delivering 3D content over the Internet. While the recipient of much hype in its early years, VRML has fallen from favor as a preferred method of transmitting three-dimensional content.

Wireless: Data or voice communication using radiowaves. In relation to the Internet, *wireless* usually refers to wireless data transmission.

index

Acquisition of customers, 51, 163–165
Adoption inertia, 35, 36
Advertising, 189–219
    bleeding-edge sites, 208–210
    broadband, 210–212
    early Web-based, 189–192
    free-PCs, 212–215
    lessons learned, 173–175, 215–219
    marketing, 160–161
    Super Bowl, 165–171
        (*See also* Marketing issues)
Advertising models
    basics, 192–199
    cost-per-thousand (CPM), 192–193
    niche sites, 202–208
    portals, 198–202
    push technology, 80–86
African American users, 44
Alexander, Pam, 177
AllAdvantage.com, 31–33, 34
Allen, Paul, 16, 20, 210–211
Amazon.com, 34, 39, 173, 248
America Online (AOL), 14, 20, 21, 22, 23, 248
Andreessen, Marc, 81, 82
AOL (America Online), 14, 20, 21, 22, 23, 248
Apfel, Jason, 147, 148
Application service provider (ASP) model, 104, 125–130

Armstrong, Arthur, 21
ASP (application service provider) model, 104, 125–130

Backweb, 73, 86–94
Barach, Michael, 47, 145
Barkat, Eli, 91–93
B2B (business-to-business) exchanges
    advertising, 199–200
    business model for Web, 6–12, 127
    ICG, 234–236
    old vs. new economy, 37
    VerticalNet, 12–15
B2C (business-to-consumer) exchanges, 15–20, 67, 128
Bernays, Edward, 175
"Beta culture," xiv, 108–109
Beta Galaxy, 108–109
Bigwords.com, 63–64
BizBuyer.com, 9–10
Bleeding-edge sites, 208–210
Bohrman, David, 210
Brands
    crucial in ecommerce, 48–50, 58–61, 70–71, 172
    recognition of, 161–163, 172–173
Broadband, 210–212
Brooks, Andrew, 53
Browsing, 45–48, 53–56
Burke, Katie, 126, 127

265

266 | index

Busey, Andrew and Jay, 56
Business failures since April 1999, xii
Business models
 ASP model, 104, 125–130
 B2B exchanges, 6–15
 differences in Web business, 1–4
 name-your-price strategy, 15–20
 pay-per-click model, 193
 pay-to-surf model, 31–34
 profitability, 26–28
 virtual communities, 20–26, 29–31, 93
  (*See also* Advertising models;
   Push technology)
Business-to-business exchanges (*See* B2B
 [business-to-business] exchanges)
Business-to-consumer (B2C) exchanges,
 15–20

Canter, Lawrence, 189, 190–191
Capital
 short-term perspective on investment,
  135–138
 sources of, 221–246
  (*See also* Venture capital)
Carlassare, Elizabeth, 58
Carter, Todd, 127
Case, Steve, 14
Castanet, by Marimba, 94–95
CDNow, 160
Charron, Chris, 24
Chemdex, 8–9
"Chinese soda," 5–6
Christian online market, 206–208
Christianity.com, 208
Clark, Jim, 25, 73
Clickmango.com, 141–142
ClickZ, 67
Client/server model, open
 Backweb as, 73, 86–94
 Marimba, 86–87, 94–99
 PointCast, 73, 80–86
CMGI, 236–237
Collison, Terry, 224, 243
Contact zone, 49, 185, 253–254
Cooper, Frank, 150
Cost-per-thousand (CPM), advertising
 model, 12, 192–193
Covisint, 7–8, 37
CPM (cost-per-thousand), advertising
 model, 12, 192–193
Crosswalk.com, 206–208

Customer issues
 acquisition, 51, 163–165
 browsing, 45–48, 53–56
 cost of customer loyalty, 51, 61–64
 customer experience, 46–58, 69–71
 demographics, 43–44
 online customers, 43–48
 retention, 173–175
  (*See also* Ecommerce)
Customer service, 52, 71

Daley, Richard, 238
Dante, Fichera, 239
DeBenedetti, Carol, 240
Demographics, customer, 43–44
Desktop.com, 126–127, 129–130
Divine Interventures, 237–239
Dolby, Thomas, 95–96
Dorman, David, 85, 86
DoubleClick, 181–182
Drebes, Larry, 126

Ecommerce, 41–71
 assumptions and reality, 41–43
 brands, 48–50, 58–61
 merchandise selection, 58–61
 online customers, 43–52
 short-term perspective, 138–146
 starting small vs. large, 37, 146–150
 wireless Web, 64–69
EBay.com, 30–31
Economy (*See* New economy)
ElectricMinds, 22, 29
Ellison, Larry, 128
EMachines, 212–213
Employees at dot.coms, 137–138
Epidemic.com, 167, 169–170
Estefan, Gloria, 202
Etail (*See* Ecommerce)
EToys.com, 170–171, 170–173, 233
Etrade.com, 182, 185
Eve.com, 58–61
Experience of customer, 46–58, 69–71
EZGamer.com, 116–118

Fads (*See* Push technology)
Fanning, Shawn, 184
Filipowski, Andrew, 237–238
Filo, David, 227
FragranceNet.com, 147–148
Free-PCs, 194, 212–215

index | 267

Fridson, Martin, 240
Fry, John, 176
FuckedCompany.com, xi, 28, 253
Furniture.com, 52–56

Gable, Tom, 179–181
Games and virtual reality, 110–118
Garden.com, 139–141
GeoCities, 23, 24
Gibson, William, 110
Gnutella, 30, 184
Go.com, 200–201
Godin, Seth, 21
Goto.com, 233, 234
Green Card advertising, 189–191
Gross, Bill, 59–60, 85, 170, 212, 231, 233

Hagel, John, 21
Hansen, Morten H., 232
Hasset, Christopher, 81
Haverty, Lawrence, Jr., 230
Hispanic users, 44, 202–204
Homepages, 23–25
Hotjobs.com, 166–167, 169, 173, 185
Hotmail.com, 32, 74
Hotwire.com, 19, 37
Howard, Ron, 210
Howell, Debbie, 140

IBelieve.com, 206–208
ICG (International Capital Group),
    234–236
Idealab!
    eToys, 170
    Eve.com, 58, 59
    free PCs, 212
    as incubator, 231–234
    Modo, 121
    PointCast, 85
Incubators, 231–240
InfoSeek, 192
Initial public offerings (IPOs)
    (See specific companies)
Innovation, software products and
    services, 106–109
International Capital Group (ICG),
    234–236
Internet time, 37, 38, 94, 107–108
    (See also Short-term perspective)
Investment
    (See Capital; specific companies)

IPOs (See specific companies)
ITag, 121–123
IVillage.com, 191, 193–194

Jackson, George, 149
Jaeger, Doug, 209
Johnson, Richard, 166
Jorgensen, Jim, 32

Kaldor, Sean, 33
Kaplan, Karen, 60
Kavner, Bob, 233
Kawasaki, Guy, 4, 5–6
Keane, Patrick, 85
Kelley, Kevin, 77
Kibu.com, 25–26
Kidron, Adam, 150
Kleinman, Neil, xiv, 108–109
Konrad, Merrill, 240

Lanier, Jaron, 110
Lashinsky, Adam, 84
Launchpad Technologies, 85–86
Layoffs since April 1999, xii
Lee, Paul, 228–229
Lenk, Toby, 170
Lessons learned, 247–256
    advertising, 173–175, 215–219
    business models, 35–39
    marketing, 184–187
    new economy, 248–252
    push technology, 99–101
    survival, 252–256
    venture capital, 240–246
Lifeminder.com, 167, 168
Lin, Hurst, 204–206
Living.com, 52–53, 56–58
Lopker, Pat, 10
Loyalty, cost of customer, 51, 61–64
Lumley, Joanna, 141–142
Lux, Larry, 210
Lycos, 23
Lynch, Stephen, 82

Machefsky, Ira, 85
Marketing issues, 159–187
    brand recognition, 161–163
    customer acquisition, 51, 163–165
    disasters, 170–171
    dot.com fatigue, 173–175
    lessons learned, 184–187

268 | index

Marketing issues *(Cont.)*:
  public relations, 175–184
  (See also Advertising)
Matson, Eric, 233
McAfee, 88–89
McGinn, Weber, 182
McNealy, Scott, 128
Merchandise, selection of, 51, 58–61
Microsoft, 73, 107, 128
Microsoft Network (MSN), 164
Middleberg, Don, 178
Mobile computing devices, 118–125
Models *(See* Advertising models;
  Business models)
Modo, 120–121, 123, 124, 125, 234
Monster.com, 166, 167, 168, 169, 173,
  185
MotherNature.com, 144–145
MSN (Microsoft Network), 164
Mullaney, Tim, 56
Murray, Dave, 182
MusicMaker.com, 115–116

Naficy, Mariam, 58
Name-your-price strategy, 15–20
Napster, 115–116, 184
Natoli, Sherry, 64
Negroponte, Nicholas, 1–2
Netscape, 75, 81, 107, 111, 135, 192,
  197, 227
NetZero, 212, 215
New economy
  April 1999 crash, xii
  cost of customer loyalty, 51, 61–64
  customer experience impact, 50–58
  lessons learned, 248–252
  as permanent, xii–xv
  public markets in, 134–138
  (See also Venture capital)
Niche sites
  advertising model, 202–208
  as business opportunities, 37–38
Niehaus, Ed, 179
Nielson, Jakob, 65, 66
Nolan, Chris, 96

O'Connor, Kevin, 182
Olsen, John, 97–99
OneClick at Amazon.com, 39
Orbitz.com, 19

Paternot, Stephan, 24
Pay-per-click model, 193
Pay-to-surf model, 31–34
PDA (personal digital assistant), 118–125
Perkins, Kleiner, 225
Personal digital assistant (PDA), 118–125
Pesce, Marc, 111
Pets.com, 142–144, 160, 173
Pitfeild, Geoff, 120
Pizza Kids, 240–242
PointCast, 73, 80–86
Polese, Kim, 94–95, 97, 101
Pop.com, 210–211
Portals in advertising model, 198–202
Priceline.com, 15–20, 37
Privacy concerns, 46–47
Profitability in business models, 26–28
Promedix, 8–9
Public relations (PR) and marketing,
  175–184, 185
Push technology, 73–101
  Backweb, 73, 86–94
  description, 76–80
  lessons learned, 99–101
  Marimba, 86–87, 94–99
  other fads, 73–75
  PointCast, 73, 80–86

Quepasa.com, 202–203, 204

Rao, Varsha, 58
Rare Medium, 151, 152, 153–154
Rashtchy, Safa, 24
Razorfish, 151, 152, 182–183
Retention of customers, 173–175
Revolution vs. fad, Internet, 75–76
Rheingold, Howard, 22, 29
Rock, Chris, 234
Rothschild, Steve, 53
Rowen, Mark, 146
Rowland, Toby, 142
Rubin, Ross, 89
Rushoff, Douglas, 241–242
Ryan, William, 179

Saunders, Vicki, 239–240
Schehr, David, 45–46
Schwartz, Peter, 155
Scout Electromedia, 119
Security concerns, 46–47

index | 269

Selection of merchandise, ecommerce, 58–61
Sephora.com, 58–59
Sharples, Clif, 140
Shatner, William, 17
Sheftel-Gomes, Nasoan, 149, 150
Short-term perspective, 133–157
   capital availability and new rules, 135–138
   ecommerce challenges, 138–146
   large startups, 149–150
   public market changes, 134–135
   rush to market, 151–154
   small startups, 146–148
   vs. long-view, 154–157
Siegel, Martha, 189–191
SINA.com, 204–206
Sixdegrees.com, 26–28, 29, 32
Skolman, Stuart, 41
Software products and services, Internet sales of, 103–132
   ASP model, 125–130
   failure, reasons for, 104–106
   mobile computing devices, 118–125
   overview, 103–104
   pricing and new product development, 130–132
   product innovation, 106–109
   virtual reality and gaming, 110–118
Spielberg, Steven, 210, 233
Stephens, Robert, 238
Stock market (*See specific companies*)
Stock options, 137–138
Sun Microsystems, 111
Super Bowl advertising, 165–170

Talal, Alwaleed bin, 150
TheGlobe.com, 23–24
3D renderings, 110–118, 212
Time, Internet, 37, 38, 94, 107–108
   (*See also* Short-term perspective)
ToysRUs.com, 171, 173
Turkle, Sherry, 233

UrbanBoxOffice (UBO), 149–150
Usability, 51, 67

Value added, 70
VC (*See* Venture capital)
Ventro, 8–9
Venture capital (VC)
   incubators, 231–240
   lessons learned, 240–246
   mechanics, 222–225
   overview, 221–222
   rush to investment, 225–230
   startup investment, xv
   (*See also* Capital)
VerticalNet, 12–15, 235
Villet, Travor, 214–215
Vindago, 118–119, 123
VirginConnect WebPlayers, 213–215
Virtual communities and business models, 20–26, 29–31, 93
Virtual reality and gaming, 110–118
VRML (virtual reality mark-up language), 110–118
Vulcan Ventures, 16, 211

Walker, Rob, 233
Walker, William, 17–18
Walsh, Mark, 12–15, 252
WebHouseClub, 18, 20
Webvan, 145
Weinreich, Andrew, 27
WELL, 21–22
Welte, Jim, 183
Wetherall, David, 236
Winer, Dave, 82
Wireless Web, 64–69, 194
Wolf, Gary, 77
Wolff, Michael, 96
Wong, Ken, 211

Xenote's iTag, 121–123

Yahoo!, 23, 24, 34, 201–202, 227, 248
Yang, Jerry, 227
Yankelovich, 16, 19
YouthStream Networks, 27–28

Z.com, 234

about the author

Sean Carton is an internationally known ebusiness speaker and writer. He is chief experience officer of Carton Donofrio Partners, a brand experience design firm located in Baltimore, Maryland. A long-time Net veteran, Sean has been writing about the Internet since 1994, when he and Gareth Branwyn wrote the best-selling Mosaic Quick Tour series . . . one of the first series of books about the Web. He has contributed to *Wired, POV, Revolution, Green,* and many other online and offline Internet publications. Sean writes a regular column for ClickZ.com. He currently lives in Pasadena, Maryland, with his wife, Lorna, daughter, Emma, and beagle, Clyde.